DANTE TO DEAD MAN WALKING

One Reader's Journey through the Christian Classics

DANTE TO
DEAD MAN WALKING

*One Reader's Journey through
the Christian Classics*

RAYMOND A. SCHROTH, S.J.

LOYOLAPRESS.

CHICAGO

LOYOLAPRESS.

3441 N. ASHLAND AVENUE
CHICAGO, ILLINOIS 60657

Scripture quotations are from the Revised Standard Version of the Bible, copyright © 1946, 1952, and 1971 by the Division of Christian Education of the National Council of Churches of Christ in the United States of America. Used by permission. All rights reserved.

Interior design by Lisa Buckley

Library of Congress Cataloging-in-Publication Data

Schroth, Raymond A.
  Dante to Dead man walking : one reader's journey through the Christian classics / by Raymond A. Schroth, S.J.
    p. cm.
  ISBN 0-8294-1431-2
    1. Christianity and literature. 2. Christian literature—History and criticism.

PN49 .S3248 2001
809'.933823—dc21

                                         2001029882

Printed in the United States
01 02 03 04 05 06 07 08 09 Sher 9 8 7 6 5 4 3 2 1

"If you love your friends . . . tell them so."
—from Myles Connolly's *Mr. Blue*

for

Jim and Cathy Dwyer

Kevin Doyle and Mary Sullivan

John and Carolyn Holl

Table of Contents

P
UTTING TOGETHER A PROJECT like this requires more wisdom and common sense than I can muster on my own. I'm especially grateful to Avery Dulles, S.J., Tom Scirghi, S.J., Mark Massa, S.J., and Fordham senior dean John Kezel, who read my original list and offered valuable criticisms and suggestions; and to patient and generous friends like Jack Deedy, Hank Stuever, Dan Degnan, S.J., Bob McCarty, S.J., John Wrynn, S.J., and Bob Kennedy, S.J., who read individual essays in progress; to the very helpful reference and circulation librarians at St. Peter's College; and to the communities and superiors at St. Peter's College, Fordham's Mitchell Farm, and Jogues Retreat in Cornwall, New York, where I moved in, talked a lot about this stuff, and wrote until it was done.

The Why and How
of This Book

SPIRITUAL IS A DIFFICULT, rich, and sometimes slippery word. The Notre Dame wit Michael O. Garvey, writing in *Commonweal* (March 12, 1999) on a new edition of *The Seven Storey Mountain*, remarked that there should be a special place in hell for both the theologian who invented the distinction between mortal and venial sin and for "the scholar who first isolated and sought to define 'spirituality.'"

For a novice in a religious order, "spiritual reading" is usually narrowly defined as a treatise on prayer, on the rules, or on some virtue, or as an edifying biography of a saint. The spirit and the flesh—one good, the other not so good—are segregated by time and place and allowed to visit one another only occasionally. When I told one religious superior during my philosophy studies that I was reading *Doctor Zhivago* on my own, he admonished me that a novel was to be read only during summer vacations.

My definition of *spiritual* is broad. The books that follow are spiritual classics in that, with the exception of a few published within the last decade, they have worked their magic on centuries and generations of readers. They speak to the human spirit, to that divine gift by which we transcend the limitations imposed by our self-absorption, our narrow-mindedness, and our moral cowardice. If we approach a book the way Karl Rahner says we should approach life—fully open to human experience and God's grace—it can transform us in much the same way that a friend, a teacher, or a coach can help us become something we have not been before.

How did I choose these titles? First, by the test of time. I consulted other lists of Great Books, reading lists, and books about reading. I drew up a rough draft and circulated it among theologians and fellow professors. Since the 1970s, at the five colleges and universities where I have taught and/or been academic dean, I have edited several short collections of faculty-written essays, such as *The Fordham Personal Reading List*, *The Rockhurst Personal Incomplete Reading List*, *The Holy Cross One Hundred Books*, and *The Loyola Personal Reading List*. In 1987, I published *Books for Believers: 35 Books That Every Catholic Ought to Read*. Because that book is now long out of print, I have updated and rewritten fifteen of those essays for this volume. In talking to friends, staring at bookshelves, and reading thousands of reviews, certain titles keep coming back. Here are fifty of them.

Second, the authors of these books, whether they are known as religious writers or not, all raised a moral or religious issue in a provocative way so that I could not put the books down without reconsidering—or at least getting a deeper understanding of—one of my fundamental beliefs. Without constructing an artificially balanced table of contents, it seemed important to touch on certain key social and moral questions of our era, such as poverty, racial justice, the status of women, nuclear arms, the crisis of the priesthood, and the problem of belief.

Third, I had to really enjoy reading a book enough to recommend it to a friend. With the individual books from the Bible, I have emphasized the value of commentaries. Some of these tomes sail more smoothly than others, but there are no "homework," castor oil, or read-it-because-it's-good-for-you titles on the list. The Newman, Gutiérrez, and Fiorenza volumes are, to a degree, addressed to specialists, but any educated person can read them selectively, for the main ideas, with great profit.

It was fascinating for me as I read and reread them all to see the same themes returning again and again, as though I had summoned the ghosts of these writers to a big book party in Manhattan and listened to them talk spontaneously over cocktails about the same topics. All are intrigued somehow by the mysterious workings of God's grace, as he freely picks the most unlikely characters—such as a whiskey priest, a murderous spouse, or a communist who has had an abortion—to accomplish his will. These authors mine the riches of the Christian intellectual tradition of the early twentieth-century "renaissance," itself inspired to some degree by the lore of the Middle Ages. They are also concerned with issues raised by two world wars and especially with the stark challenges to individual moral responsibility—what must I do today, as a believer or citizen, about a promise, a sin, a lover, a friend, my country, a child yet unborn, lest I gain the world but lose my soul?

The notes at the end of the book give bibliographic references for my favorite edition of each of these books—or, in some cases, simply the edition that for whatever reason has sat on my shelves for the past twenty or thirty years. Page references in each section refer to these editions or to secondary works also cited in the notes. I've refrained from using a scholarly approach to citing source material, but the notes should make it possible for the interested reader to follow up on a thought or to expand horizons in an area of interest.

1   The Book of Genesis

C. TENTH TO SIXTH CENTURIES B.C.

IN THE BEGINNING, God created the heaven and the earth." John, as if in response, both echoes and continues that line as he opens his Gospel: "In the beginning was the Word, and the Word was with God." In the eighteenth century, the words return in another context: "all men are created equal [and] endowed by their Creator with certain unalienable Rights." Thus, the "image of God" in man will become the basis of Western morality, and in time, the basis for the case against slavery and for all human rights.

On Christmas Eve of 1968, as Apollo 8 circled the moon and pointed its TV camera back toward Earth, with all three networks and a hundred million households tuned in, astronaut William Anders read aloud, "In the beginning. . . ."

Of all the books of the Bible—partly because it is the first and partly because it is so poetic and so involved with issues of family, violence, love, and betrayal—Genesis has been the most challenged to hold up under centuries of interpretation, use, and abuse. As a result, in the popular mind much of it's original message has been lost.

In 1999, the Kansas Board of Education voted to discourage the teaching of evolution in its schools, igniting a controversy that most people, especially in the major cities, thought had been settled years ago, and framing the discussion as if there really were a conflict between the scientific theory of evolution and the Bible's mythic account of how life began. This debate is

1

sometimes cast as if only secularists can be true scientists and as if believers shut down their brains and accept on faith what their reason tells them cannot be so. And this is in spite of the recent meeting between Pope John Paul II and spiritually minded scientists, at which the pope accepted evolution as a fact.

Reporters ask presidential candidates whether they believe in evolution or the biblical account, and the candidates back off from an intelligent response. Feminists blame Genesis for portraying the first woman as the serpent's accomplice. Capitalists and environmentalists argue over whether God's giving man "dominion" over Eden justifies strip mining or requires that we preserve the garden-earth for future generations.

The purpose of Genesis is not to teach us facts, but to use its stories to illustrate our relationships with God and one another. To appreciate the lessons of Genesis, it helps to understand that the book, once attributed to Moses, has at least three authors, each representing a different oral tradition, and each of these traditions is present throughout the book with its own emphasis or theology.

The Yahwist source (which refers to God by the name "Yahweh") is the oldest, dating from the tenth century B.C. It portrays God as personal, walking in the Garden, involved in human affairs. This author wrote the story of Adam and Eve and their sin. The Priestly source stresses God's transcendence and the observance of rules, as we see in the creation of the world and in God's resting on the Sabbath. The Elohist author (who calls God "Elohim") uses stories of angels and dreams to show God communicating indirectly with people rather than dealing with them face to face. A fourth, called the Deuteronomic tradition, comes into play in the other four books of the Pentateuch and emphasizes the law.

The book's structure consists of Israel's primeval history, including two creation accounts and the story of the Flood, followed by the three family sagas of Abraham, Jacob, and Joseph. Each demonstrates in its own way the consequences of the Fall described in the first chapters, as well as God's continual renewal of his covenant in spite of humankind's folly and sin.

Scholars comment on various themes that knit the tales together. One focuses on the verb "to beget," as the patriarchal stories are all about men whose wives are barren until God intervenes and gives them the son they need to carry on the line. Human history is seen as a fulfillment of God's command to "be fruitful and multiply," and God might even be imagined as "begetting" the world in the beginning.

Throughout the stories, we encounter a complex collection of literary forms. There are myths, such as that of the Flood, that borrow and transform stories from pagan neighbors. There is poetry, and there is narrative prose often suddenly flowing into poetry, as we see in "So God created man in his own image, in the image of God he created him; male and female he created them" (Gn 1:27).

There are long genealogies. Some stories are as long as 230 lines and some, such as the Tower of Babel, as short as 25. There are puzzling tales of deceit, brutality, and incest that the narrator seems to condone and stories in which every rational, democratic bone in us insists that God's behavior has been irrational, inhuman, or unfair.

So here are three things to keep in mind:

1. In the tenth century B.C. the Hebrews' concept of God is beginning to evolve. The story of Abraham is revolutionary in that he leaves Mesopotamia largely because he begins to perceive God as One. For a long while, that One will have the characteristics of a tribal warlord. Only much later will Jesus reveal him as Father and John's Gospel name him Love.

2. The authors do not attempt to portray necessarily good persons, but people who are as weak, mean, and deceitful as ourselves and other people we know. Somehow, through God's intervention, they nonetheless accomplish God's purposes.

3. We should not read these stories through the lens of the Enlightenment or of twentieth-century progress, but as stories told by Middle Eastern nomads for centuries before they were written down. These stories answered questions

for them, such as How did we get here? Why do we suffer? What went wrong? Is there any hope?

The first sin, for example, does not look like a sin to us. Catholic François Mauriac and unbeliever André Gide, both French novelists, were friends in spite of their deep religious differences, and when Gide would visit, they would read aloud to one another, Mauriac reading the creation and Fall from Genesis. They had a problem with the two trees in the Garden and with God's command. Did this mean that God was frightened by man's free will or threatened by the discovery of conscience?

To "eat of the tree of the knowledge of good and evil," as Adam and Eve were forbidden to do, means to know how to make adult decisions for oneself, to achieve autonomy. Today we call that "maturity" and expect every young person to achieve it. The point for the Yahwist writer, however, was that God had drawn a line and to cross it was an act of rebellion. Meanwhile, the point retains its validity for us in a larger sense: we see the human consequences of our collective decision in politics and in social behavior to deny any authority higher than our own.

A better story for our purposes, I think, is Cain's murder of Abel, with his cynical denial that we are our brothers' and sisters' keepers. This first murder flows inevitably from that "first bite of the apple" and leads inexorably to the murder on Calvary, where the forces of corrupt politics and corrupt religion join to destroy Jesus. The powers that be cannot stand the sight of infinite goodness as it is embodied in this bold man.

Some theologians prefer to consider the Crucifixion rather than the Fall in Eden as the "original sin." When we do so, we are less likely to pinpoint the offense in some mythical time and place for which we feel no responsibility. For Pilate and the Sanhedrin, the Crucifixion was just another act of violence in a world indifferent to crime and killing. We condone their act when, in our personal lives and national policies, we treat life as cheap.

The greatest story in Genesis, however, and perhaps the greatest in the Old Testament, is one that frames the book and answers Cain's question. It is the story of Joseph, son of Jacob, who was sold into slavery in Egypt by his brothers. Joseph rises in power in the Pharaoh's court by interpreting the Pharaoh's dreams and confronts his brothers thirteen years later when famine strikes Palestine and they come to Egypt for grain.

Those who feel they have been betrayed by those closest to them and are tormented by this memory, tempted to lick the wound and get even, must read the story of Joseph slowly. Joseph is able to interpret his abandonment by his family as God's providence, sending him to Egypt where he could foresee the famine and store the grain that would feed the world. "I am your brother Joseph" can be seen not just as the turning point of a beautiful story, or as a sublime moment of pre-Christian forgiveness, but as a perfect ending to Genesis and a summary of the social-moral law.

Meanwhile, back around the moon, Anders, having read four lines, passed the text to James Lovell. He read his part and passed it to Frank Borman, who concluded, ". . . and God saw that it was good."

2 The Book of Job

For the typical American, probably no book in the Bible is more foreign than the book of Job. Not that Job's experience is unusual. We need only to read the papers, watch the evening news, or answer a late-night phone call from a friend to see people we know as good, blameless men and women cut down and humiliated at the height of their creative powers. This is not necessarily the result of an unpredictable calamity such as a house fire or an economic "law" such as a business merger, but of injustice—slander at the office, a jealous rival, a malevolent boss. Business associates don't return their phone calls. When they walk into a familiar midtown restaurant, their former friends don't look up from their tables.

Our movie plots always resolve these problems. If it's a Western, the protagonist straps on his gun. If it's New York, he gets a lawyer, played by Sam Waterston, to demolish the villain in court. In an old TV program, *The Equalizer*, the hero was a tough bachelor, a former CIA operative in a trench coat who intervened in cases like these and set things right within an hour. Job, covered with sores and dirt and angry with God, keeps insisting that he has an equalizer—a witness, an umpire, a vindicator, a mediator between God and man who could explain them to each other. But he doesn't. We read Job and it offends our sense of fairness.

The book of Job is like the first chapter of Genesis (and Job is frequently compared to Adam) in that the book attempts to answer the question, Why do these terrible things happen to us?

Genesis offers two answers: the first parents crossed the line Yahweh had drawn, and Cain killed Abel and passed his violence on to all of us. Job says something different.

This story had been circulating since the second millennium B.C. Hebrew writers picked it up between 1,000 and 800 B.C. in a form that included the beginning and end, and later generations added the middle debates between Job and his so-called friends, along with other material. Our text is mostly from the sixth century B.C., during the Babylonian exile. Today's reader should study it in a Bible—such as the Jerusalem Bible or the New Oxford Annotated Bible—that has notes explaining how passages in chapters 24, 26, and 27, attributed to Job, should really be attributed to his friends. The wisdom poem in chapter 28 is probably inserted from somewhere else, and the interventions of a character named Elihu in chapters 32–37 were tacked on later.

There is general agreement that the story of Job as literature is a poetic and dramatic masterpiece. The descriptions burst with vivid imagery of the ancient world—soaring eagles, crumbling mountains, Job's God who can "pour me out like milk and curdle me like cheese" (Jb 10:10). And we recognize often-quoted passages such as the following:

> Naked I came from my mother's womb, and naked shall I return. *(Jb 1:21)*

> The LORD gave, and the LORD has taken away; blessed be the name of the LORD. *(1:21)*

> Man that is born of a woman
> is of few days, and full of trouble.
> He comes forth like a flower, and withers;
> he flees like a shadow, and continues not. *(14:1–2)*

> For I know that my Redeemer lives,
> and at last he will stand upon the earth;
> and after my skin has been thus destroyed,
> then from my flesh I shall see God. *(19:25–26)*

These are powerful lines even out of context, but the drama comes from the complexity of the characters. Job is righteous, but not always right. And his antagonists, presented as his friends, argue some truths though they are ultimately wrong.

As theology, the book of Job exemplifies a primitive, pre-Jewish folk wisdom in which God, in some passages, is the origin of both good and evil. There are only remote hints of ideas such as the afterlife that will distinguish Christianity from its Old Testament origins.

> There was a man in the land of Uz, whose name was Job; and that man was blameless and upright, one who feared God, and turned away from evil. There were born to him seven sons and three daughters. He had seven thousand sheep, three thousand camels, five hundred yoke of oxen, and five hundred she-asses, and very many servants; so that this man was the greatest of all the people of the east.
>
> *(Jb 1:1–3)*

What more could anyone want?

In the heavenly conclave, Satan challenges the Lord. This Satan is better described as an adversary whose job it is to roam the earth and catch wrongdoers than as the Satan who tempts Jesus in the desert or who stars in Milton's *Paradise Lost.* Would Job still love God if his life were not going well? Accepting the wager, the Lord gives Satan permission to test Job. His sons and daughters are killed in fires and battles. He is inflicted with a skin disease, and when he walks into town, everyone turns away.

Job's three friends, Eliphaz, Bildad, and Zophar, come to console him, but as their dialogues progress, they become increasingly antagonistic, offering specious wisdom and pressuring Job to confess that God is right and he is wrong. Job should be more humble and accept God's will. Job is suffering for the sins of his children. Job is a heretic; he is repeating Adam's sin of reaching beyond boundaries God has set. Behold the evidence of God's justice: the evil are punished and the good are rewarded in this life. The three men get nasty and accuse Job of turning his back on the poor, which is an obviously false charge.

Job's replies, laced with irony and sarcasm, also employ the language of the courtroom. He parodies a line from Psalm 8:4, "What is man that thou art mindful of him, and the son of man that thou dost care for him?" suggesting that he'd rather God not "care for him" at all but instead leave him in peace. He pathetically marshals the evidence of his good life—"I was eyes to the blind, and feet to the lame" (Jb 29:15)—and spells out in brutal detail the unpunished crimes and triumphs of the wicked. He rejects his friends' demands that he placate God by confessing to sins he did not commit. In effect, he indicts God but does not repudiate him. As a dramatic character, Job assumes heroic stature by clinging to his integrity no matter what.

How does God reply? In a whirlwind. We can hear his divine bellow across the millennia: "Don't you realize who I am?" The Creator enumerates the glories of his handiwork: the morning stars that sing together; the storehouses of snow and hail; rain that falls on uninhabited lands and deserts; lions and ravens who prey to feed their young; the ox, the ostrich, and the horse that leap like locusts; the hippo with bones like tubes of bronze; and finally, the crown of creation, Leviathan (a crocodile), whose heart is stone, who breathes smoke and fire and fears neither darts nor javelins. Job's only permitted response is, Wow, I didn't know, but "now my eye sees thee; therefore I despise myself, and repent in dust and ashes" (Jb 42:5–6).

But does this satisfy us? Hebrew scholar Moshe Greenberg notes that God's speech reverses the priorities of Genesis and Psalm 104, in which man is the summit and center of God's work. Here man stands offstage. Essayist Cynthia Ozick says that

> the poet, through the whirlwind's answer, stills Job. But can the poet still the Job who lives in us? God's majesty is eternal, manifest in cell and star: yet Job's questions toil on, manifest in death camp and hatred, in tyranny and anthrax, in bomb and bloodshed. Why do the wicked thrive? Why do the innocent suffer?

In an epilogue, Job gets a new family and his prosperity is restored. But does he not still mourn the family he lost? Was it ever right for God to take them away?

The beginnings of an answer would come in about six hundred years. God would change; he would take on flesh in a man who would call him Father and who would suffer more than Job. Unlike Job, we have a Redeemer. But that's another story.

Robert Alter

3   The David Story:
A Translation with Commentary
of 1 and 2 Samuel

1999

I F GENESIS IS SOMEHOW the foundation of our
Judeo-Christian value system, and the story of Joseph its most
inspiring tale, and if Job both goes against our sense of justice
and reminds us of what God's sovereignty might mean, the David
story, the centerpiece of the historical books of Samuel, Kings,
and Chronicles, is both the most captivating and the most trou-
bling. We think we know it because it's a Bible school and
cinema-epics favorite, but to read it slowly, especially with a
commentary, is a very different experience from watching
Gregory Peck or Richard Gere on the screen as David.

The David story, which dates from the sixth century B.C.,
repeats the motifs of Genesis: barren women are informed by a
messenger that they are favored by God to bring forth a savior.
A series of handsome young men, new Adams, taste power and
self-love and choose their own wills over that of their Creator.
The king's sons lust after their father's throne, rebel against him,
and turn on one another. And God, who mysteriously keeps loving his creatures whether they deserve it or not, grants them new
beginnings.

11

We are conditioned by our Jewish and Christian theology to see David as a precursor of the Messiah, with his kingdom as a validation of God's favor. Jesus, the Messiah, is his descendent, the spiritual fulfillment of David's kingdom. Jesus is both like and unlike David. When Jesus enters Jerusalem as king on Palm Sunday with only a week to live, he is to restore the rule that began when David took Jerusalem.

But to read the David story cold, without the thousand-years-later reassurances of church fathers that God was at work, is a shock. It is an ugly story. There are moments of reconciliation and magnanimity, such as when David, at war, comes across the sleeping Saul in his camp at night and declines to put a spear through him. For the most part, however, the whole cast—Samuel, Saul, David, and their sons and courtiers—are ruthless, clever climbers, master politicians, their antennae alert to the voices of the crowds. Their battered consciences dictate how long this opponent may be allowed to live, how quickly that one must die.

In literature, they are characters in Shakespeare's *Richard III* or *Othello*; in popular culture, they are out of *The Godfather* series or *The Sopranos*, particularly as the aged king David plots killings on his deathbed.

The story unfolds in the years right before and after 1,000 B.C., when the Israelites, threatened by raiding parties of Philistines from the coastal plain as well as by the Ammonites to the east, gradually centralized their government and called for a king to rule them, just as their enemies had done. The books of Samuel are based on generations of sources, some of which may go back to the participants themselves. A group of Deuteronomist theologians probably edited these and other historical books after the end of the Babylonian exile in 538 B.C. The diversity of the sources shows in the tension between two major themes: demanding a king was a bad idea because it went against the Lord's original plan that He alone rule Israel; yet, the Lord loved David in spite of his sins and blessed Israel through the leadership of David and his son Solomon.

The story line is more or less familiar. Samuel, son of Hannah, who had been barren, leads Israel as the Lord's prophet and judge, but against his warning, the people demand a king.

Guided by the Lord, Samuel finds and anoints Saul, who proves himself in battle and is acclaimed. Saul loses the Lord's favor and God sends Samuel to anoint David, who kills Goliath and enters Saul's court as a harpist to calm his wild moods. Saul's son Jonathan befriends David. David becomes a popular hero as he defeats the Philistines, but a jealous Saul wants him killed. To escape Saul, David joins the Philistines for a year but does not raid Israel. David passes up opportunities to kill Saul. The Philistines dismiss David, who leads an Israelite force to defeat the Amalekites, while Saul and Jonathan are killed in battle by the Philistines. David becomes king and transfers the Ark of the Covenant to Jerusalem, the new capital. He arranges for Bathsheba's husband to die in battle so he can have her as his eighth wife. Their first son dies, then the Lord replaces him with Solomon. David's son Ammon rapes his half-sister, Tamar; Ammon's brother Absolom kills Ammon and leads a revolt against their father, driving him into exile. Absolom is killed and David mourns. In 1 Kings 1 and 2, David proclaims Solomon king, blocking the ambition of Adonijah, son of another wife. Solomon arranges the deaths of his rivals and prepares to build the temple.

Robert Alter, professor of Hebrew and comparative literature at the University of California, Berkeley, in his translation of and commentary on 1 and 2 Samuel and through his literary criticism, opens up rich possibilities that the ancient text implies but does not make explicit.

For example, in 1 Samuel, Saul dies by throwing himself on his sword; in 2 Samuel, a young Amalekite reports to David that he came upon a wounded Saul after the battle and "finished him off" at Saul's request. These stories do not come from separate sources, says Alter; the young man is lying. He was looting the bodies, found Saul's corpse, and brought Saul's regalia to David expecting a reward. Ironically, Saul had lost the Lord's favor years before because he had defied the Lord's command to take no prisoners when he spared the Amalekite king; now he is asking an Amalekite to kill him. David responds by ordering the Amalekite killed for having destroyed "the Lord's anointed" (1 Sm 1:14–15). Whether or not David believes the story, this pious declaration allows David to disassociate himself from Saul's death and then to assume status himself as "the Lord's anointed," with a warning to those who might threaten him.

Alter is sensitive to poignant lines that even the careful reader might miss. Saul had given his daughter Michal to David as his first wife, then taken her back and given her to a man named Paltiel. To buttress his claim to rule all Israel, David sends Abner to bring her back: "But her husband went with her, weeping after her all the way to Bahu'rim. Then Abner said to him, 'Go, return'; and he returned" (2 Sm 3:16).

Alter writes:

> There is scarcely a more striking instance of the evocative com-pactness of biblical narrative. We know almost nothing about Paltiel. He speaks not a word of dialogue. Yet his walking after Michal, weeping all the while, intimates a devoted love that stands in contrast to David's relationship with her. Paltiel is a man whose fate is imposed on him. Michal was given to him by Saul, evidently without his initiative. He came to love her. Now he must give her up and, confronted by Saul's strong man with the peremptory order to go back, he has no choice but to go back.

We get an idea later how Michal feels about this when she repri-mands David. As the Ark is brought in procession into Jerusalem, David dances nine-tenths naked before the Ark and "exposes himself" to the servant girls in the crowd. David replies that he'll dance any way he wants. We are told that after this, Michal had no children with David, but we don't know whether David was pun-ishing Michal (or vice versa!) or God was punishing David.

Alter analyzes Ammon's rape of Tamar in all its ugly brutality. On one level, it parallels the rape stories in Genesis, though it reverses the episode in the Joseph story in which Joseph resists the advances of an Egyptian woman. On another level, it is the logical consequence of David's seduction of Bathsheba and is the next stage, after the death of Bathsheba's first child, of his pun-ishment for murdering her husband Uriah. Ammon is behaving like his father, who, because of his own guilt, will not punish him, but will helplessly watch the curse spread through his household.

Absolom becomes the avenger and later dies, yanked from his horse when his beautiful long hair gets caught in a tree branch, and his father's soldiers riddle him with their spears as he dangles there.

Alter observes that we see how David changes through his responses to the deaths of those close to him.

> Now the eloquent David is reduced to a sheer stammer of grief, repeating over and over again the two Hebrew words for "my son, Absolom." The narrator continues to refer to David only as "the king," but in the shifting conflict between the public and private roles, the latter takes over here entirely. Absolom is not the usurper who drove him from the throne but only "my son," and David is the anguished father who would rather have died, that his son might have lived.

Three thousand years later, the American Constitution separated church and state, but political life and "civic religion" nevertheless have merged the roles of president and moral leader in the same person. We debate whether or not the president's personal life has any relevance to his political leadership. The authors of 1 and 2 Samuel tell us that David slaughtered all the men, women, and children when he captured a town, and that his personal, sexual sins led to murder and precipitated the destruction of his family and another string of killings. And that he was a great king—for Israel.

15

4 The Gospel of Luke

C. A.D. 80

Though the first three Gospels, called the synoptics because they share most of the same sources, are so similar that for long passages the scenes and words are almost exactly the same, each of the three has charms and a character of its own.

Mark skips the infancy narratives and has Jesus the grown man, with power over sickness and demons, get right to work. Matthew, writing for Jewish converts, portrays Jesus as the new Moses, his Sermon on the Mount the new law for the kingdom. And the fourth Gospel, John, is an awesome blending of neoplatonism, with its poetic "In the beginning was the Word" prologue; its prayerful mysticism, in Jesus' farewell discourse at the Last Supper; and its high drama, as in the story of the man born blind and Jesus' confrontation with Pilate. Is there a moment in human history to match the tension and the consequences of Pilate's question, "What is truth?" If so, it's the scene of Pilate washing his hands and saying, "I find no fault in this man"—then sending him to his death. The same mind-set and variations on the formula have survived the centuries, reenacted every time a bureaucrat knows he is witnessing an injustice but lacks the guts to intervene: "I'd like to help you, but my hands are tied."

If I had to choose a "desert island" Gospel, however, it would be Luke. Perhaps I could get permission to take some commentaries along, too, such as Joseph Fitzmyer's definitive two-volume contribution to the Anchor Bible series, or G. B. Caird's beautifully written 1964 Penguin paperback, or Luke Timothy Johnson's 1991 volume in the scholarly and pastoral Sacra Pagina edition.

Why would I pick Luke? A Jesuit theater director told me that Luke, rather than John, is the most dramatic because it has the most human feeling, the best stories. Also, its many themes include three that are especially pertinent to today's social needs: the role of women in the church, the widening gulf between the rich and the poor, and the need for forgiveness and reconciliation in personal and international relations.

Scripture scholars offer several theories on the origins of this two-volume work that includes the Acts of the Apostles and is unified by the author's style and theme. It was composed around A.D 80. and addressed to Theophilus ("Lover of God"), who may be a Roman official, Luke's patron, or a symbolic name encompassing all his readers.

One purpose is to present a sympathetic portrait of Christianity to the Roman world following the persecution of Nero, who blamed the A.D. 64 burning of Rome on the Christians. Thus the Christianity of Luke is not a foreign superstition but a world religion, founded not by a revolutionary but an innocent, compassionate teacher and prophet, a messianic actor in a providential plan.

Luke presents himself as a historian. He is not a detached twenty-first century historian with access to archives, newspaper reports, oral histories, audio- and videotapes, and computer records. He is a believer with reports that, he says, can be traced to eyewitnesses. This is not out of the question. The New Testament events were about as distant from Luke's writing as today is from World War II. I did not witness World War I, but I can testify to some degree about the reality of General Pershing because my father, who served under him, told me stories that were true.

Luke's main sources, however, were Mark, for about half his material; "Q," a collection of texts shared by Matthew and Luke; and Luke's independent sources. These gave him the infancy narratives (mostly ahistorical meditations on Old Testament texts) and the parables—such as the rich fool, Lazarus and Dives, the good Samaritan, and the lost son—that by themselves, even for unbelievers, make the Gospel immortal literature.

Luke is a historian with a purpose. He wants to make Christianity acceptable to Gentile authorities and also to show that Jesus' mission was a necessary fulfillment of a divine plan predicted by Old Testament prophets and fulfilled in the person of Jesus. He wants us to see history as a straight line leading from Adam through the prophets to Jesus, culminating in what looks like tragedy until we, like the disciples on the road to Emmaus after the Resurrection, allow Jesus to say to us,

"Oh foolish men, and slow of heart to believe all that the prophets have spoken! Was it not necessary that the Christ should suffer these things and enter into his glory?" And beginning with Moses and all the prophets, he interpreted to them in all the scriptures the things concerning himself.

(Lk 24:25–27)

Pastorally, this is also a suggestion to contemporary Christians to understand the ordeals that they experience in the context of Christ's life.

As a storyteller, Luke also structures his narrative dynamically in several ways. To emphasize Jesus' and Christianity's continuity with the Old Testament, he begins and ends the Gospel in the temple. We begin with the priest Zechariah, father of John the Baptist, who hesitates to accept the angel's message that his wife Elizabeth will give birth. Then Mary and Joseph bring the child Jesus to the temple and hear the prophecies of Simeon and Anna about their child, "set for the fall and rising of many in Israel" (Lk 2:34). We watch the adolescent Jesus who remains in the temple to discuss "his Father's business." Finally, after the resurrection, the apostles are "continually in the temple blessing God" (Lk 24:53).

The Acts of the Apostles recounts the apostles' and Paul's journeys and sufferings and the miraculous spread of the faith through the Mediterranean world. The book seems to end inconclusively with Paul's arrival in Rome, but it is a fitting conclusion for Luke the Gentile internationalist. Rome, unlike Jerusalem, is the center of the "modern" world. Clearly, if there is a world beyond Rome, the faith will go there too.

Which Lucan themes speak to us today? All, of course. Some find in Luke's attention to women's roles arguments for the ordination of women. Theologians who speculate on the "priesthood" of Mary must draw on Luke. Luke's stories burst with interesting and assertive women characters: Elizabeth; Mary, whose Magnificat extols a God who has "put down the mighty from their thrones, and exalted those of low degree" (Lk 1:52); Anna the prophetess; the women of Galilee who support Jesus in his travels; the widow of Naim with her dead son; the sinner who pours perfume on Jesus' feet; the audacious woman with the flow of blood; the dead daughter of Jairus; Mary and Martha; the woman bent double whom Jesus straightens up on the Sabbath; the widow who badgers the judge; the women at the cross and at the tomb.

Like today, the women have a variety of roles. They are vulnerable because they lack social status and support; they are courageous individuals who see something in Jesus that others don't; they are the first witnesses to the Resurrection. In Acts, they are indispensable to the organization and spread of the church.

Second, as Luke Timothy Johnson points out, in Luke "the rich" stand for those in society who have had their consolation already and have no need of God's consolation. The poor are those who have been rejected by human standards, but are accepted by God. These include those who are crippled, lame, blind, deaf, sinners, and tax agents. Jesus the prophet proclaims the "great reversal," in which the poor Lazarus, who ate scraps from the rich man's table and whose sores the dogs licked at the rich man's doorstep, will be in "Abraham's bosom," while the rich man boils in hell.

As this is written, America enjoys an unparalleled prosperity. There are so many millionaires that, to those hooked on quiz shows and lotteries, a million dollars is no longer considered a lot of money. But the Lazaruses have multiplied and sprawl—with all their belongings in a plastic bag or in a shopping cart—in city parks, on church steps, and on subway platforms.

As this is written, Israel is deciding whether to withdraw from the Golan Heights to achieve peace with Syria, Northern Ireland is waiting for the IRA and the RUC to disarm in order to secure the peace agreement, and an American presidential election is drawn into a dispute over the fate of a six-year-old Cuban boy whose mother drowned while trying to bring him to the United States and whose father wants him returned to Cuba.

Luke's two greatest parables, the good Samaritan and the prodigal son, are both about the obligation to escape the past, to break out of categories imposed by national borders and inherited memories of past wars. They invite us to think about our personal crises in terms other than just those of our tribe, our religion, or our wounds that must be licked. They give us an opportunity to think of old enemies as brothers, rescuers, and friends.

5   The Gospel of John

C. A.D. 100

I<small>F</small> L<small>UKE IS THE</small> G<small>OSPEL</small> that we might take to a desert island, then perhaps John is the one we should take on one of those "long retreats," such as the thirty days of St. Ignatius's Spiritual Exercises, in which the goal is twofold: deep penetration into the life of Jesus, so that we may, through the eyes of the imagination, see him in action and so be drawn to him as a person; and, as a consequence, achieve that feeling of love that lifts us into contemplative prayer. This implies that, as compared to Luke, in which the classic parables, such as the good Samaritan and the prodigal son, sweep us right in, John demands more work.

This is true. Although it shares some basic content with the other three Gospels—John the Baptist, the calling of the disciples, the cleansing of the temple (John puts it at the beginning of the public ministry rather than at the end), the miracle of the loaves (John follows it with the "I am the bread of life" discourse), the Last Supper (without the institution of the Eucharist), the Passion and Resurrection—John seems to have written his narrative without depending on the others. He has added a complex literary structure based on a series of seven "signs"—changing water into wine at Cana, curing the official's son, curing the crippled man at the pool of Bethzatha, feeding the five thousand, healing the man born blind, raising Lazarus, and finally Jesus' death and resurrection. Each event builds on the other, fulfilling John's purpose that we believe that Jesus is the Messiah.

John has also added richly symbolic themes, such as the conflict between light and darkness; God's presence as symbolized by running water, which theologians would later call grace; and the relationship between seeing and believing. The most powerful theme in both the Gospel and in John's epistles is the relationship between love of God and love of one another. To look at Jesus as a flesh-and-blood person and to love him is the same as loving God. To love a friend or a spouse or a family member is the same as loving God, for God can be present to us only in flesh; and, outside of mystical prayer, God's most ready means of communication to us is through human love.

John masterfully uses ironic language throughout his work in which the words mean not the opposite of what is said but rather much more. In cryptic dialogues, Jesus' interlocutors ask what seem to be "stupid" questions so that Jesus can instruct us by correcting them; or they say much more than they mean so we readers can leap to an insight that the Gospel character, because of his blindness or lack of faith, cannot see.

For example, Jesus tells the woman at the well that he can give her "living water." In context, this means both literal running water and a union in faith with himself and the Father. She replies that she wants this because then she won't have to carry her bucket to the well. Pilate, during Jesus' trial, cynically asks, "What is truth?" as if, in a political quarrel, facts are irrelevant because expediency alone matters, or as if, in the modern philosophical sense, absolute knowledge about reality were impossible. Yet John's readers, because they are believers, see Jesus standing before this unbeliever as the embodiment of the eternal Truth, Way, and Life. At the Last Supper, Philip, after having listened to Jesus' long discourse about his union with the Father, says, "Show us the Father" (Jn 14:8). The reader wants to scream: "Philip, you idiot! Haven't you been paying attention to anything? Has the wine dulled your brain? You are looking at the Father."

Stylistically, John has two other distinguishing characteristics: there are some marvelous "sign" stories that are more complex in purpose than the healings in the synoptics, such as the man born blind and the raising of Lazarus; and there are long, abstract, philosophical passages meant to represent Jesus' deepest consciousness of his mission. In some, he is depicted as debating the "Jews," who demand to know who he thinks he is; in some he speaks directly to the Father as if in prayer. In the longest, at the Last Supper, he explains the relationship between the Father, himself, and the Holy Spirit, called the Paraclete, who will make Jesus forever present to the church following his death, resurrection, and ascension.

These passages, historically, make John the most "theological" Gospel, in that they form the foundation of the doctrine of the Incarnation as it was formulated almost four hundred years later at the ecumenical councils of Ephesus (A.D. 431) and Chalcedon (A.D 451) and of the Trinity at Nicea in A.D. 325.

The disputes with the "Jews," who appear throughout the Gospel as Jesus' antagonists and as responsible in large part for his death, have in recent years raised questions about John's so-called anti-Semitism. Some therefore resist using John in the liturgy or assume the authority to change the wording of the text so it won't seem "offensive." A better approach, it seems to me, is to properly understand the text and the author's intention so that the integrity of the text is preserved and the apparent offense is removed.

Francis J. Maloney, S.D.B., Foundation Professor of Theology at Australian Catholic University, Melbourne, suggests in his *Sacra Pagina* commentary on John that we distinguish between the *real* reader, ourselves, and the *intended* reader, the community of Christians in A.D. 100, perhaps in Ephesus. These early Christians had a background and problems that we know nothing about but that the text was intended to address.

Imagine that we pick up a letter off the street and read it. We can deduce certain things about the writer and the receiver, but it wasn't written with us in mind. John's community was a loose-knit group, mostly of Jews, who through study and discussion—and the possible influence of new members in the group, of Platonism, the Essenes, and certainly the Old Testament—were moving into a larger world. They came to the realization that Jesus was the Messiah, and as a result were excluded from the synagogue. This was a decisive blow. Most of them were Jews who, like most early Christians, still prayed in the temple. But now the term "Jews" in John's Gospel meant not the Jewish people but the antagonists of the Jewish Christians. That anti-Semites later misused the Gospel is one of the great crimes and tragedies of human history, but their crime should not seal us off from the real John.

For an example of many of these themes, let's look at John 9:1–38, the story of the man born blind.

At the Jerusalem temple for the Feast of the Tabernacles, Jesus and his disciples encounter a young beggar blind from birth. The disciples ask whether his blindness resulted from his sin or from that of his parents, a typical instance in which the disciples' misunderstanding gives Jesus a chance to set them straight. The blindness is an opportunity for Jesus to do God's work. Then Jesus utters two of those sentences typical of John that, even removed from the context, are so beautiful (in an older translation) that they take on a life of their own: "Night comes, when no one can work" and "I am the light of the world" (Jn 9:4, 5).

Jesus anoints the man's eyes with a paste of mud and spit and sends him to wash in the pool of Siloam ("which means Sent," adds the narrator in verse 7). Thus Jesus is identified again with living water, as the Messiah, and as the light that he has given to the man. The Pharisees hear of this and are angry that Jesus has cured on the Sabbath. The Jewish leaders argue that the man was not really blind and confront his parents. They affirm he was blind from birth, but as to how he was cured they say, "Ask him; he is of age, he will speak for himself" (Jn 9:21).

The narrator explains: "His parents said this because they feared the Jews, for the Jews had already agreed that if any one should confess him to be Christ, he was to be put out of the synagogue" (Jn 9:22). In this scene, the first-century readers deal with the divisions within the Jewish-Christian community.

When the Pharisees interrogate the young man, he responds, "Why do you want to hear it again? Do you too want to become his disciples?" (Jn 9:27). But it becomes clear in their dialogue that the Pharisees are blind, whereas the man who was blind sees the truth they have refused to consider.

But enough of this exegesis. There is an ancient tradition that the author of John's Gospel is John, the brother of James, both sons of the fisherman Zebedee. John is also the "beloved disciple" who rests his head on Jesus' breast at the Last Supper. He stands beneath the cross, arrives first at the tomb, and recognizes Jesus by the lake in Galilee after the Resurrection. Scholars now reject that identification. The point of the tradition is still valid: the man who loved Jesus the most is best qualified to tell us what and who he was—and is.

6 The Confessions

c. 398–400

Today, in the popular mind, St. Augustine and his *Confessions* are a hard sell.

To some critics, Augustine's negative attitude toward sexual activity, springing from a reaction to what he saw as his own overindulgence in sex as a youth, has imposed a pessimistic pall on Christian moral theology for centuries. As a result, some see Christianity as stuck with a tradition that is antiflesh, antisex, antiwoman, and antihuman.

From another point of view, today's younger generation has been sexually experienced since adolescence; goes through stages of skepticism, alienation, and searching before making a religious commitment; and accepts the idea of couples living together for years before marriage.

Augustine, of course, was carried away by lust during adolescence; went through stages of skepticism, alienation, and searching before accepting baptism; and lived with the same partner for nine years, having a son with her before his mother, who was arranging a respectable marriage for him, broke them up.

To approach Augustine as so foreign to our experience that he cannot speak to this generation would be to shut ourselves off from one of the great geniuses of Western thought and his fundamental psychological insights into "fallen" human nature and God's initiative—grace—that catches us as we are about to fall off a cliff. It is also possible, during an age in which film and TV take it for granted that sex is merely one more form of relaxation—like a beer or a cigarette—that Augustine might know something we don't.

First, it helps to see what a "book" was in the pre-Gutenberg fifth century. A scholar penned a manuscript that scribes copied and circulated. Thus, throughout the *Confessions* there is a theme of characters picking up "books," usually the Scriptures, being struck by a passage, and changing their lives to conform to what they have read. But for the most part, reading was a communal experience. Chapters from the *Confessions* would circulate as pamphlets. They would be read aloud at gatherings of Christian intellectuals, debated, memorized, spread through the "world" in conversation, and drift back to the author ten years later, in case he wanted to modify what he had said.

Augustine, who spent his last years revising his sermons and other works, was content with the *Confessions* as they were. In 397, at the age of forty-three, he had spent a year as bishop of Hippo (now Annaba, Algeria) while he was both sick and settling squabbles in his diocese, with pen in hand. He had been a Christian for only ten years and a priest—ordained almost by acclamation—for six. He probably saw himself as, above all, a writer—perhaps similar to the contemporary role of "public intellectual"—someone with insights he must spread to as wide a public as possible.

Although some call the *Confessions* the "West's first autobiography," it defies categorization. Garry Wills, in his biography of Augustine, renames this book the *Testimony*. This is a better name if we imagine a confessor as a criminal or a penitent on his knees pouring out his sins, whereas Augustine is standing tall, testifying to the power of grace. Of course many autobiographies, such as *The Autobiography of Malcolm X* and that of the Chicago social pioneer Jane Addams, *Twenty Years at Hull House*, are testimonies in answer to the question, How did you get to be the great person you are today? But Augustine's structure is more complex than this.

The text is in the genre of a prayer. Augustine addresses himself to God. In the first paragraph he says, "You arouse us so that praising you may bring us joy, because you have made us and drawn us to yourself, and our heart is restless until it rests in you." He weaves the texts of the Psalms and Prophets so naturally into his prose, several times on a page, that we do not distinguish between his words and those of Scripture. But his real audience is us, the small groups of believers in Hippo, Rome, Milan—or today in Scarsdale, Rockville Centre, Alexandria, Santa Barbara, Kansas City, or New Orleans—who will listen to these episodes and see in them our own experience.

A copper-skinned Numidian, Augustine was born in 354 in Thagaste, Algeria, of a pagan father, Patricius, and a Berber Christian mother, Monica. He had one brother and one sister, both younger than himself. Augustine was lucky to have a father who, though neither rich nor faithful, made sacrifices to get him a good classical Latin education. As a student in Carthage, he fell in with a gang called the "wreckers" and tried to compete with his peers for sexual adventures though he steered clear of their violence. He describes going to the theater as an immoral indulgence—perhaps an insight into the way a fourth-century audience entered into the "reality" of a performance, whereas a contemporary audience is too satiated to be shocked.

Not baptized, Augustine drifted from one belief—Manichaeanism, astrology, Ciceronian philosophy, Neoplatonism—to another. To make a career of teaching rhetoric, he moved from Thagaste to Carthage to Rome to Milan, with his widowed mother—who was determined that her prayers would one day lead to his baptism—in pursuit. God's instrument—for Augustine saw everyone and everything as either God's instrument or his reflection—was the famous Bishop Ambrose, whose Sunday sermons so elucidated the Scriptures and explained the church's teaching that for the first time Augustine began to see the Catholic faith as intellectually respectable. Augustine and his friends would sometimes visit Ambrose just to watch him read, silently, with his eyes traveling across the page of words feeding his mind.

The incident is significant in that it illuminates a theme in the *Confessions*—the power of the book to accomplish God's will. Indeed, the well-known story of Augustine's conversion involves three books. There are stories within stories of young men picking up books of the Epistles or books on the life of the Egyptian monk St. Anthony that challenge them to face a truth from which they have fled. Augustine's prayer had been, "Grant me chastity and self control, but please not yet" (p. 159). The story of two men who, inspired by Anthony's monasticism, gave up their plans to marry threw him into a nosedive. Why could he not muster the same courage?

Since 371, when he was seventeen, Augustine had maintained a faithful sexual relationship with a woman who bore them a son named Adeodatus, "God's gift." When Monica arrived in Milan in 385, however, she induced Augustine to send his lover, who was below his social station, back to Africa, leaving the boy behind. Monica's intention was that a more suitable marriage be arranged, but as soon as his lover was gone, rather than be celibate, Augustine found another woman to satisfy his desires. Somehow he had to break out of what he termed the slavery of lust.

In the garden by his house, he fell under a fig tree and burst into tears. As he prayed, "Oh Lord, how long?" he heard a child's voice singing, "Pick it up and read. Pick it up and read." He remembered the story of Anthony being inspired by the line, "Go and sell all you possess and give the money to the poor." He rushed into the house, picked up Paul's Epistles, opened to Romans 13:13–14, and read: "Not in reveling and drunkenness, not in debauchery and licentiousness, not in quarreling and jealousy. But put on the Lord Jesus Christ, and make no provision for the flesh, to gratify its desires." He rushed to tell his mother he had broken free.

Augustine was baptized by Ambrose along with Adeodatus and Augustine's friend Alypius. He gave up teaching to return to Africa and found a monastic community. Within a year, his mother died at age fifty-six, and three years later, his seventeen-year-old son died.

The actual *Confessions* end in Book IX with the author mourning his mother's death though she has been gone for ten years. Book X is a psychological-moral analysis of memory and of the three concupiscences of flesh, eyes, and pride with which he struggles. Books XI–XIII deal with philosophical questions such as the definition of time (What was God doing before he made heaven and earth?) and with an allegorical interpretation of the Book of Genesis.

The Confessions is more accessible if we have read a short biography of Augustine first. Rebecca West's 1933 study grants that Augustine is "one of the greatest of all writers," who has told his story with "an unsurpassed truthfulness." This does not mean that everything happened the way Augustine has told it. West points out that Augustine does not mention his brother or sister and that he is coolly silent about his father, who was not baptized until his deathbed. She calls Monica "a smooth cliff of a woman on whom the breakers of a man's virility would dash in vain." West finds it odd that, knowing the church favored infant baptism, Monica did not have Augustine baptized as a child; she concludes that the mother did not want her son to become an adult. She finds it horrible that Monica could engineer the separation of a mother and her child and later achieve the status of sainthood.

Garry Wills's *Saint Augustine* puts the idea that Augustine was a sexually obsessed pessimist in perspective. Much of this image came from Augustine's controversies, as bishop of Hippo, with the heretic Pelagius on the reality of original sin. Augustine knew that original sin was real both from Scripture and from his observation that something was "kinky or askew," as Wills puts it, in human nature. Wills cites G. K. Chesterton's observation that we see original sin at work on that lovely summer afternoon when bored children start torturing a cat. For Augustine, original sin was not sexual; sex was part of a good human nature. It's just that Augustine knew from experience that the sexual urge often seemed to have a life of its own.

It is interesting that Augustine's severe judgments on himself made him more understanding of sinners than either his contemporaries or today's politicians seem to be. He opposed capital punishment because we never know what future use God may have of sinners who repent. In the long run, as his many other writings attest, particularly his sermons and his personal history, he should be remembered as a great lover.

He was always surrounded by friends, and he poured himself out through his pen so that they—and we—could learn how God loves us all. He died August 28, 430, surrounded by bishops and refugees who had fled to Hippo, a fortified town, to escape the Vandals, Arian Christians who were raping and burning their way across Africa.

I began by calling St. Augustine a "hard sell." Yet the students in class told me recently that Dorothy Day's *The Long Loneliness* reminded them most of Augustine's *Confessions*. Day tells us in the first page that "going to confession is hard." But both confess to us because they want us to see what grace can accomplish— even when we resist.

7   Inferno

C. 1310−1314

I N EXISTENTIALIST PHILOSOPHER Jean-Paul Sartre's play *No Exit,* a man and two women are trapped permanently in one room, incapable of really knowing or loving one another, each just an object in the others' eyes. They are dead. They are in hell, and their hell is "other people."

What we know—or what the church teaches—about hell can be put in a few words: It exists; it lasts forever. It is for those who have freely chosen to be there by deliberately turning their backs on God's love. Whether there is actually anyone there or not, we may never know.

Yet the concept of hell sometimes seems right, largely because we all know or have read about people who we are sure belong there. Potential residents might include twentieth-century incarnations of absolute evil—Hitler, Stalin, Pol Pot—or some person who has injured us so grievously that only his or her damnation would satisfy our need for justice or revenge. Preachers, retreat masters, poets, novelists, and medieval painters have filled the void in the public imagination—they both terrify and thrill us by depicting the deserved sufferings of the damned.

Nevertheless, in the twenty-first century—where suffering can range from a slow death by AIDS that would make hell, or at least purgatory, superfluous, to losing a child in a drive-by shooting—the idea of eternal fire does not catch hold. We already have enough on our minds.

The image of hades, an "underworld" abode of the dead, is strong in ancient Greek and Roman mythology, in which heroes like Odysseus and Aeneas survive the ordeal of a visit. For the Jews, who did not have a fully developed idea of immortality, Sheol was a gloomy realm where all the dead, good and evil, lived on.

Some theologians have substituted the idea of annihilation for eternal punishment. The bad person, at death, would simply cease to exist; and because the immortality of the soul is a Platonic rather than a Judeo-Christian idea, the good person would receive from God the gift of eternal life.

But the twenty-first-century mind needs Dante's *Divine Comedy*, specifically its first volume, the *Inferno*, because Dante's moral vision often contradicts ours and makes us rethink the way we view the world. The Library of Congress lists 2,878 books on Dante, the ninth-largest number on any one person. Critics choosing the books of the millennium for the *Times Literary Supplement* say that the *Inferno* is the "greatest of cathedrals, with better gargoyles, and its towers are taller than the world." It "sheds light on every other work of literature written in the West, before and after."

Dante began to write the *Divine Comedy* in his midthirties, the same age as Augustine when he began *The Confessions* and James Joyce when he began *Ulysses.* Joyce's brothels, pub toilets, and committee rooms draw inspiration from Dante's hell, and whatever our objections to their portrayals, we keep reading because Job did not answer our questions as to why the unjust thrive. We have lived with lust, greed, gluttony, anger, and treason and are more than curious about their consequences.

Thirteenth-century Florence was a prosperous city-state. It was at war with its neighbors and a battleground for competing local factions, the Guelf (papal) and Ghibelline (imperial) parties. Dante's grandfather and father were urban nobility, moneylenders, and Guelfs. The father married again after Dante's mother's death, and Dante grew up with an older sister, a half-brother, and a half-sister. As a young man, he was first of all a poet-scholar. His early poetic work was inspired, he said, by the image of Beatrice, a young girl he had seen once as a boy and who, if she has been correctly identified, died in 1290. Some scholars doubt she existed, but Dante projected her as a font of metaphysical knowledge and in the *Divine Comedy* makes her his ultimate guide through the *Paradiso* and into God's presence.

After her death, Dante turned to reading both the classical masters—such as Aristotle, Cicero, and Virgil—and the Christian theologians—St. Augustine, St. Bonaventure, and St. Thomas Aquinas. He also got involved in politics, at great cost. In 1301, Dante was a leader in the White, or moderate, faction of the Guelf party. While he was out of town on a diplomatic mission, a coalition of Black Guelfs, Pope Boniface VIII, and Charles of Valois, brother of the king of France, captured Florence, put their enemies on trial, convicted Dante in absentia of graft, and condemned him to death when he couldn't pay the fine. He spent the rest of his life, until his death at fifty-six, exiled from his beloved city.

Dante began the *Inferno* in 1308 and finished it in 1312, to be followed by *Purgatorio* and *Paradiso*. The *Inferno* is many things: a synthesis of secular classical and Christian lore; Dante's own ethical vision, based on Aristotle, Cicero, and Thomas Aquinas, which he thought could renew humanity; an allegorical epic poem modeled on Virgil's *Aeneid*; a highly personal tract in which he settles scores with Florentine foes by placing them in hell; and finally, the story of the artist's journey, in midlife, into the depths of his own soul and of his emergence as a cleansed pilgrim. It is thus a challenge to every reader, written centuries before the dis-covery of the allegedly frightening secrets of the unconscious, to face the hellish aspects of his or her own personality.

The reader might begin by visiting the library shelves and pag-ing through the great variety of translations, including several new in the last few years. Some editions include the Italian on the fac-ing page, some are richly illustrated—with either abstract designs or fantastic attempts to make Dante's dreamlike journey real.

Consider the magnificent 1867 engravings of Gustave Doré, originally commissioned to illustrate the Henry Wadsworth Longfellow text, in which the nude, muscular souls squirm in pain, push giant boulders uphill, drown in the river Styx, crawl out of burning graves, metamorphose into serpents and trees, wallow in mud and excrement up to their mouths, and sprawl on the ground with their chests ripped open, their arms and legs chopped off, and their severed heads in their hands. We can understand why at one point Virgil warns Dante to discipline his curious gaze.

With Virgil as guide, we follow Dante down through the nine pits, from limbo—abode of the unbaptized just that Jesus visited after his crucifixion to liberate Adam, Eve, Abraham, and Moses—through each species of sin, from sins of lust that are least serious because they are personal and influenced by passion, to those that affect the community and are therefore most grave. The first level, therefore, is for the mere cowards, "those who lived without disgrace and without praise" (canto iii), including Pope Celestine V who was elected in 1294 at eighty but resigned after five months, under the influence of Boniface VIII, who succeeded him. Dante has no qualms about damning popes. Nicholas III is there for simony, and spots are being saved for Boniface, who died in 1303, and Clement V, the Avignon pope who died in 1314.

Among the violent, Attila the Hun swims in a river of boiling blood. But the suicides suffer even more. Their souls, separated from their bodies, are imprisoned in trees on which Harpies feed, perpetuating their pain. Then their bodies are hung on the branches, ugly reminders of the life they threw away. Among the sodomites, chained to one another in threes, Dante encounters his old teacher and addresses him with due respect. On the eighth level, among the frauds and submerged in boiling pitch, he meets the barrators (grafters), who have committed the crime of which he had been unjustly accused.

The most poignant encounter is with Homer's Ulysses. His sin, "fraudulent counsel," is one of the worst since he used his high intelligence to deceive and thus wasted his human greatness. Because he wanted to experience the world, he neglected his father, wife, and son. Surely Dante must have seen in him a potential mirror of himself. And isn't this the twenty-first-century sin: the ambitious lawyer, broker, artist, or politician who, to "have it all," leaves his or her friends and family behind?

Finally, the greatest sinners, the traitors, do not burn but freeze. They are encased in ice, utterly isolated, with the giant

Satan, king of hell, buried in ice to his waist. Satan has three faces, and in each mouth he grinds one of the three worst traitors in history—Brutus and Cassius, who betrayed the Roman state, and Judas, who betrayed the church. We see now that the fundamental ethical theme of the poem is the unity of church and state. To Dante, this means the unity of the human community against all those forces—petty crimes, exploitative money-lending, corrupt popes—that would weaken the fabric that makes us one.

We can and should argue with the *Inferno* line by line, but not shrink from those lines in which we recognize ourselves.

Michael Walsh, editor

8 Butler's Lives of the Saints, Concise Edition

1991

O NE OF THE LESSONS we might draw from the extraordinary outpouring of emotion following the deaths of Britain's Princess Diana and America's John Kennedy Jr. is the profound yearning in at least part of the public for symbolic figures with whom they imagine they can identify. Consumer culture and the communications revolution, however, have eradicated the distinction between the hero—one who, at personal sacrifice, has done great deeds for the people—and the celebrity, who is simply well-known for being well-known. As an example of how the precise use of language has deteriorated, one TV commentator loosely referred to both Princess Di and Mother Teresa, who died a week later, as "saints."

Saints have always been heroes, men and women who love God and their fellow men and women so much that they give up wealth, power, fame—everything that most people think is important—to demonstrate that love.

In time, the public, through their prayers, and the official church, through its demanding canonization process, declare these people worthy of our emulation. This process, however, has changed through the centuries. In the twentieth century, scientific historical criticism has been applied to hagiography to distinguish among several literary forms—legends, myths, tales, and

37

fables—to peel away what the pious imagination has added and to discover, as far as possible, the real person who stands behind that statue in the church or that stained-glass window.

The books behind the 1991 concise edition of *Butler's Lives of the Saints*, are the four-volume *Lives of the Fathers, Martyrs and other principal Saints, compiled from original Monuments and other authentic records, illustrated with the remarks of judicious modern critics and historians* (London, 1756–1759), published anonymously by Alban Butler, a priest-scholar and president of the English College at Saint-Omer.

Since then, *The Lives of the Saints* has gone through at least a dozen radical rewrites and editions, particularly by Herbert Thurston, S.J., and Donald Attwater, who nearly doubled the number of entries from 1,500 to 2,500. Over the years, the number of saints available for inclusion has increased—Pope John Paul II, for example, has added to the list with unusual zeal—and the number has occasionally diminished when historians have asked whether, for example, there is enough evidence to conclude that St. Christopher, St. Cecilia, or St. George ever existed. Some, like Cecilia and George, have hung on the list simply because, as patrons of music and of England, they were too popular to be let go.

The concise edition, organized by the liturgical year, limits itself to one saint for each day, and we can enjoy it most by daily reading an entry, none longer than seven pages, and then living with the idea of St. Anne Line, or St. Paul Miki and companions, as we go about our work. St. Anne Line (feast day February 27, martyred in 1601) allowed her house to be used for Mass and hid hunted priests during the English persecution. Asked in court whether she was guilty of harboring a priest, she called out, "My lords, nothing grieves me more but that I could not receive a thousand more." For this she was hanged. St. Paul Miki, S.J., and his companions (feast day February 6, martyred in 1597), including three Jesuits, six Franciscans, and seventeen others, mostly Japanese, were all crucified together near Nagasaki.

Historically, aside from their virtue, what do the saints seem to have in common? Perhaps reflecting the sociology of the first nineteen centuries, the highest number (151) are bishops or abbots, that is, established church authorities. Thirty-six are founders of religious orders, and the rest are martyrs, virgins (women religious), and widows. Few are married persons, although some enter religious life after the spouse's death. Most are from rich or noble families, but they either give all their money away or make a big point of serving the poor. The martyrs usually die horribly, and the hagiographers have an almost morbid fascination with the details of the decapitations, disembowelings, crucifixions, and exotic tortures. Everyone knows, but few believe, the legend of St. Laurence (feast day August 10, martyred 258) being roasted on the grill and inviting his executioners to turn him when he's done on one side. But many have read and believed the account of the executions of Jesuits Isaac Jogues and Jean de Brébeuf by the Iroquois, who tore out their hearts and drank their blood while it was warm. Novelist Brian Moore was inspired to write a grim novel about their ordeal.

One of the grandest lives, I suggest, is that of St. Catherine of Siena, (feast day April 29, virgin and doctor of the church, died 1380), the twenty-third of twenty-five children. She fought her parents by cutting her hair to be less attractive to a husband, and in the end they let her become a Dominican tertiary. The great battle of her life was her largely unsuccessful attempt to heal the schism between the two papacies at Rome and Avignon, where a rival, French-dominated papacy had been established. Since the age of six she had had visions; her final vision was of a ship, representing the church, crushing her. She died at thirty-three.

Another grand life is that of St. Francis of Assisi (feast day October 4, died 1226), with its repeated motif of his drifting, as a rich young man, between his old and new lives, of throwing away his garments in order to both be and look poor. A turning point was his meeting a leper begging for alms, whom he decided to kiss. We know the legends of Francis preaching to birds, but we forget that he also joined an expedition of the Crusades in 1219 and worked his way into the Saracens' camp to preach the gospel to them.

A personal favorite, because I had a statue of him in my room as a boy, will always be St. (then Blessed) Martin de Porres (feast day November 3, died 1639), the natural child of a Spanish knight and a freewoman of color from Panama. He was a black

Dominican lay brother in Lima, Peru, who cared for the poor and the sick as well as for cats, dogs, and even mice. He is the patron saint of social justice, and it was good for me as a small boy to have a black saint as a friend when there were no blacks in our neighborhood or in Blessed Sacrament School.

Because Butler-Thurston-Attwater-Walsh are as committed to telling the truth as to edifying their readers, we can't expect that the saints will always look good, at least by contemporary American standards. St. Louis IX punished those guilty of blasphemy by branding them. St. Francis Borgia, S.J., whom I had imagined to resemble an elongated El Greco, was enormously fat. St. John Vianney, the curé of Ars, the kindly patron of parish priests to whom three hundred penitents came each day in confession, was convinced that all dancing, even to watch it, was an occasion of sin. St. Ephraem (373), we are told, was not concerned about his "image": "he was of small stature . . . bald, beardless, and with skin shriveled and dried up like a potsherd; his gown was all patches, the color of dust, he wept much and never smiled."

No book has everything, so, as a former army artillery officer, I miss some information on St. Barbara, the patroness of artillerists; and the story of St. Denis, patron of Paris, who was beheaded outside the city but picked up his head and carried it all the way back to town. When a skeptic asked how it was possible for a headless man to walk that far, the believer replied, "It's the first step that counts."

Finally, any collection like this needs at least one story that demonstrates the editor's sense of humor. Christina the Astonishing (1224) had a seizure at age twenty-two, was presumed to be dead, and was carried to her funeral in an open casket. Suddenly, after the Agnus Dei, she sat up, then flew up to the rafters of the church and perched there. She went up there, she said, because she could not stand the smell of sinful human bodies. After Mass the pastor coaxed her down. She claimed that she had actually been dead and had gone to hell and seen a lot of her friends there. Then she went to purgatory where she saw even more, then to heaven—where she woke up.

Thomas à Kempis

9 The Imitation of Christ

C. 1427

T HERE'S A STORY—PROBABLY not true, but still a good story—that when the short-lived pope John Paul I died in bed of heart failure, he had been reading a controversial report on the troubles of the Jesuits. The next morning, when the nun-housekeeper found him, she discretely removed the report from his hands and replaced it with Thomas à Kempis's *Imitation of Christ.* It is testimony to this little medieval devotional manual's timeless reputation that the nun knew the public would respond, Of course! What else would a pope be reading but *The Imitation of Christ?*

This book has been almost as ubiquitous and influential as the Bible. If you had a Catholic professor in college twenty years ago, he or she had it on a shelf or a bedside table. It comforted St. Thomas More in the Tower of London as he awaited his execution, worked its way into the Spiritual Exercises of St. Ignatius of Loyola, moved Methodism's founder John Wesley to recommend it to his followers, and turned Thomas Merton toward conversion. Even fictional characters such as Agatha Christie's sleuth Jane Marple found wisdom there at the end of the day.

I had a copy when I was a Fordham student and then as an artillery officer in Germany in the 1950s, but when I had to read it as a Jesuit novice at St. Andrew-on-Hudson, I found myself fighting it. I probably resisted because when I heard the word *world,* I thought of places and scenes from the last five years of my life that had made me happy: reading the *New York Times,* crossing Brooklyn Bridge, looking for Hemingway in the cafes along Boulevard Montparnasse on Paris's Left Bank, cheering Adlai Stevenson's run for the presidency, and talking politics and books at the White Horse Tavern on Hudson Street. The implication was that these experiences of the world were obstacles to spiritual growth. For me, they made me who I was.

For Thomas, the world was both that place outside your monk's cell and an attitude, an attraction toward anything, even something good in itself, that could come between you and God.

As I reread the *Imitation* today, I still resist it, but realize the ways in which it was on target in the fifteenth century and how the world needs it now as never before. The late Middle Ages was a grim era in the history of Europe and the church. The black plague and a famine had wiped out half the population, and the Hundred Years' War between France and England reached its grisliest moment in the burning of Joan of Arc. In response to the materialism of the clergy and the dry, irrelevant intellectualism in the universities, a new spiritual movement, the *devotio moderna,* tried to recall the people to a simple, humble spirituality.

Today the AIDS plague is decimating Africa, the wars in the Balkans and the Middle East may go on a hundred more years, and in the worldwide media-manipulated consumer culture that sets the moral tone of public life, humility, self-denial, and prayerful solitude seem aberrations, vices rather than indispensable rules for personal integrity.

Thomas was born in Kempen, near present-day Dusseldorf, Germany, around 1380. He was educated at his mother's school and at a monastery of the Brothers of the Common Life, where his older brother Jan was a canon. In 1399, he followed Jan to his new post as prior of the monastery of Mount St. Agnes outside Zwolle and in 1406 was accepted into the Canons Regular of St. Augustine. He was ordained in 1413 at the age of thirty-four and would spend the rest of his life with that community.

As subprior, his job was that of novice master. It helps us to understand the *Imitation,* composed as four separate treatises between 1420 and 1427, if we see it as, in some degree, a manual for young men. Some of them were still in their teens, and like most teenagers they preferred to show off, brag, gossip, put one another down, have their own way, and hang out with their "cool" buddies rather than to keep prayerful silence, treat everyone the same, and consider others as better than themselves. These rules, especially for humility, were also basic to obedience, without which a religious order cannot control its members.

True, there is an anti-intellectualism in the advice that does not sit well today: "Certainly, when Judgment Day comes we shall not be asked what books we have read, but what deeds we have done; we shall not be asked how well we have debated, but how devoutly we have lived." An alternative spirituality, whether medieval or modern, sees love of learning and desire for God as one integrated human drive. The novice master's mind, however, sees a devotion to books as competition for a love of prayer.

Other zingers will not win Thomas any fans at the local gym or health spa: "Do not boast about your good looks nor your body's strength, which a slight illness can mar or disfigure. Do not take pride in your skills and talents lest you offend God, to whom you owe these very gifts and endowments."

Very sensibly, Thomas sees the process toward perfection as a slow one, requiring patience, wherein we must keep asking for advice and putting up with others' failings in the hope that they will put up with ours.

Yet, the most difficult passages of Book I are those that shut out the world: "Someone once said, 'As often as I have been among men, I have returned less a man.'" But that "someone," whom he does not identify, is Seneca—a Roman philosopher, not a Christian. The same chapter sings the praises of retiring to one's room and staying there. Yet anyone today who has lived in religious communities (particularly male ones) over the past thirty years knows that men who literally "shut the door to their room" shut themselves off from their own brothers and pile up tons of garbage that, once they are dead, someone else will have to throw out.

Throughout the manual, many of the instructions take the literary form of dialogues between Jesus and the disciple-reader. Others are prayers, similar to the Psalms, that the monk can make his own, such as "My God, my Love, You are all mine and I am all Yours." Several themes recur. First, we ourselves are not worth much; whatever good we have in our fallen natures is God's unearned gift. The contemporary movement to boost the self-esteem of young people by praising them regardless of their accomplishments gets no support here.

Second, whatever our powers of loving, we should focus them on love of Jesus, building intimacy with him in contemplative prayer. We sometimes experience that love in the emotional sweetness called consolation, but we should be wary of consolation—it never lasts.

Third, suffering is central to following Christ. Jesus, Kempis says, when he lived on earth, "was not for a single hour without the pain of His passion." Today, a Christologist would say that Jesus, with the full limitations of his human nature, did not foresee his suffering and death.

Fourth, we will all die, some of us much sooner than we expect. So we should live as if we were to face judgment this afternoon. "Here today, gone tomorrow! When out of sight, you are out of mind." In the Middle Ages, this was literally true. In parts of Europe, one-third of all babies died before the age of five; life expectancy was twenty-one; thirty-five was old. There were exceptions, of course. Thomas à Kempis lived to be ninety-two.

Let's say I am a twenty-nine-year-old advertising executive making $100,000 a year. Today, on the way from the office to the subway, I use my cell phone to call my parents in Florida and my girlfriend in Manhattan to try to beg off of the book discussion group she roped me into joining. In the subway car, I tune my Walkman to a jazz station and bury my nose in the *Wall Street Journal.* In my two-room apartment, I mix a martini, light a cigar, and turn on the National Public Radio news in my bedroom so there will be something to listen to as I'm in and out. I switch on my computer and my TV and read my e-mail with one eye while watching CNN with the other. As I flick through the TV channels, I pause on a quiz show, *Who Wants to Be a Millionaire?* I've brought a briefcase full of accounts home. My company is about to be bought by a conglomerate; my stock value could go up, or I could be downsized out. I flip a CD in and turn it up as I start to work.

Carelessly, I pick up and open the book for that discussion group I failed to get out of. It says:

> The rich of this world will vanish like smoke and their past joys will no longer be remembered. Even in life they did not enjoy their riches without some distress, some anxiety, or a touch of sadness, for the very objects that afforded them delight were the same that brought them pain and sorrow. And this is only just and proper since the pleasures they unrestrainedly desired and pursued were never capable of bringing complete enjoyment, since they carried with them the seeds of bewilderment and bitterness.

What do I do now?

Ven. John Henry Newman

10 The Idea of a University

1851, 1873

I F THERE IS ONE THEME that dominates the story of Catholic higher education in the United States, it is the search— and now the struggle—for identity.

In the mid- and late-nineteenth century, the mission of Catholic colleges was clear: put Catholic young men, most of them second-generation Irish and Italians, in a rigorously controlled Catholic environment. Teach them classical literature, catechism, and Christian manliness, and protect them from the hostile Protestant culture.

In the early twentieth century, these colleges became rudimentary universities, adding law and medical schools so Catholics could become lawyers and doctors like their Protestant counterparts. When veterans returned to college after World Wars I and II, the universities expanded more, tacking on business and evening schools, and the seminary atmosphere began to erode. Vatican II, the cultural and sexual revolutions, and the civil rights and antiwar movements forced Catholic institutions to confront secular society, and they decided to compete for excellence according to the same rules of academic freedom and scholarship as state and secular private schools. Whether this transformation made them less Catholic than before depends on our idea of a university. This returns us to John Cardinal Newman's classic answer to a question that resists a conclusive answer.

Newman was born in 1801, the eldest of six children and son of a banker. In 1816, following an illness and the failure of his father's bank, Newman underwent a spiritual crisis and committed himself to celibacy. Newman's own education was at Oxford University, and he was a tutor at Oriel College, where he embraced Anglican fundamentalism. Ordained an Anglican priest in 1825, he also became a university preacher.

A member of the Oxford Movement, a group of Anglican intellectuals attracted to Roman Catholicism, Newman entered the Catholic Church in 1845, studied in Rome, was ordained a priest, and introduced the Oratory of St. Philip Neri, originally founded in Rome in 1564, into England in 1848. He was then, and for the rest of his life, a controversialist. As a writer, lecturer, magazine editor, novelist, poet, and the author of *Essay on the Development of Doctrine* (1845) and of his spiritual autobiography, *Apologia pro vita sua* (1864), Newman argued the Catholic case to a non-Catholic world. Whether or not he won the controversies of his day, his style and insights entered the mainstream of English literature, and his influence lives on in G. K. Chesterton, Evelyn Waugh, James Joyce, and Graham Greene.

In 1851, Archbishop P. Cullen asked him to establish a Catholic university in Dublin so that Catholic boys could have the same opportunities there as Protestants had at Trinity University. To establish the philosophical foundation for his project, Newman delivered five lectures in 1852 that were later published as pamphlets. These, along with other lectures on allied subjects, were collected and published in 1873 as *The Idea of a University*.

If his arguments lack clarity, it is because there was no clear agreement between Cullen and Newman as to what the university was supposed to accomplish. When Newman went to Oxford, its standards were not high. Unlike more advanced universities, it was not dedicated to research or to teaching, but to socializing the sons of the ruling class, preparing them to run the empire. Ireland was more like the United States; its sons would not be running an empire, but needed to break into the middle class. So was this to be a university for the Irish, many of them farmers, or for English Catholics who might not get into Oxford? As one critic suggested, Newman would have been most pleased if his university had become the place where the upper-class Catholics of Evelyn Waugh's *Brideshead Revisited* would send their offspring.

Newman's first principle is that a university without theology in the curriculum is not a real university because it does not deal with all of human knowledge. He presumes, more than an academic would today, that most reasonable people believe in God. Not to include the Creator as integral to human understanding is to exclude the truth that actually makes all knowledge one. A political economist, for example, may argue that accumulating wealth is the key to happiness. But what about the Christian gospel's refutation of that idea? The role of theology as an integrating element—a theory popular in American Catholic colleges in the 1950s and early 1960s—is at the heart of Newman's university.

Second, the liberal arts are, by definition, not "servile" or "useful." They are not professional or commercial. Today, bluntly, they don't—unlike accounting and computer science—get you a job. They do something more important: they form a habit of mind that lasts throughout life. And chief among those concepts valued in liberal arts are freedom, moderation, and wisdom. In the non-Catholic civilized world they cultivate the "ladies and gentlemen," citizens of the world. At the Catholic university, they do the same thing. But Newman insists that you study the liberal arts not for what you will do with them, but for what they will make of you if you master them.

He gives very few examples. Today I would be tempted to argue that reading Tolstoy, Mauriac, and Newman may not get you an accounting job, but it will make you a more interesting person with things to think about alone on long drives with the radio off. Newman did, however, adapt his vision to Irish reality; while he was rector he set up an engineering program and a medical school.

Third, liberal knowledge does not make men and women better persons. He says: "Quarry the granite rock with razors, or moor a vessel with a thread of silk; then may you hope with such keen and delicate instruments as human knowledge and human reason to contend against those giants, the passion and pride of man."

This comes as a surprise. We know that Nazi SS officers could listen to Beethoven symphonies and turn on the gas ovens at the same time. But we—or I—cling to the idea that if they had really been made to think deeply about Bach and Beethoven and Mozart, they might have seen their victims as human beings.

Fourth, remembering his days as an Oxford tutor, Newman believed in the educative powers of the community. He said that if he had to choose between a standard nonresident university where professors gave exams and one without professors, in which the young men all lived together and talked about their ideas, he'd take the free-flowing friendships. This would not necessarily be a morally better system, but it would make for a better education.

A high point of the *Idea* is Newman's classic definition of a gentleman. He does not argue that this is the goal of Catholic education. A gentleman is a product of a civilization; if he can be a Christian too, so much the better. A gentleman is "one who never inflicts pain" and

> carefully avoids whatever may cause a jar or a jolt in the minds of those with whom he is cast . . . his great concern being to make everyone at their ease and at home. . . . [H]e is tender toward the bashful, gentle toward the distant, and merciful toward the absurd; he can recollect to whom he is speaking; . . . he never speaks of himself except when he is compelled, never defends himself by a mere retort; he has no ears for slander or gossip, is scrupulous in imputing motives to those who interfere with him, and interprets everything for the best.

We should record that, whatever the rightness of his ideas, the university Newman founded did not work. It had little support from the cardinal or the Irish people. Newman left in 1858. In 1879, he was named a cardinal, and he died at the age of eighty-nine in 1890.

Today, Newman's name does not live in Catholic universities but in Newman Centers, Catholic outposts on large non-Catholic campuses where like-minded Catholics can gather for liturgy and mutual support. On Catholic campuses, theology is no longer the integrating discipline—there is none. In the curriculum, theology or religious studies is one department among many—English, history, political science—supplying two required courses for the core and competing with every other discipline for influence. However, theology departments are often leaders in their cutting-edge research and scholarship, university activities that Newman saw as secondary.

His idea that the liberal arts are valuable in themselves hangs on by its fingernails. Schools do attempt moral formation, but by retreats, liturgies, and social-action programs more than through the curriculum. The suggestion that the student should also become a gentleperson is seldom heard.

Henry David Thoreau

11   Walden

1854

Martin E. Marty takes the title of his history of American religion, *Pilgrims in Their Own Land*, from Jacques Maritain's *Reflections on America*: "Americans seem to be in their own land as pilgrims, prodded by the dream. They are always on the move—available for new tasks, prepared for the possible loss of what they have. They are not settled, installed. . . ." In fact, says Maritain, some aspects of this American mood are close to "Christian detachment, to the Christian sense of the impermanence of earthly things."

Maritain knew the United States mainly from his years here during World War II and as a Princeton professor in the 1950s. I'm not sure our "Christian detachment" is still very strong, yet the ideal lives in writers whom we respect even when we cannot emulate them.

On July 4, 1845, the twenty-eight-year-old Harvard graduate, pencil maker, surveyor, and schoolteacher Henry David Thoreau made his ritual break with the small-town society of Concord, Massachusetts. With secondhand wood and borrowed tools, he built himself a ten-by-fifteen-foot cabin, about as big as a college dormitory room, and planted a bean field in a cove at the end of Walden Pond. So far, he had failed to fit in at Concord, the bustling little center of the philosophical-literary movement called transcendentalism.

"I went to the woods," he says, "because I wanted to live deliberately, to front only the essential facts of life, and see if I could not learn what it had to teach, and not, when I came to die, discover that I had not lived."

In a sense, he was doing what monks do when they enter a monastery or what laypersons do on a spiritual retreat, though Thoreau would probably not call his retreat spiritual or his detachment Christian. As Marty says, in leaving the Unitarian Church, Thoreau turned nature into a church, thus becoming the forerunner of a type of churchless spirituality for those who claim to hear not only a different drummer but even an individualistic personal drummer, those who turn soul-searching into an entirely private affair.

Walden deals, as Perry Miller says, with some "Eden of the soul in which at least one American held off the pressure of materiality and mediocrity." Paradoxically, however, few private persons have had so broad or lengthy a public impact. Known for his knowledge of little Concord, which was deep enough, he implied, to give him a knowledge of the whole world, Thoreau also traveled more widely than most men of his time. He explored Canada, the Maine woods, the streets of Manhattan, the long beaches of Cape Cod, and the wilds of Minnesota, and no one recorded more beautifully the details of what he saw: the flying squirrel, the playful diving loon, the mist on the surface of the lake, the woodchuck stealing across his path, the sound of raindrops on the cedar splints that covered his roof.

On Walden Pond for two years he took his cold, early morning dips, took notes on epic battles between the black and red ants, measured the depth of the pond, and chronicled the cosmic croakings of the frogs, the bong of the church bells, and the rumbling of the iron horse, which made the "hills echo with his snort like thunder." To his ears, those frogs were communicating with other frogs all across the country, and in those church bells he heard the vibratory hum of pine needles as if they had become the strings of a harp. In his notes he leads us to see, as Prof. Bob Brown used to tell us at Fordham, "the macrocosm in the microcosm," the omnipresent divine creative spirit in every atom of God's creation.

"I love to be alone," he wrote in the journals that he later distilled into *Walden*, but nearly every day he sauntered into town for banter with the local folk or for lunch at his aunt's house, and back at the lake he crowded into his hut as many as thirty visitors at one time.

In thirty years of teaching, I have found that Thoreau has his ups and downs among students. Thoreau represents to young people, particularly in late adolescence, most of what they don't want to be: alone, intellectually arrogant, unemployed, short, disappointed in love, ill at ease with young women, celibate, a writer whose books went unsold. Thoreau was dead of tuberculosis at forty-five, and is resented to this day by the descendants of the townspeople who saw him as a strange young fellow with no steady job who accidentally or deliberately set one of their fields on fire.

Some of the students' resistance is prudent—we swallow no author whole. Thoreau did not have everything we look for today in a mature, well-integrated person. Critics can trace his excessive aggressiveness, independence, and resentment of state authority to his social failures and his resistance to the authority of his parents.

But so what? With Thoreau, as with most great artists, the truth and power of his writing transcend the limits of his personality. And few lives, short as his was, had more singleness of purpose.

Thoreau's "steady job" was indistinguishable from his life. Though semiskilled as a teacher, naturalist, and lecturer, he was above all a writer, subordinating all other activities—job, social life, friendships—to his journal, the raw material of his essays and books. The best of these, *Walden*, may well be the greatest American book, a greatness of which his contemporaries were unaware. Of the 1,000 copies printed of his first book, *A Week on the Concord and Merrimack Rivers* (1849), 706 cluttered the attic of his parents' home, and *Walden* was barely noticed.

To "notice" *Walden*, we must learn to join Thoreau on a walk and pay attention to other things as well: the gentle rain that waters his bean patch, his kinship with the badger and the loon, the embrace of the water as we join him for a swim. We will discover that he teaches us to deal with the fundamental human experience, what it means to be an individual person, "to live deep and suck out the marrow of life."

More than any other book except perhaps the Gospel of Luke, *Walden* offers the message Americans most need, incentive to get a grasp of oneself as a free individual. This is not the "rugged individualism" of the Darwinists in which only the strong survive, nor is it the individualism that Alexis de Tocqueville describes in *Democracy in America* in which, in today's terms, the upwardly mobile middle class withdraw with a few close friends into their gated communities and the warmth of their whirlpools. Rather, this is the individualism of personal integrity, the willingness to march to a different drummer, and, as Thoreau did, to spend at least one night in jail to protest an unjust war.

Patterned around the seasons of one year, *Walden* takes on the rhythm of nature's own death and rebirth as, in the climactic chapter, spring cracks the pond's ice and Thoreau says: "I left the woods for as good a reason as I went there. Perhaps it seemed to me that I had several more lives to live, and could not spare any more time for that one."

He had heard the "different drummer" again and was stepping out to be himself somewhere else.

In his 1939 essay, "Walden," E. B. White writes Henry a letter after his own visit to the pond, where, he reports, the full, clear croak of the frog, hoarse and solemn, still bridges the years, but there are two beer bottles in the ruins of the old hut.

I have been to Walden three times, twice with students to walk along the edge of the water through the pines to Henry's cove for a swim.

One time I walked into Concord, past Emerson's house, to Sleepy Hollow Cemetery and sat quietly by Henry's grave and contemplated the cricket perched confidently on his little stone.

12   "The Second Inaugural Address"

1865

IT WAS A MISERABLE DAY in Washington on March 4, 1865, very much like the November day on which Abraham Lincoln had been reelected, as if the heavens were reaffirming their cold indifference to the Union and its leader. In fact, it had been raining for several days, so the crowds that had been coming into Union Station from around the country made their way through the chill drizzle and the gray wind, slopping through mud almost a foot deep in some places.

For selected guests, there would be two ceremonies: the swearing in of the vice president in the Senate chamber and then the public inauguration of the president on the steps outside. Before the Senate ceremony, Andrew Johnson, who had suffered a bout of typhoid fever, had unfortunately downed a glass of whiskey to settle his nerves and, in his address, rambled on semicoherently for over an hour. Once Johnson finally took the oath, Lincoln whispered to the parade marshall, "Don't let him speak outside."

The war had finally turned in the Union's favor. Within a month, Richmond would fall and Lincoln would personally follow the troops into the defeated southern capital. Three days later, Lee would surrender his army to Grant at Appomattox. On April 11, Lincoln would give a speech implying that some Negroes

55

might be given the vote. One man in the crowd, infuriated by what he heard, was John Wilkes Booth.

Although he would make no predictions about when the war would end, Lincoln sensed it would be soon. He saw these weeks as a true turning point in American history and his inauguration as the time to spell out the spiritual principles on which the nation should be rebuilt. Then there was a deeper challenge: to somehow bring rational order, through a philosophy—or rather a theology—of history, to the horrible events of the last four years. Why had those 364,511 boys died? Why had so many returned from battle without arms and legs?

It was like the scene in John's Gospel in which the disciples asked Jesus why the man was born blind. Was it the result of his sin or that of his parents?

Early in his political career, Lincoln's enemies had tried to undermine him by calling him a deist, but it would be more correct to call him, as did Mary Lincoln, "not a technical Christian." Highly rational, self-educated, deeply read in Shakespeare and the Bible, he thought for himself rather than take his religion from frontier preachers. He believed in the "doctrine of necessity"—that our actions are predetermined by a higher power. He told a skeptical friend to take all of the Bible he could on reason and the rest on faith and he would "live and die a happier and better man."

Happiness, in the ordinary sense, had long eluded Lincoln. All his life he struggled with a deep depression brought on by extreme anxiety, overwork, and exhaustion. It was aggravated by a seemingly endless succession of handicaps and tragedies—the poverty and illiteracy of his parents; rejections by Mary Todd's family; the deaths of his sons Eddie at four and Willie, in the White House, at eleven; the progressive madness of his wife; the petty betrayals of politicians. In his dreams, he saw the collective suffering of a shattered nation that had become a phantom vessel with himself at the helm. It was moving swiftly toward a distant shore where God's mysterious will would prevail, but only after the sin of slavery had been purged.

The strain of the war, as the last photos taken by Alexander Gardner testify, had turned him into a gaunt and haggard man of sorrows. But as the president approached the podium, the sun burst through the clouds and, as a witness wrote, "flooded the spectacle with glory and with light."

Lincoln's high-pitched voice carried clearly over the vast crowd as he delivered what Alfred Kazin describes in *God and the American Writer* as "the most remarkable inaugural address in our history—the only one that has ever reflected literary genius." It was also the most religious. It presumed an America whose citizens knew the Bible almost as well as he did, in which people did not see themselves as absolutely autonomous individuals but as joined by fate and a common history, even though this history had taken separate paths at Fort Sumter.

It also presumed what is called the American "civic religion," in which, whatever the constitutional separation of church and state, the president still represents some kind of a religious and moral center as, unlike England, we combine the head of state and the ceremonial leader in the same person. Thus, though Lincoln was not a Presbyterian, he took his sons to the Presbyterian church every Sunday.

I urge the reader to take up the text and, either in the privacy of his or her own room or with a few friends, read it slowly aloud as if projecting it to an audience. This will take six minutes. If anyone with feeling for the United States can do this without choking up emotionally at least once, I will be surprised.

His text does several amazing things. First, Lincoln attributes the cause of the war to the evil of slavery and condemns the whole system of slavery more vehemently than he has ever done before. One-eighth of the whole population, he says, have been colored slaves. The Confederacy sought to spread slavery even if this would destroy the Union by war; the Union wished to restrict slavery, even at the cost of war. How could this war be justified?

> Both read the same Bible and pray to the same God, and each invokes His aid against the other. It may seem strange that any men should dare to ask a just God's assistance in wringing their bread from the sweat of other men's faces, but let us judge not, that we be not judged. The prayers of both could not be

answered. That of neither has been answered fully. The Almighty has His own purposes. "Woe unto the world because of offenses; for it must needs be that offenses come, but woe to that man by whom the offense cometh." If we shall suppose that American slavery is one of those offenses which, in the providence of God, must needs come, but which, having continued through His appointed time, He now wills to remove, and that He gives to both North and South this terrible war as the woe due to those by whom the offense came, shall we discern therein any departure from those divine attributes which the believers in a living God always ascribe to Him?

While stating the immorality of slavery—an idea that did not have general acceptance even in the North—Lincoln did not claim God's endorsement for the Union's cause. It is, in some ways, the realization of Job: that God is God, and we are not to question his ways. Thus it may be that God is punishing both the North and South, each of which had its own responsibility for this national sin.

Lincoln continues:

> Fondly do we hope, fervently do we pray, that this mighty scourge of war may speedily pass away. Yet, if God wills that it continue until all the wealth piled by the bondman's two hundred and fifty years of unrequited toil shall be sunk, and until every drop of blood drawn with the lash shall be paid by another drawn with the sword, as was said three thousand years ago, so still it must be said, "The judgments of the Lord are true and righteous altogether."

In short, he did not try to comfort his audience with assurances that their side had always been right.

Then he concludes with the sublime plea for reconciliation that we love to hear, but have yet to learn to live: "With malice toward none, with charity for all, with firmness in the right as God gives us to see the right, let us strive on. . . ."

Kazin does not think it right that "under the smug Republican administration of Calvin Coolidge, a great temple in Washington was built around a statue of Lincoln seated on a throne." This, along with the fact that Lincoln was killed on Good Friday, and that the funeral carried his body to every major city between Washington and Springfield, made Lincoln the kind of religious object that he specifically rejected.

Lincoln told the New York political boss Thurlow Weed, who complimented him on his address, that he himself thought the speech was perhaps the best he had produced, but not immediately popular. "Men are not flattered by being shown that there has been a difference of purpose between the Almighty and them."

Fyodor Dostoyevsky

13 The Brothers Karamazov

1881

I N *CLASSICS REVISITED*, a collection of short essays that appeared in the *Saturday Review* in the 1960s, Kenneth Rexroth claims that Dostoyevsky is out of date, that the long conversations in *The Brothers Karamazov* in which the characters spin out their views on moral issues are not only tiresome but irrelevant, and that the moral dilemmas of Ivan Karamavoz have been "dissolved rather than solved by time."

To him, the book is a tragedy without a hero and a detective story without detectives, a murderer, or even a murder. And it has no message.

To the rest of us, it is the greatest novel ever written and the one most worth rereading. It is a most challenging and satisfying religious experience. As a young lawyer said to me some years ago, "Everything is there."

Perhaps Rexroth's debunking has the good effect of allowing readers to approach this formidable volume with more confidence, rather than on bended knee. After all, like the novels of Dickens, who influenced Dostoyevsky's style, *The Brothers Karamazov* first appeared as a serial in a journal. Written for everyone, the novel is on its first level a thrilling narrative in which four brothers—all complex, divided characters—struggle to solve personal problems revolving around their love affairs and their relationship with their murdered father.

Some would argue that it is a "philosophical" novel—or an existentialist tract—with the philosophy emerging from the conflicting personalities and worldviews of the characters, not merely from the author's desire to teach or preach.

It also helps to understand the ways in which the story grows out of Dostoyevsky's early life, his religious ideas, and his conversion experience. Born in 1821, only a few years after Napoleon and his army had been driven from Russian soil, Dostoyevsky grew up in a Russia that was in a state of continual upheaval, experiencing the effects of both patriotism and oppression in ways that would finally come to crisis in the revolution of 1917.

His father was a poor, drunken military doctor who tyrannized his serfs until his sudden death when Fyodor was eighteen. Some biographers have perpetuated the story, widely believed at the time, that he was killed by his serfs; but a series of investigations failed to prove it. Freud himself, writing about Dostoyevsky, suggested that the father's "murder" and the Oedipal myth that every man desires his father's death were at the basis of his personality, but a recent biographer, Geir Kjetsaa, says Dostoyevsky admired his father greatly and that similarities between the author's father and the brutal elder Karamazov are merely superficial.

At twenty-one, Dostoyevsky was arrested as a revolutionary. He was sentenced to be shot but was granted a reprieve at the last moment and was sent to Siberia for four years and to the army for another four. Prison was a transforming experience, both artistically and spiritually. He learned to identify with criminals—including an ex-officer who had been accused, unjustly, of having murdered his own father—and to find greatness in men the rest of the world despised. He also studied the New Testament, renewed his faith, and came to believe in the redemptive value of suffering.

His work is the product of a stormy life. He was epileptic, addicted to gambling, a poor man with a divided character in which his conservative Christian principles warred with his desire to do evil. One contemporary wrote of him: "I cannot consider Dostoyevsky either a good or a happy man. He was wicked, envious, vicious, and spent the whole of his life in emotions and irritations." Dostoyevsky portrays in the Karamazov brothers the battle with conflicting emotions that tore him, and that tear every human, in different directions. Flesh, intellect, spirit, and animality all play their part as God and the devil battle for the souls of Dimitri, Ivan, Alyosha, and the illegitimate Smerdyakov.

The story springs from the murder by one of the brothers of the elder Karamazov, a cruel drunk. In the investigation and trial, the novel develops the ways in which each of the brothers, contaminated by the evil strain in the family, shares in the responsibility for the crime. One is tried, another actually did the deed, but another—the guiltiest—subtly disposed him to strike.

Dostoyevsky has told us that the chief problem he is dealing with is one that has tormented him all his life: the question of God's existence. For if God does not exist, the world is but a "vaudeville of devils" and "all things are lawful," including crime. Does Rexroth include the question of God's existence among those that have lost fascination? More likely, the question retains its force, but today, rather than conclude that moral anarchy follows God's disappearance, one might build an ethic on humanitarian respect for one's fellow persons.

I sometimes think that too much is made of the famous chapter, often excerpted for classroom use, called "The Legend of the Grand Inquisitor." Here, Ivan, the rationalist, embittered by the injustice of life and the suffering of children, asks us to imagine a debate between Christ and an agent of the Inquisition. Dostoyevsky has Ivan express, through the monologue of the grand inquisitor, the most powerful arguments against Christ and against Dostoyevsky's own beliefs. Christ, he says, misunderstands human nature and thus cruelly asks for what man cannot give. He argues that man prefers the certitude offered by institutionalized religion to the anxiety that comes with free, unconditional faith.

Some interpreters claim that the inquisitor "wins" the debate. But we must remember who tells the story: it is Ivan, the cold, skeptical rationalist. He does not represent the author's rejection of religion. Furthermore, the issues raised are not meant to be answered in a debate, but rather in the lives of the characters as the whole novel unfolds. A more interesting chapter, I suggest, is the later one in which Ivan receives a nocturnal visit from the devil—a suave, accommodating, seedy, middle-aged gentleman as clever in conversation as Ivan himself. Here Dostoyevsky again employs the literary device of the "double," a second character who is in many respects the other side of his protagonist.

At the heart of Dostoyevsky's purpose is the saintly Russian monk and mentor of the nineteen-year-old novice Alyosha, Fr. Zossima, who exemplifies and teaches about the absolute demands of love as he teaches the need to forgive and accept forgiveness. Here love is "harsh and dreadful" and exacts an enormous cost from the lover. "What is hell?" Zossima asks. He then answers his own question: "The suffering of being unable to love."

At the end, the brothers—those who are still alive—go on to new futures. Alyosha, who has become a hero to a group of schoolboys, gives a eulogy for a boy who has died and bids his young friends farewell as they cry "Hurrah for Karamazov!" Dostoyevsky told a friend that he planned a sequel in which Alyosha, as the main character, would become a revolutionary but return to the religious life. By now we know enough about human nature to realize how open-ended his and everyone's future is.

Meanwhile, Dostoyevsky's influence lives on—in Andre Malraux's *Man's Fate,* in the author's sympathy with his characters; in Rebecca West, who uses Dostoyevsky's orthodox Manichaeanism to penetrate the Slavic character; in Norman Mailer's apocalyptic worldview and in the divided personalities of his criminal characters; and in Dorothy Day, who loved *The Brothers Karamazov* and pondered and adopted the implications of Fr. Zossima's "harsh and dreadful love."

63

14 The Story of a Soul

1898, 1958

I KNOW I WOULD NEVER have read the autobiography of the Little Flower if Dorothy Day had not pushed me in her direction. Like everyone else at Blessed Sacrament School in Trenton, New Jersey, in the 1940s, I had grown up trained to venerate the "little" St. Thérèse (as distinguished from "big" St. Teresa of Ávila). We had a Little Flower statue at home and the holy cards with that photo of the sweet, round face that, I was not surprised to learn later, had been so doctored and gussied up by Carmelites promoting her cult that all the individuating character had been washed out. I granted some validity to her "little way" spirituality of everyday life, but I presumed she was a devotion one outgrew.

Her eighty-nine-city tour of the United States in the fall of 1999, while hitting the world circuit, gave me second thoughts. The news reports told of forty thousand packed into a soccer stadium to see her in Brazil and fifteen thousand in one day at St. Patrick's Cathedral. They described her visit as if she were a live person arriving in a limo rather than a reliquary. The ornate wooden box, encased in Plexiglas, held a few small pieces of her bones retrieved from her tomb for her canonization in 1925. As one devout welcomer put it, "She's there for me. The other great saints and mystics—I could never live up to that. She's like me— plain, ordinary." She also has a Web site.

Dorothy Day explains in *Thérèse* (1960) that she first heard of Thérèse of the Child Jesus and the Holy Face, her proper title, in the 1920s in Bellevue Hospital, where, still a non-Catholic radical and unmarried, Dorothy gave birth to her daughter, Tamar. The nurse gave her a St. Thérèse medal for her baby. In 1928, a year after Dorothy's baptism, her confessor gave her a copy of *The Story of a Soul*. Dorothy had read the *Confessions* of St. Augustine and *The Imitation of Christ* and was initially turned off by the picture of the nun's "sweet, insipid face" and the book's "colorless, monotonous" style. Still involved with the Communist party and its interpretation of the class struggle, she asked what Thérèse had to do with the world conflict in which she was involved. It took her some years to see that "in these days of fear and trembling of what man has wrought on earth in destructiveness and hate, Thérèse is the saint we need."

No one would call *Story of a Soul* great literature. Rather, written in the last years of her life at the insistence of her religious superiors, one of whom was her older sister Pauline, it is a combination of three documents, each a different literary form: a family memoir of her childhood, a short essay on her personal spirituality, and a manuscript addressed to her prioress on convent topics such as sacrifice and prayer. The first editions were heavily edited by the Carmelites, with changes in a third of the text. An original version of her work was not available until the 1950s.

Born into a prosperous family in Alençon, France, in 1873, Marie-Françoise-Thérèse Martin, was the youngest of nine children (two boys and two girls died before her birth). To judge by the story she unfolds, she seems to have been preoccupied with religion for her entire short life, as she died at age twenty-four in 1897. Clearly, as an amateur writer, she is influenced by the spiritual-literary convention in which even ordinary events are interpreted as God's direct intervention. Dorothy Day's book puts the family history in the broader context of the Franco-Prussian War, the class struggle in France, and the Martins' efforts to create a family in which it was easy to be good. That four of the five daughters entered the Convent of the Discalced Carmelites in Lisieux and the fifth, after several tries, became a Visitation sister is evidence that they succeeded.

Thérèse divides her life story into three phases: the years before her mother's death from cancer when Thérèse was four; her
eight years of withdrawal, mysterious illness, hypersensitivity,
and scrupulosity; and her sudden "conversion" in 1886, following which she got over her sensitivity, began to practice charity
more zealously, became interested in the apostolate, and was so
determined to enter the convent that in an audience with Pope
Leo XIII, although she had been forbidden to speak, she blurted
out her request for permission to become a Carmelite at fifteen.

Again, because a pious memoir is so narrowly focused, it helps
to read another book, such as Day's or Peter-Thomas Rohrbach's
The Search for Saint Thérèse, for additional analysis of events in her
life that she may not have fully understood or, because the work
is dedicated to her prioress, the controversial and not-universally-
loved Mother Marie de Gonzague, events that she left out.

For three months in 1883, when she was ten, Thérèse was
seized by an undiagnosed illness—convulsions, comas, and hal-
lucinations. She says she never lost control of her reason during
the episodes and later became convinced that the devil himself
had caused them. Today we might say that she was still suffering
from the death of her mother and that the departure of her sister
Pauline to join the convent was depriving her of her mother-
substitute and best friend, and she was suffering a nervous
breakdown.

Life in the convent where Thérèse spent the last nine and a
half years of her life and developed her "little way" spirituality
has been compared to the opening sentence of Tolstoy's *Anna
Karenina*, in which "every unhappy family is unhappy in its own
way." As Thérèse and other readers of Thomas à Kempis knew,
religious houses are Eden after, not before, the Fall; although the
nuns elected Mother Marie de Gonzague to six three-year terms,
she was a mercurial, autocratic tyrant who split the community by
her favoritism. She humiliated sisters, including Thérèse, in
order to "test" them, yet could be manipulated by those who gave
her the loyalty she craved. When Pauline was finally elected to
replace her, Thérèse was torn between factions following the former prioress and those following her own sister. As a result, and
because she was reserved, seemed cold and aloof, had three

sisters in the convent, and didn't play politics, there was always a group of nuns who just didn't like the future saint.

When she expresses her spirituality in one word, it is *love*. She sees no opportunity for "sensational acts of piety" such as preaching and martyrdom, but even a little child can love. "That shall be my life, to scatter flowers—to miss no single opportunity of making some small sacrifice, here by a smiling look, there by a kindly word, always doing the tiniest things right, and doing it for love." Some of the opportunities, to someone not in a convent, do seem small: she goes out of her way to convince a nun she doesn't like that she does like her; she puts up with the nun who sits behind her in church making odd noises with her teeth; she doesn't complain when the nun at the wash tub accidentally splashes her. Although she really believed writing letters was a distraction and didn't do much good, she wrote fifty-two letters in her last year, many to two "spiritual brothers," missionaries in China and Algiers, who counted on her for prayers. She has been named a patroness of foreign missions.

But her routine daily suffering was real: at the end of the day she would collapse with fatigue, she slept on a straw mattress, and the house was deathly cold. When death first introduced itself in a rush of blood to her mouth in the middle of the night, she rejoiced that she would soon see God. But God kept her waiting many months as tuberculosis reduced her to skin and bones. She never complained. As heaven approached, she told us she would spend her heaven doing good on earth. The popularity of her autobiography and the "shower of roses"—answered prayers—after her death caused the pope to waive the fifty-year waiting period and canonize her twenty-eight years after her death.

Pope John Paul II has named her a Doctor of the Church, presumably not for her scholarship or writing but for what he considers the wisdom of her basic ideas.

From Dorothy Day's point of view, she has been canonized by the masses.

What stands out in her life? Her holiness does, of course, and the holiness of her entire family. That is not an ordinary thing in this day of postwar materialism, delinquency, and all those other words that indicate how dissatisfied the First World is with its economy of abundance while the Third World sits like Lazarus at the gate of Dives. When the whole world seems given over to preparedness for war and the show of force, the message of Thérèse is quite a different one.

Henry Adams

15 Mont-Saint-Michel and Chartres

1904

The whole Mount still kept the grand style; it expressed the unity of Church and State, God and Man, Peace and War, Life and Death, Good and Bad; it solved the whole problem of the universe. The priest and the soldier were both at home here, in 1215 as in 1115 or in 1058; the politician was not outside of it; the winner was welcome; the poet was made happy in his own spirit, with a sympathy, almost an affection, that suggests a habit of verse in the Abbot as well as in the architect. God reconciles all. The world is an evident, obvious, sacred harmony. Even the discord of war is a detail on which the Abbey refuses to insist.

THE MOUNT IS MONT-SAINT-MICHEL, a rocky island abbey on the coast of France, familiar today in its magnificent travel posters, the medieval community alone and braving the ocean tides that regularly cut it off from the rest of the world. Between the eighth and seventeenth centuries, a series of abbots and architects constructed a collection of medieval churches, monasteries, and fortresses there. When Henry Adams visited, it was a public monument, a tourist attraction. A few years before, it had been a prison.

Today the word *medieval* does not resonate easily in the public mind, which associates it with all that is backward, primitive, and antimodern. But at the beginning of the twentieth century, for many intellectuals and particularly for Catholic ones, respect for the Middle Ages suggested an alternative system of values to both the depersonalizing materialism and technology of the Gilded Age and the disillusionment following World War I. Catholics familiar with the college reading lists of the 1940s and 1950s will remember James J. Walsh's *The Thirteenth, Greatest of Centuries* (1907), in which Walsh—a young Fordham graduate, former Jesuit, and medical doctor—traveled throughout Europe collecting evidence that the century of Thomas Aquinas and Dante was a golden age offering a vision with which the drifting twentieth century could regain its course.

It is an interesting irony of American cultural history that an Irish Catholic apologist such as Walsh and Henry Andams, a member of America's most distinguished family, not known for Catholic sympathies, could share a profound insight on the origins of modern Western civilization: that this mount, a monastery, "solved the whole problem of the universe."

The visitor to Mont-Saint-Michel in our opening quote was not a religious leader but Henry Adams, great-grandson of President John Adams, grandson of President John Quincy Adams, and son of Charles Francis Adams, the ambassador to Great Britain during the Civil War. Henry Adams was, arguably, America's first great historian. In the tradition of Francis Parkman and George Bancroft, Henry was a New England patrician intellectual; he was also a scientific historian with his head and hands in the archives. His *History of the United States of America* (9 vols., 1889–1891) is one of the monuments of American historiography. He breaks the family mold by cutting away from the Unitarian-Protestant milieu in which he was raised and by rhapsodizing about a Catholic medieval abbey and the thirteenth-century cathedral of Chartres. The cathedral, he asserts, embodies the spirit of the Blessed Virgin Mary not just as a symbol of a primitive faith but also as an emblem of unity for the modern world.

Born in Boston in 1838 and educated at Harvard, Henry Adams made the image of the Virgin Mary the object of universal scholarly attention. He toured Europe, worked as a journalist, was active as a liberal republican, and edited the *North American Review*. He returned to Harvard to teach medieval history, and he wrote two novels, *Esther* and *Democracy*, which satirizes the corruption of Washington political life.

The suicide of his wife Marian in 1885 threw Adams into depression. Though he described himself as a "cave dweller," he roamed the Pacific with his friend, the painter John LaFarge. He visited the World's Columbian Exposition in Chicago in 1893 and the Paris Exposition in 1900, where he encountered the dynamo, a symbol of technology's dominance of the fragmented modern world. Meanwhile, he found solace in his friendship with Elizabeth Cameron, wife of Adams's friend Senator Don Cameron. One critic suggests that Adams's longings for Elizabeth, as well as his sorrow over his lost wife, inspired his extraordinary idealization of the Virgin of Chartres.

Today, Adams's reputation rests on the two masterpieces— *Mont-Saint-Michel and Chartres* (1904) and his autobiography, *The Education of Henry Adams* (1907)—representing his philosophical response to a world he feared was falling apart. The Virgin represented the unity for which he longed, the dynamo the multiplicity he dreaded.

The heart of *Mont-Saint-Michel and Chartres* is in the first ten of its sixteen chapters. Here, imagining that he is addressing his young niece, or that he is a tour guide, or that he is a medieval townsperson or a modern historian, Adams leads us through most of the cathedrals between Normandy and Paris, culminating in Chartres. He moves back and forth through the centuries, concentrating on the eleventh and the thirteenth.

His goal is that we should share his awe of the art he describes and get on our knees to a symbol we have lost. In doing so, he has adopted the literary style of a travel writer: Behold this. Notice that. In fact, though he has meditated on everything he has seen, he writes from the art books stacked on his desk.

To measure the devotion of the cathedral builders in a way that the 1904 American mind could grasp, Adams tells us how much money they spent. Between 1170 and 1270, he says, the French built eighty cathedrals and nearly five hundred churches in the cathedral class, property that was valued in 1840 at $1,000 million dollars. Just as the French in the nineteenth century invested in the railway system, the thirteenth invested in the Virgin. She was the Queen of Heaven and she would repay them, with forgiveness and protection, in the world to come.

The Virgin Mary that Adams discovered in the architecture and stained-glass windows of the Chartres cathedral was by no means the Gospels' humble girl of Nazareth but the ultimate Queen, a living presence who personally directed the architects who built her shrine according to her regal taste. Chartres belongs, says Adams, not to the Trinity but to Mary and her son. Under her inspiration, a Gothic church is not gloomy, but brilliant with light, joy, and the mercy she dispenses to the multitudes who pour through the doors. The imagery of suffering and fear has no place here. "At Chartres Christ is identified with his Mother, the spirit of love and grace, and his church is the Church Triumphant."

I have never been to Mont-Saint-Michel, but Adams's purpose as a writer is not to take me there but to make me think about what it means. Now I want to go. I have been to Chartres; as a twenty-year-old student during my junior year abroad I joined a pilgrimage of thousands, on foot, from Paris to the shrine.

I remember the first sight of the two unmatched towers piercing the horizon. They typified, says Adams, "the aspirations of man at the moment when man's aspirations were highest." I did not know that, according to the critics, the smaller, older, simpler spire was the one we pilgrims were "expected to recognize as the most perfect piece of architecture in the world."

Adams is full of statements like that. *Mont-Saint-Michel*—because it presupposes familiarity with or thirst for medieval poetry (which he quotes in French and translates himself), architecture, and scholastic philosophy and theology—is not a classic for everyone. But even obscure passages occasionally reward our attention with charming legends, such as the story of the nun who fled the convent for a life of sin and returned years later to find that, because she had said a prayer every day, the Blessed Virgin had filled in for her as sacristan, and no one had even noticed that she was gone.

In the last six chapters the theme changes. We leave the magnificent rose windows of Chartres behind. In Adams's interpretation, the institutional church, to shore up a belief system that piety could not sustain, replaces the intuitive faith inspired by art with the intellectual rationality of the systematic philosophy represented by Abelard and St. Thomas Aquinas. In this context, the Virgin and St. Francis of Assisi, with their emphasis on feeling, intuition, and mystical spontaneity, become subversive, "heretical" figures, symbols of a genuine spirituality that rational Christianity could not accept.

Adams described his book to a friend as "my declaration of principles as head of the Conservative Christian Anarchists; a party numbering one member. The Virgin and St. Thomas are my vehicles of anarchism. Nobody knows enough to see what they mean, so the Judges will probably not be able to burn me according to law."

Adams died in 1918. In 1912, he had booked passage on the *Titanic* for its return voyage to England, and he saw in its sinking, says a biographer, "the whole shipwreck of modern life" that he had predicted. Adams wrote to a friend, "The sum and triumph of civilization, guaranteed to be safe and perfect, sinks at a touch, and drowns us, while nature jeers at us for our folly."

We hear the cries of the drowning—and there is no Virgin to rescue them.

16 Orthodoxy

1909

In the 1970s when I was book review editor of *Commonweal*, the liberal Catholic weekly for which Chesterton had written in the 1930s, I assigned a new biography of this great man to a Catholic philosopher and university president who had a lot of wit and learning and who could, I had found, write perceptively on just about any topic sent his way. He accepted the assignment and sent in an essay in which he confessed that he had not read much Chesterton before, but that on the basis of this biography, he was sure his reputation was overrated.

Our courageous articles on social injustice in Latin America—one of the defining moral crises of the century—had been welcomed by respectful silence; but our slight on Chesterton inspired a comparative deluge of outrage.

Here is evidence, if we needed any, that Chesterton, who had seemed dead for forty years, was still very much alive. New biographies continue to appear, and a quarterly journal, *The Chesterton Review*, knits his enthusiasts into a community of admiration. When I edited *The Loyola Personal Reading List* in 1995—twenty essays by faculty on the five books that had most influenced them—two contributors ranked Chesterton's *Orthodoxy* at the top. One of them was inclined toward traditional Catholicism; the other was a leading liberal theologian.

We have known Chesterton at different ages in his many roles: as poet, author of the stirring "Lepanto"; as mystery writer, creator of Fr. Brown, who unmasks a criminal posing as a priest when the criminal argues faith against reason; and as historian and philosopher. Chesterton's biography of Thomas Aquinas is considered one of the best.

Yet, when I ask colleagues if they have read *Orthodoxy* and they reply enthusiastically that they have, it seems that they read him long ago when they were young. In some ways it is a young person's book. To one who was young in the 1950s, orthodox Christianity—specifically Catholicism, to which Chesterton converted—seemed to be engaged in an intellectual shoot-out. It struggled to draw a bead on its enemies and knock them off with a turn of a phrase. Chesterton did that well, and one could cheer him on.

And it's a young person's book in that it recounts a teenaged G. K.'s passage from paganism at twelve to agnosticism at seventeen. His reading of all of the enemies of Christianity, such as the evolutionists Spencer and Huxley and the freethinker Tom Paine, led him to the conclusion that if Christianity had thrown these naysayers into such contradictions and conniptions, "it must be an extraordinary thing."

Born in London in 1874 and educated at St. Paul's School, where he had a reputation as a not-so-quick thinker who didn't work hard enough on his studies, Chesterton studied art for two years and then English literature at University College. In 1901, he married Frances Blogg. He had fallen in love in 1896, but in her mother's judgment, he had lacked the stability and income to wed. His parents had not taught him how to dress or wash or keep himself neat or keep appointments. Now it was up to her.

In his early twenties, he kept a notebook, its entries the seeds of his more than one hundred books and plays. One entry explains why Chesterton would ultimately be remembered for his friendships with such public intellectual figures as H. G. Wells, George Bernard Shaw, and Hilaire Belloc as well as for his writings: "My great ambition is to give a party at which everybody should meet everybody else and like them very much." As Maisie Ward says in her 1943 biography, "G. K. liked everybody very much, and everything very much. He liked even the things most of us dislike. He liked to get wet. He liked to be tired."

A waiter in the pub where Chesterton worked on his writing while drinking a lot of beer was amused by the way in which the young man, who had been thin but was putting on weight, sat at his table, wrote a paragraph, read it, then laughed out loud at what he had written. As a columnist-polemicist, he sometimes turned out ten thousand words a week. He could be careless with facts, but to him the facts were less important than the main idea.

The essence of Chesterton's literary style is the paradox, a statement that is both true and false at the same time, but that when properly grasped will lead the reader to a higher understanding. Indeed, the essence of Christianity is crystallized in a series of paradoxes: we die in order to live; we give all, yet we receive more than we could ever give away; we devote ourselves totally to the Other, yet we are the freest persons in the world.

To enjoy *Orthodoxy* it helps—it is indispensable—to visualize the author in his study at the turn of the nineteenth century with a pile of "modern books" on his desk, which he considers "a pile of futility." He says,

> By the accident of my present detachment, I can see the inevitable smash of the philosophies of Schopenhauer and Tolstoy, Nietzsche and Shaw, as clearly as an inevitable railway smash could be seen from a balloon. They are all on the road to the emptiness of the asylum.

He compares the brilliance of these masters unfavorably to the more basic wisdom of Joan of Arc.

> I thought of all that is noble in Tolstoy, the pleasure in plain things, especially in plain pity, the actualities of the earth, the reverence of the poor, the dignity of the bowed back. Joan of Arc had all that and with this great addition, that she endured poverty as well as admiring it; whereas Tolstoy is only a typical aristocrat trying to find out its secret.

It also helps to have read at least parts of St. Augustine's *Confessions*, which Chesterton listed as a must-read classic, not because G. K. is burdened with the saint's solemnity, but because both are conversion stories—young men looking very systematically for the truth, lining up the adversaries, conceding their attractions, then embracing the God they have found with their total being.

As a note, it's interesting to compare their conclusions on sex. Augustine's life was a long struggle for chastity, putting off God because he could not end a sexual relationship. Chesterton, happily married, just cannot argue himself into accepting the Catholic Church's position on the virtue of celibacy. He concludes his opinion must be wrong, but he's going to hold it anyway.

Today, *Orthodoxy* is best read not so much as a coherent essay, but for the flashes of insight that jump off the pages of its nine chapters. In "The Ethics of Elfland," he suggests that the logic of fairy tales, because they allow for the imagination, may be a more reliable source of truth than rational argument. He observes the patterned, repetitive behavior of nature and wonders whether this pattern has its source in some greater will.

> I had always vaguely felt facts to be miracles in the sense that they were wonderful: now I think them miracles in the stricter sense that they were willful. I mean that they were, or might be, repeated exercises of some will. In short, I had always believed that the world involved magic: now I thought that perhaps it involved a magician. And this pointed a profound emotion always present and subconscious; that this world of ours has some purpose; and if there is a purpose, there is a person. I had always felt life first as a story: and if there is a story there is a storyteller.

Chesterton also draws some ethical conclusions, for example, "We should thank God for beer and Burgundy by not drinking too much of them."

Politically, Chesterton was neither liberal nor conservative, but, as he described himself, "a rebel." With his friend Hilaire Belloc and other prominent Catholic intellectuals, he embraced distributism, an economic theory in which wealth, particularly productive property, must be widely distributed rather than concentrated in the hands of a few capitalists. No matter how large the needle or small the camel, he says in *Orthodoxy*, Christ's words "must at the very least mean this—that rich men are not very likely to be morally trustworthy." Tell him that the rich should be trusted in politics because they cannot be bribed, and he will tell you, "The fact is, of course, that the rich man is bribed; he has been bribed already. That is why he is a rich man."

By 1936, he had finished his *Autobiography*, but the machine of his huge, overweight body was running out of steam. Physically, his heart was too small. As Maisie Ward says, "The thought of a Chesterton whose heart was too small presents a paradox in his own best manner."

As he lay dying, he came to for a moment and said, "The issue is now quite clear. It is between light and darkness and every one must choose his side." Two priest friends at his bedside sang the Salve Regina as he passed away. Chesterton's pen lay on the table beside his bed. One of the priests, Fr. Vincent McNabb, picked it up and kissed it.

17 Dubliners

1914

THE FIRST IMAGE IN James Joyce's *Dubliners* is of a dead priest. The narrator of the story "The Sisters" is a young boy who has, over the years, befriended old Fr. Flynn, who has been cared for by his two sisters during his long illness—a paralysis. Just what caused the paralysis we don't learn until the last page, but through the boy's memories, we see him visiting the ailing father, listening to the priest's basic catechism stories that detailed all the ways a person could go wrong and sin.

At the end of the story, as the boy listens to the sisters talk about their brother at the wake, we discover with him that Fr. Flynn was scrupulous, obsessed by guilt over trivial matters. When he somehow broke a chalice during mass, he lost his mind and became physically and emotionally paralyzed until his death. Laid out in his coffin, he looks better in death than he did in life, and his hands hold the chalice he had dropped years before. Thus Fr. Flynn becomes a vehicle for many things—the paralyzing force of Catholic guilt, the refusal of Catholic people to see the clergy as they are, and the overwhelming inescapable impact of a specific kind of cultural Catholicism on Joyce's imagination.

The story also forecasts themes in many of the thirteen stories to follow: the paralysis of characters trapped in stultifying poverty, Irish history, and religious traditions; long-suffering women in the service of self-centered men; a corrupt church clinging to a

79

public respect it does not deserve; and the central character, usually a male, coming to an awful moment of awareness—an "epiphany"—in which he or the reader sees a shattering truth to which the story has led us.

In many ways, the most decisive moment in the young James Joyce's life was his rejection of the church. Only by separating himself from the stifling milieu of Ireland and of the church could he achieve freedom as an artist. So, in 1904, Joyce exiled himself to the Continent with his longtime companion, Nora Barnacle, whom at the time he refused to marry. Nora was a young woman from Galway who met his sexual needs but was in no way his intellectual equal.

Joyce lived in Italy, Trieste, Switzerland, and eventually Paris, surviving as an English teacher or by begging from benefactors. Thus, for most of his fifty-nine years, James Joyce was a geographical and psychological exile, but his creative imagination never left Dublin. He had the map of Dublin in his heart and in his head, and his characters roamed its streets, riverbanks, fields, pubs, churches, boarding houses, and brothels in search of sex or a pint, with the epic seriousness of Odysseus sailing home to Greece. Still in his midtwenties, he wrote the stories that would lead to *Dubliners*, *A Portrait of the Artist as a Young Man*, *Ulysses*, and *Finnegans Wake*, all of which would make him, by general agreement, the greatest writer of the century.

In rejecting Ireland and the church, Joyce was separating himself from a miserable life. His mother, Mae Murray, a religious girl who sang in the church choir, bore sixteen children, ten of whom survived. His father, John, a gifted tenor and an admirer of Charles Stewart Parnell—who was supposed to lead the Irish to home rule until his adulterous love affair was exposed—was a once-prosperous, often brutal man who drank away the family's fortune. The family moved around Dublin twelve times, always into smaller quarters. Joyce was educated at the best Jesuit schools and read voraciously, but he cut the lectures and walked the city streets, frequenting prostitutes and working out epiphanies for *Dubliners* in his head.

In exile, Joyce suffered poverty, hunger, joblessness, rotting teeth, increasing blindness, and regrets that he had married someone who couldn't understand his stories. He was unfaithful to Nora and squandered money from patrons on expensive restaurants and drink. When the publication of *Ulysses* in 1922 made him famous, he became, his brother Stanislaus said, "too moneyed and pampered." He turned in on himself, feared dogs, thunder, madness, and loneliness, and neglected the needs of his son and daughter, then in their twenties.

Commenting on this period, biographer Edna O'Brien asks:

> Do writers have to be such monsters in order to create? I believe that they do. It is a paradox that while wrestling with language to capture the human condition they become more callous, and cut off from the very human traits which they do glisteningly depict. There can be no outer responsibility, no interruptions, only the ongoing inner drone, rhythmic, insistent, struggling to make a living moment of both beauty and austerity.

One of the several miracles of *Dubliners*, which Joyce began writing in 1904 soon after his mother's slow death from cancer, is that the stories transcend the anger and bitterness that mark the work of other alienated writers. Whatever their pitiful corruption, his characters remain complex and human, even sympathetic, though some will never understand their own pettiness and stupidity. Because "Ivy Day in the Committee Room" was considered insulting to King Edward VII, and the word *bloody* and the real names of pubs and pawnbrokers are sprinkled throughout the text, censorious printers and publishers held up publication until 1914; reviews were mixed, and a year later only 379 copies had been sold, 120 to Joyce himself.

Ulysses, which marks a turning point in twentieth-century literary consciousness, is best read in a graduate course with a professor and a guidebook, but *Dubliners*, the creation of a twenty-three year old with the wisdom of an old man, is deceptively simple. I can think of few works that are more enjoyable to teach. Each story leads us along to a subtle moment of revelation, then goads us to go back for another look, a second reading that takes nothing for granted, especially with details such as the implied eucharistic symbolism in "The Sisters," when the boy eats crackers and drinks a glass of sherry at Fr. Flynn's wake.

In "After the Race," young Jimmy Doyle falls in with a group of car racers—French, Canadian, Hungarian, and, later, American—as they go out on the town to celebrate their victory. Jimmy has been spoiled by his father with an English Catholic college and Cambridge education and has been given enough money to hang out with social climbers and invest his savings in the auto business. The evening moves quickly, and the next thing we know they're on the American's yacht, singing, dancing, eating, drinking a lot—and playing cards. Jimmy is losing track of things: "They were devils of fellows, but he wished they would stop: it was getting late." They drink. They cheer. At daybreak Jimmy has lost it all. The announcement of "daybreak" is the realization that these fellows were "devils" indeed.

"Grace" opens with Kernan, drunk and bleeding, sprawled on the floor of the pub's basement men's room. The scene is Joyce's evocation of Dante's *Inferno.* His friends get him home and, with his wife's cooperation, plan to save him from his irresponsible ways by getting him to make a Jesuit-preached retreat with the famous Fr. Purdon. They celebrate their decision in his sickroom with a bottle of whiskey. At the church, Purdon takes his sermon from the obscure text "Wherefore make unto yourselves friends out of the mammon of iniquity so that when you die they may receive you into everlasting dwellings." This "learned" Jesuit tells his audience of businessmen that Jesus intended these words for professional men like themselves. The spiritual life, he says, is like keeping a businessman's accounts. In short, the worldly priest's vision is no loftier than their own. Kernan's kneeling in church is little better than his falling down the pub stairs.

"The Dead" is one of the greatest stories in English literature. While it echoes the themes of Ireland's decay and the individual's obsessive self-absorption, it ends the book with an uncharacteristic possibility of redemption. Gabriel Conroy and his wife, Gretta, attend the annual party presented by his aunts for their family, music students, and friends. That Gabriel wears a new invention, galoshes, to protect him from the snow, is Joyce's signal that he has shut himself off from water, symbolic of experience and of life.

They sing, dance, mingle. Gabriel cuts the goose and delivers a carefully prepared, pompous speech. After the dinner, they return home through the softly falling snow, Gabriel full of himself and feeling very amorous toward his wife. In the bedroom, she appears distracted, and he learns that, prompted by a song at the party, she has been thinking not of him but of a young man, Michael Furey, who loved her and died years ago. Gabriel suddenly sees himself as a ludicrous, fatuous fellow; but he is also granted a new vision of reality and his place in the universe, reminding us of Matthew 5:45, in which we must be children of our Father who is in heaven, "for he makes his sun to rise on the evil and the good, and sends rain on the just and on the unjust."

The snow is falling all over Ireland.

It was falling too, upon every part of the lonely churchyard on the hill where Michael Furey lay buried. It lay thickly drifted on the crooked crosses and headstones, on the spears of the little gate, on the barren thorns. His soul swooned slowly as he heard the snow falling faintly through the universe and faintly falling, like the descent of their last end, upon the living and the dead.

18 Kristin Lavransdatter

1920–1922

K RISTIN LAVRANSDATTER IS a very difficult woman. She is a difficult young thirteenth-century woman when her admirable father, Lavrans, arranges a good marriage with Simon Dare, son of a knight. She willfully goes against her father and plunges into a love affair with Erland Nikulausson, an older knight with political ambitions, an unstable free spirit who will guarantee her years of turmoil and pain. And she is a difficult woman all her life as she raises eight sons sired by Erland, as she abandons him and he abandons her, as she harbors her grudges and lists her offenses, waiting for the time when a secret can become a weapon.

Over three generations, she grows into an older woman, a widow who has seen a lot of blood, outlived the men who loved her, and moved her children into adulthood and freedom. She finally comes to a spiritual peace over her sins.

She is no saint. There are long stretches when she is not even a good person, but she is a heroine. Perhaps, if enough contemporary critics would take another look, they would find her one of the most complex and challenging characters, man or woman, of twentieth-century literature.

Meanwhile, it is hard to imagine a Catholic writer who had more influence on the consciousness of educated Catholic readers from the 1930s to the 1950s than Sigrid Undset. Her reputation was sealed by the 1928 Nobel Prize for literature, based on the whole body of her work, of which her medieval sagas are the best.

My fellow professors and many parents of today's students recall devouring the *Kristin Lavransdatter* trilogy, comprised of *The Bridal Wreath*, *The Mistress of Husaby*, and *The Cross*, as one of the transforming emotional experiences of their lives. And I remember Jesuit seminarians, after two years in the novitiate, where novels were outlawed and affections usually held in check, rushing to take Kristin to their rooms for at least a vicarious share in her romance. In the freezing cold and snow of thirteenth-century Norway, the men and women in this book quarrelled among themselves all day, then came into the great houses from the storm, slept together under bear skins by the fires, exchanged secrets, conceived children, and carried on, forgetting nothing, deciding whether it was better to kill the offender or to forgive.

Reread today, this passionate family saga sometimes seems every one of its 1,100 pages, especially in the 1929 translation that attempts to replicate a medieval speech pattern with vocabulary that includes "vouchsafe," "I trow," "meseems," "bethinks," and "I wot" (there is a more recent translation). Yet, for the patient reader, there is never a dull page, and to complete it is both to glimpse the cultural force of medieval Christianity in the farthest reaches of western Europe and to participate in a life, the outward ambition and the inward struggle, of one of the most fully drawn women of modern literature.

Born in Denmark in 1882, Sigrid Undset absorbed from her father, a renowned archaeologist who died in 1893, a love of Scandinavian history. She grew up in Christiana (renamed Oslo in 1925), Norway, thought of becoming a painter, but went to a commercial college and worked for ten years as a typist and secretary at the German Electric Company. This gave her an extraordinary opportunity to study human nature, to discover every corner of the city in intimate detail, and to make observations that she could transform into the material of her fiction.

In 1912, she married, in a civil ceremony, an artist named Anders Castus Svarstad, a divorced man with three children who was thirteen years older than she. She gave birth to three children of her own, the second of whom was retarded, but whom she would never consider putting in an institution. As her marriage to Anders fell apart, she put all her energy into caring for six children and trying to start a career as a novelist.

On one level, in lectures and articles, she was establishing herself as an emancipated woman, but her priority was the woman's role as wife and mother. She wrote: "Any woman who becomes a good mother is greater than most ministers of state, for she is indispensable in her work, whereas many ministers can be replaced with advantage."

Though she had received a routine Lutheran religious education, her family and friends were indifferent or skeptics. In her travels to Rome and France, she found herself moved by the spectacle of the Catholic liturgy and medieval architecture, but she was a realist, not a romantic nostalgist. The inner logic of the Catholic Church's teaching appealed to her. As it compared to the doctrine of Protestant sects, she said, "If one takes away the form given to it by the church of Rome, all Christianity has the effect on me of an unsuccessful omelet."

She struggled with her religious commitment while she was writing *Kristin*. In order to finish the novel, she would put the children to bed and then sit up writing until 3:00 A.M. with a pot of hot coffee and a pack of cigarettes. In 1924, she delivered her manuscript to the publisher and joined the church.

Small wonder that *Kristin* is a tale of a woman with seven children, a bad husband, a hard-won faith, and a will driving her to accomplish as a mother what the men could neither do nor understand.

Kristin, daughter of the industrious landowner Lavrans Bjorgulfsson and his pious but withdrawn wife, Ragnfrid, is, above all, a strong and willful young woman. Yet, along with her profound sensuality and her sensitivity to nature, there is a strain of mysticism, a longing for union with God that again and again forces her to confront her selfishness, her dishonesty, and her attempts to manipulate the lives of others.

Betrothed by her father at fifteen to Simon Dare, she falls in love with Erland Nikulausson, who is under the ban of the church because he has two children by another man's wife. By deception, she overcomes her father's resistance and helps to bring on and cover up the suicide of Erland's paramour, who had demanded that he marry her.

Already pregnant when they marry, Kristin takes charge of Erland's estate, Husaby, and bears him eight sons. Erland conspires against the king, is imprisoned, and loses his lands. Released by the intervention of Simon Dare, he returns to Kristin's estate. But with her guilt and self-righteousness she drives him first into infidelity, then away from her home. However, when the rumor is spread by a small-minded, slandering priest that the eighth son is not his, Erland comes back to defend her honor and dies in a fight. Kristin enters the religious life and dies nursing victims of the plague.

In 1940, when the Nazis occupied Norway, they made a point of destroying Undset's books. During World War II, in which her son died serving in the ambulance corps, Undset fled to America, where she became acquainted with Willa Cather and wrote and spoke against Nazism, Fascism, and Communism. In 1942, she gave an address to Catholic writers, published in *Truth and Fiction* (1942), in which she answers some of the same criticisms that would later be aimed at Flannery O'Connor:

> Tell the truths you have to. Even if they are grim, preposterous, shocking. After all, we Catholics ought to acknowledge what a shocking business human life is. Our race has been revolting against its creator since the beginning of time. Revolt, betrayal, denial, or indifference, sloth, laziness—which of us has not been guilty of one or more of these sins some time or another? But remember you have to tell other and more cheerful truths too: of the Grace of God and the endeavor of strong and loyal, or weak but trusting souls, and also of the natural virtues of man created in the image of God, an image which is very hard to efface entirely.

Helen Alvare, a writer for *Crisis Magazine* (February 1999), says that she gives *Kristin Lavransdatter* as a cautionary tale to every young woman under her influence the day she turns sixteen. "Reading Kristin is about as close to learning from experience as you can get without the experience." The point: sex before marriage and sexual infidelity are the sources of incalculable damage not just to the couple but to others as well.

I'm sure Sigrid Undset, who died in 1949, would agree. But Kristin, having finally both confessed her sins and forgiven those who "trespassed against her," would have no regrets.

François Mauriac

19 Thérèse

1927–1935

I MET FRANÇOIS MAURIAC twice. The first time was in 1953. As a student spending my Fordham junior year in Paris, I attended a meeting of a study group called Le Conference Olivain, and Mauriac was the guest of honor. Then sixty-seven, he looked old and frail, but was extremely animated, with deep piercing eyes. Although he had won the Nobel Prize in literature the year before, he was there less as a novelist than as *l'homme politique*. His Christian national conscience was raised on political and colonial issues, such as those of Algeria and Indochina, which would soon become our Vietnam.

As he spoke, his voice—a thin, raspy whisper, the result of X-ray treatment for throat cancer in 1932—combined with his gesticulating fingers to hold us in moral awe. Wringing his thin hands, he told us we must all become more engaged in the issues of the day. In post–World War II "Catholic" France, in which no more than 10 percent of French Catholics practiced their religion, his was the voice of liberal, intellectual Catholicism, one of the great "Catholic Renaissance" trio of philosopher Jacques Maritain, Georges Bernanos, and himself. During the 1930s and 1940s, they demonstrated that on public issues one could think for oneself and still be a faithful Catholic; they stood against Fascism, Nazism, and anti-Semitism in their various forms,

89

whether in Franco Spain or Vichy France or within a too compromising church.

What made Mauriac so enormously credible that night was not so much his fame as that voice, his badge of suffering, which also gives excruciating authenticity to his novel *Thérèse*. If a Mauriac novel is sometimes painful to read—though equally impossible to put down—it is because the author has fearlessly poured himself, in all his psychological and moral weakness, into its pages. His readers feel this and respond. Appearing at the height of his career between two of his most admired works, *The Desert of Love* (1925) and *The Vipers' Tangle* (1932), *Thérèse* was chosen by a jury of French literary critics as one of the twelve best novels of the half century.

Born in Bordeaux in 1885, Mauriac grew up among the ancestral estates of pine trees and vineyards that set the scene for *Thérèse* and other novels, and followed him, as if he were encased by a wall, the rest of his life. In 1913, he married Jeanne Lafont, a banker's daughter, and his son Claude was born the following year. When World War I broke out, he tried to enlist, but was rejected as too weak and sick. In 1922, after years of struggling as a poet, journalist, and novelist, his fifth novel, *The Leper's Kiss*, finally brought him recognition. As his reputation grew in the 1920s, the Catholic right attacked him for his morbidity and sexual passion, so he decided to deal more indirectly with religious themes; meanwhile, his own marriage was in trouble because of his infidelity. Finally, he was rescued from his crisis of faith by a Jewish-convert priest, who, as Mauriac described it, found him bleeding in a ditch and carried him on his shoulders to the inn, the Solesme monastery, and who then accompanied him to Lourdes.

As a novel, *Thérèse* consists of four parts—Thérèse Desqueyroux, Thérèse and the Doctor, Thérèse at the Hotel, and The End of the Night. Each of these parts was originally published as a novella between 1927 and 1935. These stories may be appreciated independently but achieve their full impact as parts of a coherent narrative. Thérèse has been accused of poisoning her husband, Bernard—an oafish, self-righteous lawyer-landowner interested in nothing beyond shooting parties and his family's acquisitive ambition. The attempted-murder case has been dismissed merely to protect Thérèse's father, who wants to run for the senate.

Mauriac makes no attempt to justify what Thérèse has done; he respects her too much to portray her simply as a victim, when a real sinner, within whom grace must do battle for the sake of even small victories, can be both a more challenging and, in the long run, more inspiring heroine. He also declines to tell us to what degree she is actually guilty, in a personal rather than a legal sense, of trying to dispose of Bernard. She becomes a fascinating figure, in Bordeaux and in Paris, to those who learn her story. In moments of intimacy, they try to ask, "How could you . . .?" revealing, of course, that dark spot in every human heart that, unconstrained by conscience, suspects that a well-placed drop of arsenic would bring them freedom and peace.

Though spared prison, Thérèse is condemned to exile within the extended family, sentenced to play a role that will protect the family's reputation. She will appear with her husband in church on Sunday and once a week ride with him through town. After the families have arranged her half-sister's marriage and con-solidated their estates, Thérèse, in the public mind a psycholog-ical invalid, will disappear, on an allowance, to Paris.

Thérèse is a scandal on two levels. First, the heroine is a crim-inal who deliberately tried to free herself from a miserable life by adding arsenic to her husband's medicine and who indeliber-ately poisons a number of other relationships by her charm. Second, she is a sinner in a "Catholic" novel who never repents. Mauriac refuses to spare us the unrelieved pain of sharing the heroine's misery—her psychological abandonment, her failing heart aggravated by her chain smoking, her paranoia—by inject-ing a sentimental rescue scene with a sacramental confession, following which the loving God who has been waiting in the wings for his cue rushes onstage and embraces the dying penitent.

In the conversational prologues to his stories, Mauriac con-fesses to his readers that he would have preferred to write a differ-ent ending to the last part, The End of the Night, in which Thérèse awaits death by heart failure after a tormented reunion with her daughter. He would have modeled his heroine on St. Locusta, a poisoner in the reign of Nero who became a saint.

But he could not; his intellectual honesty prevented him. He had never met a priest capable of leading someone like Thérèse back into the church.

Yet, in one of the novel's few explicitly religious scenes, Thérèse watches the Corpus Christi procession—which Mauriac remembered with great fondness from his youth—from behind half-closed shutters as the procession wends its way through the town with the young, stiff, unpopular curé, his lips moving in prayer, bearing the "mysterious object" in his hands. The townspeople flee the procession lest they have to kneel as it passes, and Thérèse is repelled by the sight of her husband in the procession, treading behind, one of the few men taking part but "doing his duty" nonetheless.

Later, Thérèse, in a fit of depression, is about to commit suicide by drinking chloroform, but she remembers that procession and prays that if the "Something" in the priest's hands did exist, "Let him prevent the criminal act while there is still time." At that moment, the maid bursts in to announce that old Aunt Clara has been found dead in bed! Mauriac explains nothing, nor need he. The reader decides that God has intervened, taking Aunt Clara in place of Thérèse, in response to an atheist's prayer.

Critics have sensed in *Thérèse* Mauriac's attempt to rebel against the stultifying provincial cage of his boyhood, and he has acknowledged that as a novel of revolt "it was my cry of protest. . . . And I might say, although I have never thought of poisoning anyone, that Thérèse Desqueyroux was I myself." Each generation of readers, both men and women, will find something of themselves in Thérèse. Perhaps prewar French intellectuals noted, as we do, that the novel's most intelligent character, the emancipated woman, is the most "immoral" in public esteem. She is the most alienated from religion, and yet, paradoxically, the most saintly, as she endures suffering and, as Mauriac says, never ceases, "in spite of her wretchedness, to react against the power she exercises to poison and corrupt those around her." Meanwhile, the most odious characters, the bourgeois Bordeaux landholding families who humiliate her, are the most outwardly pious.

For the rest of his life, while scathing in his condemnation of Pharisaism, Mauriac never scorned or retreated from the humble

Catholic piety he had learned as a boy. Intellectually, he had long been tormented by André Gide's question, "Why do Catholics not love the truth?" The election of John XXIII and the decrees of Vatican II convinced him for the first time that "the Spirit" was visibly alive in the church, but he was far from being swept up by every element of 1960s liberalism. He had met Teilhard de Chardin and preferred the personal Christ of Cardinal Newman to the cosmic Christ of Teilhard. Nor did he add his voice to the protests against Pope Paul VI's encyclical, *Humanae Vitae*; he was too aware of his own generation's obsession with sex to criticize a defense of chastity. Mauriac died on August 31, 1970.

I met him for the second time, in Paris, on Boulevard Raspail in the early 1990s. Not in the flesh, I confess, but in a life-sized bronze statue that had been planted right there on the street, with his hand reaching out as if to grab the elbows of passersby. "Don't just stand there," he said in his raspy voice. "We are sinful people in a sinful world. So we must speak up."

20 Death Comes for the Archbishop

1927

Edgar Allan Poe, in the last years of his life, 1846–1848, following the death of his young wife, sought solace in conversation with the French Jesuits at St. John's College, now Fordham University, in the Bronx. He would wander onto the campus and spend hours talking French and philosophy with one of the scholastics, then join the fathers for a glass of wine. What he admired in the fathers was not so much their piety as their worldliness: they knew good literature, good conversation, and good wine; and, most important, they were kind to poor Poe.

Willa Cather's *Death Comes for the Archbishop* gives us a reinforcing insight into the same generation of French priests, not all Jesuits, who made their way, often in reaction to the inhospitable politics of the French New Regime, as missionaries to the New World. Her two main characters—for the archbishop is by no means the sole focus of her narrative—arrive in the Southwest, the primitive form of what would be the diocese of Santa Fe, to take over the vicariate of New Mexico. First evangelized by the Spaniards in 1500, now long in decline, this wild turf is by no means ready for the rational French mind to bring order, rebirth, or reform.

The young bishop, Jean Marie Latour, thirty-eight, in a buckskin jacket with fringed cuffs, is handsome, elegant, intelligent,

94

and severe. His companion and boyhood friend, Fr. Joseph Vaillant, is exceptionally ugly, weather-beaten, short, skinny, and bowlegged, yet bursting with warmth and joy. For almost forty years, under their care, the desert faith will bloom, fade, and bloom again.

Fathers Jean and Joseph are ascetic and prayerful without sacrificing their French appreciation for good sense, good food, and good wine, even when the good food is a simple onion soup Joseph has prepared with loving hands for a two-man feast. Meanwhile, they must negotiate a place for their French missionary version of the church among three other local cultures: decadent Spaniards, superstitious Indians, and pioneer Americans.

As the new bishop rides his mule hundreds of miles through desert storms from one outpost parish to the next, he discovers an "American" church as primitive and violent as the frontier itself. One Mexican priest dances the fandango every night, hunts and plays poker with Americans, enjoys the steady companionship of a rich widow, confirms infants at their baptisms, and has not said Mass at the remote mesa-top Indian church at Acoma in years. He is to be removed.

Latour is embarrassed to find a huge early-seventeenth-century church on this desert mesa clearly built on the backs of the Indians to feed the ego of its Spanish pastor. Then he hears the story of the tyrannical, greedy Friar Baltazar, whose Indians endured him because his "miraculous" painting guaranteed rain for their crops. Finally, at a feast for fellow priests, Baltazar accidentally slays a servant boy who spills the soup, and the once docile Indians bind and carry the fat padre to a precipice and toss him off.

When Latour and Vaillant seek shelter in a storm, their ornery host's slave-wife warns them to flee before he slits their throats. A dissident priest who has sired a son and rules a string of parishes like a dictator warns Latour that if he tries to introduce European civilization to the Southwest, an "early death" awaits him.

Clearly Cather's narrative is not about the archbishop's death—which comes in her final pages gracefully, beautifully, in 1899 when Latour is in his seventies—but how an extraordinary, good man who is not necessarily a hero or a canonizable saint leads a life dedicated to serving God. And it is about his friend Joseph, who must leave him to establish the church in the riotous mining camps of Colorado.

Cather, a devout Episcopalian who grew up in Virginia and in Red Cloud, Nebraska, was educated at the University of Nebraska when it had only four buildings, and broke into journalism as a favorite fiction writer for S. S. McClure's muckraking magazine. She had been thinking about this book, her favorite creation, since visiting Santa Fe in 1912. The late but already legendary Archbishop Jean Baptiste Lamy, whose bronze statue stood outside the French Romanesque cathedral he had had built in this Spanish town, gradually became a spiritual presence in her life. As she explained in a letter to her many readers in *Commonweal*, she came across a rare book, Fr. William Howlett's *The Life of Right Reverend Joseph P. Machebeuf* (1908), filled with documentation and letters on the lives of the first generation of French missionary priests. With few changes, Lamy and Machebeuf became her Latour and Vaillant.

Like Lamy/Latour, Cather too explored the landscape on horseback (and sometimes in a Cadillac) and absorbed it into her consciousness until she could bring it back to life with her pen. On Latour's pastoral travels the western landscape looms up before him, wind sweeps down from the mountain and howls over the plateau. He looks out over distant mesas, through glittering sheets of rain, and sees far-off mountains bright with sunlight. He knows now what the first dawn of creation must have looked like "when the dry land was first drawn up out of the deep, and all was confusion." On other days, however hot and blue the sky, cloud formations—some dome shaped, some flat, some like Far East cities—hang over the mesas as if part of them, "as the smoke is part of the censer, or foam of the wave."

Though deceptively simple in its structure—a series of distinct episodes told chronologically, which Cather called a narrative rather than a novel—*Death Comes for the Archbishop* is rich in allusion to European Catholic literature and art. It includes references to the journey motif of Dante's *Divine Comedy* and of John Bunyan's *Pilgrim's Progress;* to the medieval collection of saints' lives, *The Golden Legend;* to the frescoes in the Paris Panthéon of

Sainte-Geneviève; and to the sixteenth-century woodcuts of Hans Holbein the Younger, specifically the series *Dance of Death*, in one of which a skeleton comes for an archbishop.

Today, applying the perspective of 150 years, we might ask whether a representative of French civilization had the right idea in imposing his culture, including a Romanesque cathedral, on the American frontier. Historically, the original Archbishop Lamy, who had experienced an Indian raid and one of whose priests had been killed, did not oppose the campaign that his friend, the famous scout, Colonel Kit Carson (whom Cather portrays sympathetically) led to either tame or exterminate the marauding Navajos and Apaches. Nevertheless, we love the book partly because it is a Western, part of our national myth wherein the frontier forms the American character while we struggle to bring the deserts, mountains, and plains under our control.

Ultimately, this is a story of loneliness and spiritual friendship, of two religious men who love one another, who might have done great work for God if they had never met, but whom God brought together and sent to the American Southwest.

97

21 Mr. Blue

1928

"And then," he declared, "think of the beautiful lives they would live up on these clean heights. Think of the customs they would build up, and the literature they would create. Can't you picture a group of laboring men gathered together out over some cornice after their day's work, gazing into the sunset, and making the tales and legends of a new race of people? Can't you imagine the women putting up their fragrantly clean washing in the lofty winds of a May morning? Can't you see the new games the children would play, the new gaiety in their hearts? Poor people with these horizons! Poor people with the whole beautiful world beneath them! Poor people up here in the skies!"

U<small>P HERE" IS THE ROOF</small> of a 1920s thirty-storey midtown Manhattan skyscraper, where our rhapsodic dreamer, J. Blue, already lives—in a large packing case, with the word *Courage* painted in red on the side. He's sounding off, as he tends to do, to our narrator, whose name is never used, but who identifies himself in a footnote as M. C.

Today, one of the thrills of living in New York is to take the elevator to the top of some of the tallest buildings in the world, such as the World Trade Center or the Empire State Building, or even some of the more modest heights such as the Beekman Towers overlooking the East River, and look down on the other rooftops. With their penthouses, swimming pools, trees, and garden patios, one can imagine J. Blue, the penniless, handsome, slender, black-haired twenty-nine year old, spelling out his dream of poor people all living in tent cities on skyscraper roofs. We remember that Blue liked to make and fly his own box kites, so we can also imagine him racing across the roof to launch one of his creations while his startled friend cringes, terrified he'll see his eccentric pal topple off into oblivion.

Today we look out and try to imagine a New York in which thirty stories made a tall building; we look up, and our chances of sighting a box kite in the Manhattan sky are slim.

When *Mr. Blue* first appeared during the era for which it was written—ten years after World War I, at the height of the Roaring Twenties (when if someone wasn't rich it was presumed he or she wasn't trying very hard), and the year before the bottom fell out in the Great Crash—hardly anyone noticed. But somehow the depression, World War II, the religious revival of the 1950s, and the cultural revolution of the 1960s each enabled us to find a kindred spirit in this solitary but warmhearted figure. This modern Thoreau, when he had money, gave it away and went against most of the values that prosperous Americans held dear. No matter what his suffering, he constantly exuded joy.

Blue's creator, Myles Connolly, had just the background that could give birth to this unusual character. Born a Boston Irish Catholic in 1897, he went to Boston Latin School and Boston College, served in the Navy in World War I, wrote for the *Boston Post*, wrote for magazines, and went to Hollywood, where he wrote or produced forty motion pictures and was known as a brilliant conversationalist with charming manners. Besides *Mr. Blue*, he wrote four other novels before his death in 1964.

As narrator of *Mr. Blue*, M. C. takes on the voice of the standard, benevolent, mediocre Christian American pragmatist who can't help evaluating everything in terms of investment, profit, and loss. Business, he says, "is the backbone of our civilization." He would like to "get together some money—50 million, say," and then do some good with it. Blue's writing ability, his sincerity, he speculates, "under astute management, could have been made to pay dividends."

Then the author allows Blue to speak for other values that, obviously, Connolly holds dear: America's need for a saintly witness who, without sounding like an angry prophet, goes against the values of his culture; the need for church artists to throw aside past models—no more imitation Gothic cathedrals like St. Patrick's in New York—and to embrace new art forms, such as film. He has Blue say, in one of his letters, that the new masses have no time for the printed word. "If you want to reach the masses, you have to reach them through pictures." Children can be taught to love, to transcend their culture, through film: "Here is a destiny for an art second to none in history. For it is given to the motion picture to save the soul of civilization." Connolly writes this before films with sound or color, TV, and video, and before commercials were considered a sophisticated art form.

Structurally, the novel takes three forms: the narrator's occasional meetings with Blue in New York and Boston, interrupted by months and weeks in which Blue disappears then reemerges with a new home and a new idealistic dream; a long story within the story, in which Blue describes the great apocalyptic film he would love to make; and Blue's letters, eleven documents collected after his death, that spell out more of his sublime spirituality.

Briefly, Blue is rich. He inherits five million dollars from an uncle and spends it on houses that he fills with servants. He builds a factory that manufactures toy balloons, ties fifty- and hundred-dollar bills to them and sends them off into the sky. From then on he has nothing. Sometimes he prays to the Virgin Mary for rent, sometimes he begs at back doors; at the end he gets a job in a Boston lumberyard where he befriends poor blacks and other working men.

His film idea is a futuristic fantasy in which a totalitarian state, the International Government of the World, enslaves all humankind, destroys the food supply, reduces the survivors to automatons fed on two liquids piped into their steel-encased-skyscraper one-room apartments, and kills every last Christian. But one last secret priest conspires to grow grain, bakes bread, makes a host, and offers a Mass that will bring Christ back into the world. Indeed, Christ appears in judgment; it is the end of the world! M. C. has to tell Blue that he doubts the picture will have much box-office appeal.

Blue dies, as we would expect, like Christ, giving his life for a poor black man about to be run down by a rich man's limo.

But we have the letters he has left behind. One answers "conservative historians" who describe men with the passion for greatness as crazy.

These conservatives are partly right: play life safe, and you'll keep out of harm. Be careful, be cautious, and you'll never die on St. Helena. Your failure is measured by your aspirations. Aspire not, and you cannot fail. Columbus died in chains. Joan of Arc was burned at the stake. Let us all live snugly—and life will soon be little more than a thick, gelatinous stream of comfortability and ignorance.

Of his love of conversation he says:

If one loves anything—truth, beauty, women, life—one will speak out. Genuine love cannot endure silence but must break out into speech. When it is great love, it breaks out into song. Talk helps to relieve us of the tiresome burden of ourselves. It helps some of us find out what we think. It is essential for the happiest companionship. One of the minor pleasures of affection is in the voicing of it. If you love your friends, says the song, tell them so.

22 Out of My Life and Thought: An Autobiography

1933

IN THE EARLY 1980S when I was dean of the College of the Holy Cross, I promised a student friend, Pat Rogers, that if he succeeded in joining the Peace Corps and was sent to Africa, I would go and see him there.

So it was that a few years later my plane landed in Libreville, capital of Gabon, a small former French colony on the western coast, just below Cameroon. The next day I was rumbling into the interior along a dusty, potholed road in a crowded taxi on the way to Pat's little village. He had already built a schoolhouse and now was constructing a dispensary out of cinder blocks that he and the native workers made themselves. I did some token work for a day, hauling cement in a wheelbarrow, then we journeyed deeper into the jungle, up the Ogooué River, to visit one of the continent's— even the world's—truly sacred places: Dr. Albert Schweitzer's jungle hospital at Lambaréné.

There's a story that is probably true about Albert Einstein's traveling alone on a train. A stranger spots him and, anxious to meet so famous a person, can't help introducing himself. They have a cordial conversation for several minutes, and finally the stranger stands to leave, filled with awe by the experience. He grasps Einstein's hand and says, "I can see that you really are the greatest man in the world, Dr. Schweitzer; this is the greatest moment of my life."

The story has several versions. In the 1950s, Einstein and Schweitzer looked somewhat alike, with their flowing white hair and moustaches, and they were friends. In one version, Schweitzer, mistaken for Einstein, offers to sign Einstein's auto-graph. But the story symbolizes the esteem in which Schweitzer, with the help of *Time* and *Life* magazines, was held. What a life! A brilliant theologian, an organist and a world authority on Bach, and a medical doctor, he leaves the world behind and, accompa-nied by his wife, Hélène Bresslau, a nurse and scholar, sets up a revolutionary hospital and a leper colony for the native people, deep in what was then called "darkest Africa." His life, like that of Mother Teresa in the 1990s, seemed to represent a radical good-ness that we could admire from a distance but to which we could not aspire.

Out of My Life and Thought, written in 1932 when Schweitzer was certainly a renowned person but not yet the mythical figure of the 1950s, is not, perhaps, as compelling a literary autobiogra-phy as *The Seven Storey Mountain*. This may be because Schweitzer is a less self-conscious, more matter-of-fact writer. At fifty-seven, he had already proved himself as a scripture scholar, musicologist, and medical missionary; so he includes a chapter in the French and German editions of his book on Bach and how to play him:

> Bach is played altogether too fast. Music which presupposes a visual comprehension of lines of sound advancing side by side becomes for the listener a chaos, if too rapid a tempo makes this comprehension impossible. . . . Bach calls for phrasing which is full of life. He thinks as a violinist. His notes are to be connected with one another and at the same time separated from each other in a way which is natural to the bow of a violin.

The next chapter is on how to build an organ.

As a theologian, he is best known for his unique interpreta-tion of the motivation of the historical Jesus. Born in Upper Alsace (then German, now French) in 1875, son of a Lutheran pastor, Albert earned doctorates in philosophy and theology at Strasbourg, where he had a reputation for developing theories that did not always jibe with those of his professors. *The Quest of the Historical Jesus* (English translation, 1910), written when he was only thirty, critiques the work of the previous generation of liberal Protestant scripture scholars who interpreted Jesus as an ethical teacher who had replaced the Jewish idea of an apocalyptic messiah with that of a spiritual, rather than historical, kingdom. This idea, says Schweitzer, is not supported by the older Gospels, Mark and Matthew. Rather, he says, Jesus thinks eschatologically. That means there must be a period of tribulation and suffering before the messianic kingdom is ushered in. Therefore, he offers his own death as atonement for the other believers, to save them from the end-time suffering. That's what he means by "lead us not into temptation," also translated as "do not put us to the test."

Obviously, the end time didn't come. Does this mean that Jesus misunderstood his own mission? Yes, says Schweitzer, but his ethical message of love remains valid in spite of the ancient system of thought from which it emerged. He concludes *Quest* by saying,

> As one unknown and nameless He comes to us, just as on the shore of the lake He approached those men who knew not who He was. His words are the same: "Follow thou Me!" and he sets us to the tasks which He has to carry out in our age. He commands. And to those who obey, be they wise or simple, He will reveal Himself through all that they are privileged to experience in His fellowship of peace and activity, of struggle and suffering, till they come to know, in their own experience, who He is.

"I wanted to be a doctor that I might be able to work without having to talk." In 1905 Schweitzer announced his startling decision to go to medical school and then to equatorial Africa, but he had been thinking of it for years. "It struck me as incomprehensible that I should be allowed to lead such a happy life, while I saw so many people around me wrestling with care and suffering." When he and Hélène arrived at Gabon in 1913, it was clear that the natives' misery—leprosy, malaria, sleeping sickness, dysentery, ulcers, pneumonia, heart disease, hernia, and elephantiasis—was even worse than they had supposed. In one typical year, 1934, he performed 622 major operations.

In a radical departure from European medical practice, with its emphasis on sanitation, Schweitzer, convinced that the natives would not come otherwise, designed his hospital to replicate village life. The rooms opened on the jungle, animals had access, and the patient's family accompanied the sick person, sleeping on the floor and cooking his or her meals in the open.

Between 1913 and World War II, he returned to Europe several times, once because he was Alsatian, interned during World War I. During these breaks, sometimes lasting several years, he traveled, lectured, and gave organ recitals to raise money for the hospital; continued his scholarship on the mysticism of St. Paul; and developed his fundamental philosophy, called "Reverence for Life."

As he explains in *Out of My Life and Thought*, two themes dominate his philosophy. First, the Reverence for Life, which he saw as the universalization of Jesus' love ethic, does not distinguish between levels of life; animal, insect, and plant life are sacred, too, and we must make a conscious decision to sacrifice them for a greater good. Schweitzer would see the germ that causes sleeping sickness in the microscope and regret that he had to kill that germ. Second, he saw himself as contrary to the spirit of his age in his insistence that men should rationally think through issues for themselves, subverting national propaganda and the advertising industry, which, even in 1930, was bombarding the public to buy their "boot polish or soup tablets." In short, he was resisting modernity. In practical matters, he resisted even his daughter, who joined him at Lambaréné and wanted electric lighting installed.

The Lambaréné that Pat and I visited over twenty years after Schweitzer's death in 1965 had kept the original home, little zoo, and hospital as he had left them, but added a thriving modern hospital as well. Why has the "greatest" man's reputation faded? In Scripture studies, form criticism, which deals with the Gospels' various literary forms and the audiences to which they were directed, has replaced his historical approach. His philosophy was never systematic enough to attract fellow philosophers. Visiting journalists to Lambaréné, in search of a saint presiding over the Garden of Eden, found an authoritarian man who referred to the Africans in his employ as "children," and who sometimes, in frustration, even hit them. But he was convinced that they would be better off under a colonial government with an agrarian and handicraft economy, rather than being taught reading, writing, and mathematics and engaging in international trade. But he also used antibiotics and DDT sparingly, for the same reasons that we use them sparingly today.

We visited the graves where he and his wife are buried side by side. The night before, I had awakened shaking uncontrollably in a cold sweat. I told Pat that our dorm had gotten cold that night. He said the night had not been cold. I had caught a fever that, fortunately, quickly passed. If I were to return to Africa today, the scourge would be not just the malaria, which I briefly feared had struck me that night, but AIDS.

According to the *Manchester Guardian Weekly* (February 12–21, 2001), there are more than 332 million men, women, and children infected with HIV in developing countries. Drugs that would keep them alive are priced at $10,000 to $15,000 in the West. Generic copies of these drugs could be manufactured in the third world to cost $200 a year per patient. The international drug companies sued to prevent distribution of cheaper drugs, then withdrew the suit. If they can't pay our prices, they said for a while, let them die.

My heart sinks.

Georges Bernanos

23 The Diary of a Country Priest

1936

My parish is bored stiff; no other word for it. Like so many others! We can see them being eaten up by boredom, and we can't do anything about it. Some day perhaps we shall catch it ourselves—become aware of a cancerous growth within us. You can keep going a long time with that in you.

So BEGINS THE PRIVATE JOURNAL of a young man, newly ordained and serving a bleak parish in the French countryside, who does not know that he has but a short time to live.

Every so often the story of a priest's death reminds us of how far most people are from an intimate, or even adequate, understanding of the personal turmoil—the struggle between the lighter and darker sides of the self—that renders the emotional lives of many priests somewhere between a purgatory and a hell.

Sometimes, though rarely, a priest kills himself, subject to the same despair as someone who has never had the consolation of belief.

In Paris, a distinguished theologian, a curial cardinal who was once an intellectual liberal but is now more famous for his rigid orthodoxy, is found dead at the foot of the stairway of a house in the red-light district. Why did his life end here? An errand of mercy? A midnight acting out of a compulsion long held in check? In Brooklyn or Arizona, a popular parish priest ends up stabbed or bludgeoned to death in a seedy motel room or the front seat of a car, victim of some secret inner struggle or a murdering hustler who has exploited him.

Good novelists make public the secret lives of men and women whose professions depend on those masks that make them mysteries to the rest of us—they lay bare the souls of presidents, princes, and priests. But popular literature has not done well in making the priest an understandable human being, perhaps because few novelists know priests well and because so few priests have the skill, discipline, or personal courage to write novels.

When the great French novelist and political writer Georges Bernanos was a boy, he asked God for two things: for the necessities of life and for glory. He loved God, and the church, and St. Thérèse of Lisieux, and the French monarchy, and of course his large family; but his prayers were answered only some of the time. To survive on a struggling writer's income, he often moved his family—to Majorca, to South America during World War II, back to France after the war, and to Tunisia. The "glory" rose or faded depending on the popularity of his political stands—conservative Catholicism in the 1920s, criticism of Franco Spain, resistance against Vichy and the Nazi occupation—and whether or not his novels sold.

He said he had no more theological training than his Jesuit-school catechism, and he was the struggling father of six when he wrote to a friend in 1935 about his plan to write the diary of a country priest who "will have served God in exact proportion to his belief that he has served Him badly. His naivete will win out in the end, and he will die peacefully of cancer."

So simple an outline of so complex a work! Bernanos brought to it, if not theology, a profound spirituality formed in steady dialogue with God since his youth, an obsessive fear of death heightened by his battle experiences in World War I, his own suffering from illness and poverty, and his artistic vision.

Today readers may shrink from *The Diary of a Country Priest*, perhaps influenced by the stark images of the Robert Bresson film, because it is "gloomy." As Peter Hebblethwaite says, there is more joy in it "than a hasty first reading might suggest. But it is a hard-won joy, not excluding suffering and apparent failure. It is the paradox of the Beatitudes."

Through the ingenious diary form we see the young curé as the curé sees himself, foolish and inexperienced, stumbling and bumbling his way from one apparent failure to another as he makes his rounds of his country parish. We also see him as he really is— or at least as Bernanos would have us see him, the hero-saint in a contemporary reenactment of Christ's agony in the garden.

Through the diary we also learn what he calls "the very simple trivial secrets of a very ordinary kind of life." We share the priest's recollections of his own impoverished background; sense in him the makings of a poet, an intellectual with powers of analysis that will never come to fruition; and deal with the relatively limited but powerfully drawn group of characters who constitute his world.

In the Curé de Torcy, his older friend and spiritual mentor, we hear Bernanos's other voice—the monarchist, the realist, the man of a previous generation who, if he does not romanticize the medieval church, at least longs for its unity, its vision of the well-ordered Christian society. He warns his young comrade: "A true priest is never loved, get that into your head. And if you must know, the Church doesn't care a rap whether you're loved or not, my lad. Try first to be respected and obeyed."

This "lad" does not ask for love; he only seeks to give it—by ministering to a corrupt village lorded over by a corrupt aristocracy in a château where the count is having an affair with the governess and the countess hates her adolescent daughter for surviving when the countess's son has died in infancy.

Meanwhile, the curé makes his rounds in constant pain—the cancer, which he mistakes for tuberculosis, is eating away his stomach in the way that spiritual decay is eating away at France.

At the novel's climax, the curé, with the fearless honesty that can come only from humility, confronts the countess, forces her to deal with her hatred, and brings her peace. But she dies of a heart attack that night. The daughter and the villagers spread the rumor that the curé is a rash fool who turns the heads of young girls and who drinks. Indeed, the curé is trapped by alcoholism, not from indulgence, but rather from the tainted blood of his poor peasant family and his miserable diet of stale bread and foul wine. The curé dies in Lille where he has gone, much too late, to consult a specialist and to visit a seminary friend who has left the priesthood.

Knowing he has not long to live, he stays up all night and pours himself into his diary:

> I can understand how a man, sure of himself and his courage, might wish to make of his death a perfect end. As that isn't in my line, my death will be what it can be, and nothing more. Were it not a very daring thing to say, I would like to add that to a true lover, the halting confession of his beloved is more dear than the most beautiful poem. And when you come to think of it, such a comparison should offend no one, for human agony is beyond all an act of love. . . .
>
> God might possibly wish my death as some form of example to others. But I would rather have their pity. Why shouldn't I? I have loved men greatly, and feel this world of living creatures has been so pleasant. I cannot go without tears.

24 The Power and the Glory

1940

Ⲓⲛ HIS ESSAY ON FRANÇOIS MAURIAC and the religious novel, Graham Greene observes that "after the death of
Henry James a disaster overtook the English novel. . . . For with
the death of James the religious sense was lost to the English
novel, and with the religious sense went the sense of the importance of the human act." Greene means that it matters greatly
that the novel's character exist not only to the person the character is addressing in the story, but also in the eye of God. "His
unimportance in the world of the senses is only matched by his
importance in another world."

For years, my favorite Greene novel to teach has been *The
Quiet American* (1955). On one level it is the story of an English
journalist in Saigon, dependent on the ministrations of his
Vietnamese mistress yet determined to be "detached" from what
is happening to her country. On other levels it is a prescient
attack on American foreign policy and a tract on divine grace at
work even when it is denied.

But in *The Power and the Glory*, which John Updike says is gen-
erally agreed to be Greene's masterpiece, the reader is forever
conscious of that "eye of God," the profound dignity which the
Creator has bestowed on the fictional creature, even though the
creature knows nothing other than what he considers his own
absolute unimportance.

111

The unnamed priest in *The Power and the Glory*, a fugitive from Mexico's atheistic state during the anti-Catholic persecutions of the 1920s, is a "bad priest," something he tells himself and anyone who will listen, again and again. He is a "whiskey priest," sipping brandy under stress, and the father of a daughter in a remote village, conceived in five minutes of lust seven years before. Yet, in Greene's *ex opere operato* theology—which affirms that the sacraments are valid regardless of the disposition of their minister—this "bad priest" "puts God in people's mouths." Though in sin himself, unable to confess for years, he hears confessions and baptizes, preaches and says Mass in village huts even as the police arrive and order everyone out into the town square. Either they must betray the priest in their midst or a hostage will be taken and shot.

Born in 1904 in Berkhamsted, Hertfordshire, where his father was a housemaster at the school, Greene graduated from Balliol College, Oxford, in 1926 and converted to Catholicism in order to marry Vivien Dayrell-Browning in 1927. When he undertook the journey that would lead to his greatest work, he had been a book reviewer and film critic for the *Spectator;* an editor and critic for the literary magazine, *Night and Day;* a novelist (*A Gun for Sale*, 1936; *Brighton Rock*, 1938) and travel writer (*Journey without Maps*, 1936, on his trip through Liberia). His *Night and Day* review of nine-year-old Shirley Temple in *Wee Willie Winkie*, in which he focused on her sexuality, her "dimpled depravity," brought a libel suit from Twentieth Century Fox that Greene lost.

The suit, it seemed, was a good time to leave the country, to travel through Mexico and produce a journalistic book on the persecution of the church. The war between the Mexican state and the Catholic Church had gone through several phases since the middle of the nineteenth century, but the constitution of 1917 had imposed a thoroughly secular culture, and in the persecutions under president Plutarco Elías Calles (1924–1928), foreign priests and bishops were banished, Catholic institutions were suppressed, and Mexican priests and religious were imprisoned and executed.

Fr. Miguel Pro, S.J., completed his theology training in Europe and returned to Mexico in 1926 as a hunted criminal.

Churches had been closed and priests were forced to marry or flee. Yet the thirty-five-year-old Pro secretly said Mass and served communion to hundreds at a time. Arrested in 1927 with one of his brothers, he was dragged into the prison yard and shot. His last words, "Viva Cristo Rey!" entered Mexican history and legend. Greene had long been fascinated with the idea of martyrdom, including that of the English seventeenth-century Jesuits such as John Gerard, author of *The Autobiography of a Hunted Priest*, and Edmund Campion, of whom Greene's friend Evelyn Waugh had written a biography. Reacting to news that five bishops had been killed in Spain, Greene commented that Catholics should not trumpet their complaints about priests and bishops who had been executed: "You don't complain about a death of that kind. It should be taken for granted."

By the time of Greene's five-week trek through Mexico in 1939, persecution had abated, but Greene, whose philosophy of travel led him to experience a place at its worst and who was often sick with fever, quickly learned to hate the country, largely because of the hate he saw there. He wrote in his travel book *The Lawless Roads*, "I've never seen a country where you are more aware all the time of hate. . . . There has always been hate, I suppose, in Mexico, but now it is the official teaching: it has superseded love in the school curriculum."

None of this comes through in Greene's fugitive priest, an unattractive, plump little man with big eyes and little wit. He has every reason to hate his persecutors, but hates only the failures he sees in himself.

If for some of us Adam and Eve's disobedience or Cain's killing Abel is the primordial sin, for Greene it is Judas's kiss. In his other novels, such as *The Third Man* or *The Quiet American*, the plot hinges on a moment of this ultimate sin—betrayal. The priest knows throughout the book that the fang-toothed, miserable half-breed who follows him from town to town will turn him in for the reward, yet he cannot hate him. He gives him his mule, some brandy, and a sandwich.

The priest was once an ambitious cleric with his eye on a church career. He feels guilty of pride because he stayed to serve his people when the other priests fled, and will not even allow himself the comfort of being a martyr. He spends the last hours of his life alone in his cell drinking brandy, weeping and drunk, making his confession to the imagined presence of an old, disgraced, and married ex-priest who could not muster the courage to come to his cell. His greatest sin, he thinks, is that he could not love every soul in the world as much as he loved the daughter he barely knew. If he had lived differently, he tells himself, if he had not started to drink, or had not given in that one time to lust, or if he had only a little more self-restraint or courage, he would not face God empty-handed when he goes before the firing squad tomorrow. He might have been a saint.

Greene's purpose is not to redefine sainthood. Rather, he wants us to see human beings, no matter how miserable, through the eyes of his priest. And he wants us to see the priest and love him as a true human being. In 1960, a Catholic teacher from California wrote to Greene:

> Last year, on a trip through Mexico, I found myself peering into mud huts, through village streets, and across impassable mountain ranges, half-believing that I would glimpse a dim figure stumbling in the rain on his way to the border. There is no greater tribute possible to your creation of this character—he lives.

The execution of Greene's unnamed "whiskey priest," inspired as it was by the execution of Miguel Pro, still shocks, partly because it takes place in neighboring Mexico even within the lifetime of Americans still alive. But, while the corpse is still warm, a new fugitive priest knocks on a Christian's door in town, seeking refuge and risking all to deliver the sacraments.

Where do these priests live and die today? We usually find their stories in the pages of the *National Catholic Reporter* or the London *Tablet*—formerly in communist eastern Europe, but now in the third world, victims of genocidal tribes, and murdered by death squads for daring to criticize the state. A Vatican commission has identified 13,000 Christians who in some sense, in the twentieth century, have sacrificed their lives for the faith.

Rebecca West

25 Black Lamb and Grey Falcon: A Journey through Yugoslavia

1941

O_N JUNE 28, 1989, the Serbian leader Slobodan Milosevic, to celebrate the six hundredth anniversary of the Battle of Kosovo that the Serbs lost to the Turks in 1389, called a million people together on the site of the defeat, the Field of Blackbirds. It was a signal of what was to come. The Albanians' ancestors had been in Kosovo for over a thousand years, but as greater Yugoslavia was disintegrating, the Serbs, dreaming of a "greater Serbia," were preparing to spread the chaos by driving the Albanians out.

The Kosovo epic myth, which seems to have guided Serbia's destiny at various turning points—such as the opening of World War I, precipitated by a Serb terrorist's assassination of Archduke Ferdinand at Sarajevo in 1914—is that Czar Lazar knew he would lose the battle to the Turks on the fateful day that opened western Europe to the Ottoman Empire. He fought anyway because it was "better to die in battle than live in shame."

Exploiting that myth, Milosevic drove his country into war, laid waste Kosovo, and endured a NATO bombing campaign that guaranteed both his defeat and Serbia's shame. Meanwhile, how Europeans and Americans would respond to Milosevic's aggression depended on how much history we knew, what books our leaders had read, what lessons we drew from the past, and how many of us had anything close to a map of Yugoslavia in our heads.

As the crisis developed, President Bill Clinton was reading Robert D. Kaplan's *Balkan Ghosts* (1993), which, as the president understood it, followed the "ancient hatreds" thesis that the people of this region had been fighting amongst one another for so long that it was futile to intervene. Thus, *Balkan Ghosts* was to Clinton what Michael Harrington's *The Other America* had been to Kennedy, Johnson, and the Great Society. Kaplan had been influenced by Rebecca West's *Black Lamb and Grey Falcon*, which he called "this century's greatest travel book," though it would have been more accurate to call it one of the century's greatest books of any kind.

Clinton, faced with evidence that Muslims, Catholics, and Orthodox Christians had lived in harmony for a long time, later regretted having swallowed Kaplan's interpretation. But if he had read Rebecca West's book, in all its 1,181 pages, he would have come away with a different message—along with its analysis of ethnic conflicts, it is above all a warning about the rise of Nazi Germany and an essay on international moral responsibility.

In 1985, because the map of Yugoslavia had never been clear in my head, I took a boat from Vienna down the Danube to Budapest, then an all-night train across the mountains of Yugoslavia into Split, the largest town on the Dalmatian coast, in a journey that would continue down the coast to Dubrovnik, and end in a flight to Istanbul. It was an exploration of that historic corridor where Eastern and Western civilizations had clashed.

It was also a search for a woman and her book. I had used an anthology of Rebecca West's work, *Rebecca West, a Celebration*, in journalism class, and I had never met a writer who so beguiled me by her fluent and provocative style and her audacious judgments.

In her biography of St. Augustine (1933), West dealt with both the Calvinism of her earlier religious training and what she considered the irreparable harm done by Manichaeanism. She also addressed the tension in her relationship with her illegitimate son Anthony West, the offspring of her ten-year affair with H. G.

Wells, through her analysis of Augustine's relationship with his mother, Monica.

In her political and crime reportage, with her ability to sit in a courtroom and observe little details and make moral judgments based on her knowledge of history, West established herself as one of the best journalists of the postwar period. At the Nuremberg trials, her pen restores the individuality of disgraced defendants who, in the public mind, had become faceless zeros. Streicher is a "dirty old man of the sort that gives trouble in parks;" Goering is "soft," with "the head of a ventriloquist's dummy," or like a madam of a brothel seen "in the late morning doorways along the steep streets of Marseilles."

Wounded by the realization that her father, a flamboyant journalist named Fairfield, had deserted her family when she was a child, and by her affair with the womanizer Wells, Rebecca West—a name chosen to indicate her sympathies with the rebellious heroine in Ibsen's *Rosmersholm*—made the moral issue of loyalty and betrayal the basic theme of her autobiographical novels, her postwar journalism, and her epic, *Black Lamb and Grey Falcon.*

In some ways, the country she and I saw was the same, with its handsome, high-cheekboned, olive-skinned men and beautiful peasant women, its string of monasteries and churches and lively religious faith, its dazzling blue Adriatic lapping the rocky beaches. Each coastal town was at one time an independent principality fighting off the domination of Rome, Venice, or Turkey, establishing its identity by its walls, its *corso,* and its cathedral.

But West's Yugoslavia was less than twenty years old as a nation, a contrived coalition of the kingdoms of the Serbs, Croats, and Slovenes that tried to give equal treatment to the three religions, with each group still refusing to compromise for a national unity. It was also the eve of a Nazi occupation. My Yugoslavia was a beautiful tourist attraction, with its economy in ruins, adrift in the wake of Tito's death, and divided into eight peoples, five languages, and three religions.

My Dubrovnik was a unique treasure, a thousand-year-old fortified coastal town surrounded by walls and battlements dating to the twelfth century in some places, a city small enough to walk around slowly in an hour, but large enough to burst with restaurants, jewelry stores, and families crammed into back streets and alleys. West's Dubrovnik was an exemplar of the moral cowardice she deplored in contemporary Europe. Though a Catholic power, it bought its peace with the Ottoman Empire, "the devouring enemy of Christendom." While the rest of Europe fought the Turks, Dubrovnik bribed them.

On the first level, West's book is a narrative of her Easter-season trip with her husband, the banker Henry Maxwell Andrews (referred to only as "my husband"). Their other companions included the Jewish poet Constantine and his German wife Gerda, whom Rebecca and Henry despise and whom Rebecca uses to symbolize and typify the incipient Nazi mentality. Here she may also have anticipated the 1970s' "new journalism" by creating some "composite" characters.

Second, it is a history of each locality she visits. A high point is her minute-by-minute account of the Hapsburg Archduke Franz Ferdinand's suicidal visit to Sarajevo that invited his own assassination in 1914. The archduke was a profligate hunter who had reportedly killed 59 boars in one day, 2,150 small game on another day, and, in his lifetime, 3,000 stags. West imagines the many thousand ghosts of his furry and feathered victims assembled at Sarajevo to watch Franz get his.

The horrifying high point of the book recounts the time in Macedonia when she is permitted to witness a bizarre ritual in the countryside in which gypsies gather around a huge blood-splattered rock and, in the presence of a child, slaughter a lamb.

Now the man who was holding the lamb took it to the edge of the rock and drew a knife across its throat. A jet of blood spurted out and fell red and shining on the browner blood that had been shed before. The gypsy caught some of it on his fingers, and with this he made a circle on the child's forehead. . . . "He is doing this," a bearded Moslem standing by explained, "because his wife got the child by coming here and giving a lamb, and all children that are got from the rock must be brought back and marked by the sign of the rock." . . . Under the opening glory of the morning the stench from the rock mounted more strongly and became sickening.

West interprets this as a message to Western liberals on the eve of World War II, a warning against what she considers "the lie," the Pauline doctrine of atonement exemplified by superstitious peasants who slaughter black lambs to please "the gods," in which the proper price of any good thing is pain. It is a refutation of the false message in a Slavic poem about a falcon who tells the Czar on the eve of Kosovo that spiritual salvation follows from military defeat.

Sacrifice, West argues, is a dangerous idea, and one that does not necessarily lead to a more moral resolution of a conflict. When absolute love entered our history in the person of Jesus, she says, we killed it. Now, in the face of the Nazi menace, our desire to "sacrifice" ourselves, to work for personal salvation at the expense of the world community—which is how she interpreted the attitude of English pacifists—was preventing us from confronting Hitler. Ironically, the Serbs, for whom she felt sympathy in the 1930s, turned out, in the minds of many interpreters, to be the Nazis of the 1990s.

During her trip, in a Serbian monastery, West found the headless body of Czar Lazar lying in state and actually touched his blackened, shriveled hand.

26 Brideshead Revisited

1945

T̲HE SCENE—MOROCCO, 1926. The narrator, Charles
Ryder, searches for his old college friend to tell him his mother is
dying.

> So I set out after dinner, with the consular porter going ahead
> lantern in hand. Morocco was a new and strange country to me.
> Driving that day, mile after mile, up the smooth, strategic road,
> past the vineyards and military posts and the new, white settle-
> ments and the early crops already standing high in the vast, open
> fields, and the hoardings advertising the staples of France—
> Dubonnet, Michelin, Magasin du Louvre—I had thought it all
> very suburban and up-to-date; now, under the stars, in the
> walled city, whose streets were gentle, dusty stairways, and
> whose walls rose windowless on either side, closed overhead,
> then opened again to the stars; where the dust lay thick upon the
> smooth paving-stones and figures passed silently, robed in
> white, on soft slippers or hard, bare soles; where the air was
> scented with cloves and incense and wood smoke—now I knew
> what had drawn Sebastian here and held him so long.

Evelyn Waugh himself has told us in the preface to the 1960
edition that the central theme of *Brideshead Revisited* is "the

operation of divine grace on a group of diverse but closely connected characters." In a 1947 memorandum to prospective scriptwriters at MGM, he defined grace as "the unmerited and unilateral act of love by which God continually calls souls to Himself." And indeed part of the joy in reading *Brideshead* is theological; it is a story about people in whose lives God really matters—whether they believe in him or not, whether they have formally slammed the door in his face or turn to him the way a hungry, stray cur curls up on the porch of a stranger's house in the rain.

But the first delight in reading Waugh is in his brilliance as a writer. Charles Ryder—through whose eyes we view the back streets of the Moroccan village, the drunken pub-crawling of Oxford boys, and the palatial Brideshead English country estate in its glory and its decline—is an artist, a painter of both aristocrats' country homes and exotic jungles in Latin America. What he sees we see and feel as well.

Author of more than twenty-seven novels and travel books, Waugh, born in 1903, dropped out of Oxford in 1924, married in 1927, and began making his living as a teacher and writer. Two years later his wife left him for another man, and in 1930 Waugh entered the Catholic Church. For seven years he traveled around the world and wrote, earning a strong critical reputation as a satirist, particularly with *Scoop* (1938), about the war in Ethiopia, which journalists revere as by far the funniest send-up of their profession. In 1936, his first marriage annulled, he married Laura Herbert and settled down to raise six children. During World War II he joined the Royal Marines. Then, injured slightly in a parachuting accident, he was given six months off to finish writing *Brideshead Revisited.*

As the story opens, a thirty-nine-year-old army captain, Charles Ryder, revisits the Brideshead estate in the last days of World War II to find it taken over and vandalized by the army. This takes place under the command of a coarse and stupid lieutenant named Hooper, the symbol of "Young England," a generation with no comprehension of the upper-class values represented by the house and by the old Catholic family who had lived there. So Charles' mind goes back twenty years to when this family first came into his life.

At Oxford, Charles is first attracted to Lord Sebastian Flyte, "the most conspicuous man of his year by reason of his beauty, which was arresting, and his eccentricities of behavior, which seemed to know no bounds." Charles is "in search of love in those days," and he finds it in his friendship with Sebastian, who leads Charles into the strange network of his family: the pious, manipulative mother who struggles to maintain the family's and the estate's integrity; the ineffectual older brother, the Earl of Brideshead; Julia, the beautiful and ambitious sister; and Cordelia, the plain but clever younger sister, who, we sense, often serves as Waugh's voice in her comments on the disintegrating fortunes of this odd bunch. Meanwhile, the father, the Marquis of Marchmain, has long ago fled his wife's control, escaping to Venice with his mistress.

Surely Sebastian has been symbolically named for the martyr-saint whom Renaissance artists like Mantegna loved to paint with a beautiful body pierced by dozens of arrows. Waugh's Sebastian, however, has self-inflicted wounds. His college drunkenness is the first step down into a brutally depicted alcoholism that drives him from friends, family, and England to poverty and sickness in North Africa. Indeed, Sebastian's drunkenness is so forcefully described that George Orwell concludes that Sebastian's condition and the family's unwillingness to deal with it is the novel's real theme.

For several reasons, some literary critics find Waugh and *Brideshead* hard to swallow. A snob, Waugh tends to identify the truths of Catholicism with upper-class values. For Edmund Wilson, the novel is a "Catholic tract," destined to be a best-seller, but disastrous as literature. For Catholic Sean O'Faolain, it fails to make its theme sufficiently universal. If God's love is the source of happiness, why are some of the most Catholic characters so unhappy? And even the contemporary, post–Vatican II Catholic, in an era of relatively easy annulments and a general confidence that all persons of good will are saved, may not react like Waugh's generation to Julia's marrying a divorced man or the suspense over whether Lord Marchmain will come back to the faith on his deathbed.

Yet, the controversy adds to *Brideshead's* appeal. For one thing, Waugh's satire, which bites both the middle and upper classes, can be hilarious whether or not we share his aristocratic prejudices. Lady Marchmain, for example, justifies the gap between the rich and the poor by believing that the rich may sin by envying the poor, and that it is the "achievement of Grace to sanctify the whole of life, riches included." In the book's funniest scene, Rex Mottram, the middle-class Canadian politician on the make who intends to move up in society by marrying Julia, goes to a Jesuit for instruction in the faith. He has no beliefs or even questions of his own; he will say or sign anything, no matter how odd or incomprehensible, and pay any fee, just to be called a "Catholic" and have it over with.

As readers, without completely suspending critical judgment, we must allow ourselves to enter fully into the author's world and mind. In the final scenes, Lord Marchmain dies. Julia, who has made a bad marriage outside the church and is carrying on an adulterous affair with Charles, turns away from Charles. Cordelia, who has found the ailing Sebastian in a monastery near Carthage, tells how his suffering has made him holy, and Charles, an agnostic who has bitterly resented the Marchmains' religion, attempts to pray. If we can bring the openness of faith to this story about the mysteries of grace, these closing scenes might come not as a nostalgic indulgence but as an occasion of grace as well.

Alan Paton

27 Cry, the Beloved Country

1948

SOUTH AFRICA IS ONE of the most beautiful countries I have ever seen. When I arrived in the summer of 1991, I could relish its beauty—from the top of Table Mountain in Cape Town, to the hills viewed from the tower of the Great Trek Monument in Pretoria, to the wealthy white neighborhoods of Johannesburg and the Zulu tribal huts surrounding Pietermaritzburg in Natal— without my conscience telling me I shouldn't be there.

And I could walk through the shantytowns of Cape Town, climb a rock to peer over the wall surrounding Nelson Mandela's house in Soweto, and attend the African National Congress rally, where I got within two feet of Mandela, knowing that apartheid was dead. Black-on-black violence still waged, particularly among the Zulus, but one by one the old segregation laws were being voted out. The future of this bleeding, lovely land was largely in the hands of the people of color who filled the soccer stadium that afternoon.

Alan Paton was the author of several books in addition to *Cry, The Beloved Country*, only one of which, *Too Late the Phalarope*, received wide attention. His works include a biography and two autobiographies, one published after his death from cancer in 1988. Although some considered him a conservative in his later years because he opposed international sanctions, he had devoted his life to fighting apartheid. We can imagine him hoping to hold on until he could see the sun rise on the country he loved and over which he had taught the world to weep.

Born in Pietermaritzburg in 1903, he studied at Natal University and then taught school in a rural village, Ixopo, for three years. At the age of thirty-two, he was made principal of the Diepkloof Reformatory, which housed four hundred black delinquents near Johannesburg and where the boys were locked twenty in a cell every night, with one bucket and no access to toilets or sinks. Young Paton reformed it, unlocked the cells, made it a school that taught trades, and allowed trustworthy boys to visit families and work in the city. After World War II, he traveled to Sweden, England, Canada, and the United States to study prisons and reformatories and, during his travels in 1946, began to write what would be his first published novel, *Cry, the Beloved Country*.

Its success inspired Paton to return, in 1948, to the coast of Natal to devote himself to writing. That year, however, the National Party came to power and instituted its apartheid policies. These put into law the rigid segregation of the races and the white minority's control over South Africa's economy, education, land, wealth, and social life.

The story is simple and fairly well-known, especially since it became a Broadway musical drama, *Lost in the Stars*, by Kurt Weill and Maxwell Anderson, and twice a film (1951 and 1995). An elderly black Anglican priest in a remote Natal village, Stephen Kumalo, receives a letter from a fellow priest in Johannesburg, the booming industrial gold-mining capital a full day's journey to the northwest, telling him that his sister Gertrude is "very sick."

Gertrude's illness is symbolic of a larger social evil. The Johannesburg mines have been draining the young people from the countryside. Abandoning farms and village life, they have been lured into an exploitative semislavery in the big city. They are paid only a few shillings, live in shantytowns, receive no education, and fall into prostitution and crime. To the mine owners and ruling whites, they are not persons but items on their ledgers. The young blacks were also objects of fear—in political rhetoric Americans will remember the threat of street crime in the 1960s and 1970s. To the whites it was better to keep them uneducated and therefore as subservient cogs in their economic wheel.

"Old" (he is sixty) Kumalo takes the train to the big city, which he has never seen before. He is also in search, we learn, of his son, well-named Absalom, and younger brother John, who had been swallowed by the city years before.

Guided by the younger priest, Msimangu, who wrote to him about his sister, Kumalo travels, as if in Dante's hell, in search of his lost sister, son, and brother. Each is lost in a different way. His brother John has become a big-voiced political demagogue. Gertrude has become a prostitute and has given birth to a son. Absalom is a thief who did well at the reformatory (the one Paton reformed), but got a sixteen-year-old girl pregnant. He then quit his job and returned to a life of crime.

Absalom is also a murderer. He shoots, in a botched robbery, the most interesting character in the novel, into whom Paton has poured much of himself, but whom we, as readers, know only through those who mourn him and in writings he has left behind. Arthur Jarvis, son of James Jarvis, the landowner who controlled the farmland around Kumalo's village, was an idealistic young Johannesburg mining engineer whose studies had convinced him that the mine owners' policies violated Christian principles. Supported by his wife, he was ready to risk his job and future to fight for the blacks, explaining the real causes of street crime and reforming the educational system. Absalom and two friends break into his house and shoot him in a panic.

At this point *Cry* becomes a different book. It changes from a story of a father searching for a lost son to one of two fathers who have lost sons discovering the real meaning of their sons' lives and discovering each other.

James Jarvis has never seen eye-to-eye with his son on the racial issue. As he journeys to Johannesburg, like Kumalo, in search of his son, and sits in his son's chair in the home study where he did his writing, he reads the son's unfinished essays, with their radical ideas:

> The old tribal system was, for all its violence and savagery, for all
> its superstition and witchcraft, a moral system. Our natives

today produce criminals and prostitutes and drunkards, not because it is their nature to do so, but because their simple system of order and tradition and convention has been destroyed. It was destroyed by the impact of our civilization. Our civilization has therefore an inescapable duty to set up another system of order and tradition and convention.

On the wall of his son's study, Jarvis is taken by the pictures of Christ crucified and of Abraham Lincoln and by the hundreds of books about Lincoln on his son's bookshelves. He turns to another manuscript by his son: "The truth is that our civilization is not Christian; it is a tragic compound of great ideal and fearful practice, of high assurance and desperate anxiety, of loving charity and fearful clutching of possessions. Allow me a minute . . ." Those were his last words.

Jarvis takes a Lincoln volume from the shelf and opens to the "Second Inaugural Address." Now he begins to understand his son.

Kumalo's faith is tested like Job's. Why would God bring these sons, black and white, together, only to destroy them both? The two fathers meet. Absalom is arrested, tried, and sentenced. Both fathers return to the remote hills of Natal. Arthur Jarvis' senseless death achieves a union that in life he could never have foreseen.

Although in 1953 Paton helped found the Liberal Party to challenge the Nationalist government's racial policies, some critics, particularly Africans of the next generation, did not share what they saw as Paton's sentimentality, his emphasis on love and reconciliation. But he understood the need for a show of black force, as in the great 1976 demonstrations of the Soweto schoolchildren after which nothing would be the same again.

The title comes from a chapter in which the author enters the minds of white people overcome by fear of native crime. They hold meetings, call for more police, and talk of cutting up the country into "separate areas, where white can live without black, and black without white. . . ." An unnamed narrator laments:

Cry, the beloved country, for the unborn child that is the inheritor of our fear. Let him not love the earth too deeply. Let him not laugh too gladly when the water runs through his fingers, nor stand too silent when the setting sun makes red the veld with fire. Let him not be too moved when the birds of his land are singing, nor give too much of his heart to a mountain or a valley. For fear will rob him of all if he gives too much.

Thanks to writers like Alan Paton, love has begun to cast out fear.

28 The Seven Storey Mountain

1948

THOMAS MERTON'S LAST RECORDED WORDS, in a TV talk at an ecumenical conference in Bangkok in December 1968, right before his accidental death by a bathroom electrocution, were, "And now I shall disappear."

He could not have been more wrong. In the more than thirty years since leaving us, Merton, the author of fifty books, including the recent publication of his personal journals in seven volumes, is more present to the church and the world than ever. Articles and books about him pile high on editors' desks; the same public appetites that devoured 600,000 copies of *The Seven Storey Mountain* when it first appeared, and millions of copies since, still hunger for his words. His readers survived World War II and entered the cold war, says his friend and editor Robert Giroux, and were looking for the spiritual reassurance that could come from a well-told life story of an eloquent young man who had apparently found peace in a Trappist monastery.

His contemporary and fellow convert, Avery Dulles, S.J.— whose own memoir, *Testimonial to Grace*, is a spiritual gem—testified in his 1994 Merton lecture at Columbia University that Merton's turnaround fit the pattern of young men of his generation driven to the church. Depressed by the hollowness of modern civilization, they read St. Augustine's *Confessions*, *The Imitation of Christ*, Dante, modern Catholic philosophers such as Jacques Maritain

129

and Etienne Gilson, admired the glorious art and architecture of the Middle Ages, and embraced the dogmatic faith that had inspired these marvels.

But perhaps the most powerful element of the Merton mystique is the idea that the monastery is a haven—a home that gives "that peace which the world cannot give" (Jn 14:27).

Early in his *Blue Highways* journey through America's back roads in search of his country and himself, William Least Heat Moon pulls his van into a Cistercian monastery in Georgia. Though a nonbeliever, he joins the monks at meals and prayer and engages two in conversation about their vocations. Browsing in the monastery bookstore, he picks up Merton, and a monk virtually commands him, "That's the one to read." Millions of believers and nonbelievers have been saying that for over fifty years.

Like Thoreau, in his solitude Merton seems to personify so much of what Americans fear; yet in his asceticism, in his hard-won peace of soul, he also represents what Americans most need.

I have read *The Seven Storey Mountain* in the 1950s, the 1980s, and in 2000 and have found it a period piece, a nostalgic reminder of what seemed most attractive about Catholicism—the mysteriousness of the ritual, the order of its intellectual system—in an era grasping for a sign of stability before the 1960s swept the order away. I also found it one of the great American autobiographies. Like the stories of Jane Addams, Dorothy Day, and Malcolm X, it is a conversion story, mingling witness and confession, testimony that our lives do not tumble along haphazardly, but develop, often to our surprise, according to some inscrutable plan.

> On the last day of January 1915, under the sign of the Water Bearer, in a year of a great war, and down in the shadow of some French mountains on the borders of Spain, I came into the world. Free by nature, in the image of God, I was nevertheless the prisoner of my own violence and my own selfishness, in the image of the world into which I was born.

So he begins. His mother, an American, died when he was six, and his father, a New Zealander who painted "like Cezanne," died when Tom was sixteen. Young Tom spent his early years in France and England, went to Cambridge, where he flirted with communism, and came to Columbia in 1935. There he met friends who, he later believed, had been sent by God for a special purpose.

> God brought me and half a dozen others together at Columbia, and made us friends, in such a way that our friendship would work powerfully to rescue us from the confusion and the misery in which we had come to find ourselves. . . . All our salvation begins on the level of common and natural and ordinary things. . . . Books and ideas and poems and stories, pictures and music, buildings, cities, places, philosophies were to be the materials on which grace would work.

His friends, such as Robert Giroux and the poet Robert Lax, helped make him a writer, but he might have remained silent after entering the monastery had not his abbot convinced him to undertake his memoir. For the rest of his life he was a writing machine. Though he rose at 3:15 every morning, prayed the seven hours of the office with the other monks, worked in the fields, planted hundreds of trees, served as novice master for ten years, and dealt with visitors, he wrote for at least two hours every day and involved himself more and more in the issues of race and of a war that was waging, it would seem, so far from his monastery garden.

"We are no longer living in a Christian world," he said in *Commonweal* (February 9, 1962). He meant that in the nuclear age the ethical restraints that once characterized the Christian West had been "discredited as phony and sentimental." "It is pure madness to think that Christianity can defend itself with nuclear weapons. The mere fact that we now seem to accept nuclear war as reasonable is a universal scandal."

This was an intellectual evolution his 1948 readers had not foreseen. And readers of any of the recent biographies and posthumously published journals know that he was, and became, a much more complex, even contradictory, person than the young convert who, in *The Seven Storey Mountain*, warned his readers a bit too often that hell was not so far away.

Partly because of Trappist censors, his book passed over, or merely hinted at, some of the more embarrassing periods of his preconversion life, such as his love affair at Cambridge and his illegitimate child who died during the war. Readers of his spiritual books, who might have heard that he had withdrawn in his later years from the main monastery residence to live in a Walden-like hut in the woods, knew little of the friends who would frequently meet him outside the hermitage with a six pack or of his six-month fling with a student nurse from Louisville half his age. He mused in his journal, "In a month I'll be fifty-three, and no one in his right mind would get married for the first time at such an age. . . . Yet this afternoon I wondered if I'd really missed the point of life after all. A dreadful thought."

To some readers these words are scandalous, to others, evidence that Merton, unlike some religious, never shrank from the hard questions.

None of this detracts from our fascination with his ascent up the metaphysical seven steps of Dante's *Purgatorio* to peace, as he saw it in 1948. The most powerful passages include his description of Columbia professor Mark Van Doren as the great teacher who came to class loaded with real questions that he cared about. He described his experience of working with Baroness Catherine de Hueck at the interracial Friendship House in Harlem, the neighborhood he saw as a "living condemnation of our so-called 'culture' . . . a divine indictment against New York City and the people who live downtown and make their money downtown." He carefully worked out a moral decision to join the army as a noncombatant, and then flunked the physical for not having enough teeth.

After forty years, the one episode I remember best from my first reading is the scene in which a mysterious stranger comes to young Tom's New York apartment, explaining that he knew someone who had read his recent review in the *Times* and that therefore Merton might give him money to get home to Connecticut! Merton had just been making the Spiritual Exercises of St. Ignatius, not with a guide, but reading them on his own, and he had been meditating, legs curled up in Zen fashion, on the rules for giving alms when he heard the knock at the door. His visitor, he concluded, might well be an angel. You never know when God is going to knock and give you a chance to practice what you've been praying about.

29 Letters and Papers from Prison

1951

As the twentieth century drew to a close and institutions subjected themselves to the scrutiny appropriate for moments of high historical consciousness, the toughest questions posed to religious leaders in Europe and North America were: Where were you when Hitler came to power? How did you respond as his power grew? The questions embody their own presuppositions: that religious belief has ethical and political consequences, and that silence in the face of injustice violates not just secular ethics, but the gospel.

The life and writings of the German Lutheran theologian Dietrich Bonhoeffer, introduced to many of us in seminary seminars and reading groups through John A. T. Robinson's *Honest to God* (1963) and Harvey Cox's *The Secular City* (1965), had enormous influence in the 1960s. We turned to him partly because his insights spoke directly to the critical issues that challenged believers and ex-believers in those years, such as moral responsibility, ecumenism, and God's silence in a world in which secularism and atheism seemed to have triumphed. But, above all, Bonhoeffer had unique credibility. He took part in the plot to kill Hitler and was hanged at the Flossenbürg concentration camp in 1945 in the last days of the war. He was thirty-nine.

Like St. Thomas More, he spent his last months in prison writing. He had already published the challenging commentary on the Sermon on the Mount, *The Cost of Discipleship* (1937), with its attack on the concept of "cheap grace," forgiveness which borders on spiritual laxity. His posthumously published *Letters and Papers from Prison* became primary documents in the so-called "Death of God" debate and in modern Christian theology's attempt to express itself in a voice the Vietnam generation would heed.

Both Bonhoeffer and St. Thomas More were theologians, controversialists, patriots, and prison writers who were executed because their consciences set them against the state. But was Bonhoeffer a martyr and saint? Lutherans do not canonize their spiritual models, so the question will not come up in a formal way, but those who knew him loved him and testify to his generous, sensitive, and joyous personality as well as to his heroism. If the title "martyr" adheres to his reputation, it will be a sign that German public opinion has dealt well with its memory of World War II. But in one way Bonhoeffer's story is more interesting than Thomas More's: More's end emerged from a straight line in his character, his devotion to duty. Bonhoeffer changed; to conspire against Hitler he had to forsake some of his deepest principles, because those principles did not speak to his ethical situation.

Born in Breslau, February 4, 1906, son of a psychiatry professor at the University of Berlin and of a mother whose grandfather had been chaplain to the emperor until his views differed with his majesty's, young Dietrich was raised in a big family of three brothers, a twin sister, and three other sisters. As a student at Tübingen and Berlin, he was influenced by historian Adolf von Harnack and the new theology of Karl Barth. From the beginning, his outlook was pastoral, ecumenical, and international.

Before becoming a lecturer in systematic theology at Berlin in 1931, he was an assistant pastor in Barcelona and an exchange student at Union Theological Seminary in New York, where he toured America and learned Negro spirituals in Harlem. Later, from 1933 to 1935, he was assistant pastor of a German church in London. But the Nazis' coming to power in 1933, particularly with their anti-Semitism, gave the young professor-pastor's life a decisive focus.

From his return to Germany in 1935 until his arrest in 1943, Bonhoeffer was a leader of those German Protestants called the

Confessing Church who opposed the Nazi regime. When he was arrested, the Nazis suspected he was a dangerous conspirator. They would not grasp the full extent of his involvement until a bomb went off a year later. He directed a semisecret seminary in Pomerania where students from around Germany shared a common lifestyle and piety, traveled to England and America to establish contact with anti-Nazis abroad, and eventually joined a conspiracy, along with other members of his extended family, to overthrow Hitler.

The Cost of Discipleship attempted to cut through the obstacles, such as excessive dogmatism and a preachers' personal opinions, that institutional religion had put between Jesus' words and his listeners. It is a step toward a Christology that would give believers strength to follow Christ and accept the consequences of their decision. In 1939, during a visit to New York, Bonhoeffer was urged to stay in America like other French and German intellectuals in order to escape the war. He wrote to his friend Reinhold Niebuhr, "I will have no right to participate in the reconstruction of Christian life in Germany after the war if I do not share the trials of this time with my people."

Meanwhile, some of his religious principles changed. He had accepted the traditional Lutheran distinction between politics and religion, but he began to see the Nazi regime as a false, corrupt faith and Hitler as the Antichrist, similar to the way in which Thomas More had understood Luther, and as a threat to the world's basic values. As a disciple who had meditated on the Sermon on the Mount, he was at heart a pacifist. He yearned to visit Gandhi and learn how to apply his nonviolent resistance to Germany. He saw the ecumenical movement as a force for peace and disarmament, and he knew that he himself could never bear arms. How could he put aside, or rather, overcome, these convictions? He was able to do so partly because his mind was concrete and practical and these ideas did not work, and partly because he loved and felt personally responsible for the German people.

For the next years, Bonhoeffer brazenly led a double life. To escape the draft he joined the Abwehr, a branch of military intelligence that was plotting to remove Hitler. He lived at the Benedictine monastery of Ettal near Munich, where he worked on his book *Ethics*, fell in love, and became engaged to Maria von Wedemeyer. Ten weeks later, when he was at his sister's home, the Gestapo knocked on the door.

Letters and Papers from Prison is neither a systematic nor a coherent literary work; rather, it is a collection of those documents—after many were destroyed lest they fall into Nazi hands—that survived his two-year imprisonment, mostly in the Tegel military prison in Berlin. The early letters to his family are cautious, because he knew the authorities would read them. Later, especially to his best friend Eberhard Bethke, a Congregational minister, he could pour out his heart as he rethought his whole theology.

Bonhoeffer doesn't complain about his suffering but chats about nineteenth-century literature, modern art, and the Handel and Monteverdi he has heard on the wireless. He says he expects to be released, speaks of enjoying a cigar and imagining himself on a warm beach, describes the terror of the Allied bombing, and worries about his outward image of calm when he is actually plagued by the *tristitia*, sadness, that characterizes prisoners. He urges Eberhard to attend the Good Friday liturgy at St. Peter's if he gets to Rome. Then on April 30, 1944, the tone shifts. His friend would be disturbed, he suggests, if he knew how Dietrich's ideas were taking shape.

Bonhoeffer rejects the emphasis on "inwardness" in spirituality, the tendency of journalists, psychiatrists, novelists, and confessors to probe human secrets as if the real person were the one we can never see. He rebels against the concept of "religion." By this he means elements of institutional religion, such as an excessively metaphysical theology, that get in the way of real Christianity. It means using God to fill in the gaps in human knowledge, trying to show that we need God to explain mysteries such as death and guilt that we do not otherwise understand. Ancient Greek drama used the deus ex machina, a god dropped onto the stage in the last act, to solve a problem. Religion uses God as a "stopgap," while Freud, Marx, Darwin, and all the advances of modern science push God to the margins of human experience rather than allowing him to become the center.

We should find God not at the end of life but in the center, in health and vigor as well as in suffering. This is possible in the revelation of God in Christ. "Christ is the center of life, and in no sense did he come to answer our unsolved problems." We encounter Jesus by experiencing him "as one whose only concern is for others." Thus our faith becomes not a religious relationship to a supreme Being "but a new life for others, through participation in the Being of God." The new role of the church should be to give away its endowments to the poor, "not lording it over men, but helping and serving them."

On July 20, 1944, young Colonel Claus Schenk, Count von Stauffenberg, left his briefcase carrying a time bomb in Hitler's conference room. The bomb went off, but Hitler lived. Von Stauffenberg was shot that night. By October, Bonhoeffer was transferred to a maximum security prison because Hitler might want him tortured to get other conspirators' names. In February, he was moved to Buchenwald. In April, as he finished a prayer service, two men in civilian clothes interrupted. "Prisoner Bonhoeffer, get ready to come with us." He turned to a friend and said, "This is the end . . . for me, the beginning of life."

He lived on in ways he could not have foreseen. The provocative term "religionless Christianity" found a home in theological discourse because, whatever its imprecision, it caught something that many believers had experienced. And his description of Jesus as the "man for others" made its way to Fr. Pedro Arrupe, General of the Society of Jesus, and became the motto for Jesuit educators throughout the world. If Jesuit schools do well, they send forth "men and women for others."

30 The Long Loneliness

1952

MY FIRST ENCOUNTERS WITH Dorothy Day, like everyone else's, were indirect. When I was a Fordham student in the 1950s, there was a strange unshaven guy stationed at the Third Avenue gate in baggy old clothes with a rope for a belt. He was handing out radical religious pamphlets to students on their way to or from their homes in the Bronx and Westchester or to local pubs. To us he was "a bum"; in reality he was Ammon Hennacy, friend of Dorothy Day, and a legendary character, in retrospect, of the Catholic Worker movement.

One of my friends in the American Civilization program, Jerry Holden, was doing his thesis on the Catholic Worker, so we talked about it a lot. Just as we graduated in 1955, Dorothy Day and twenty-four followers were arrested in City Hall Park for refusing to go along with New York's cold war air-raid drills, based as they were on the premise that the Soviet Union was about to send an atomic warhead missile our way and we'd better go underground if we wanted to survive.

Day, Hennacy, and the others were hauled into court, and they offered their defense. They undertook their protest

> not only to voice our opposition to war, not only to refuse to participate in psychological warfare, which their air-raid drill is, but also as an act of public penance for having been the first

people in the world to drop the atomic bomb and to make the hydrogen bomb.

Of the greatest American women, Jane Addams, Eleanor Roosevelt, and Dorothy Day, Eleanor Roosevelt was the only one to attract the historians at the end of the millennium. But the influence of Dorothy Day, in many ways, draws on the power of the other two and will last on a level that the others cannot touch.

Jane Addams and Dorothy Day established institutions—Hull House in Chicago and the Catholic Worker house in the Bowery, respectively—to meet the needs of the inner-city poor. Both lost national popularity when they followed through on the international implications of their values, from fighting poverty to embracing pacifism. This was similar, in a way, to Martin Luther King Jr.'s losing part of his constituency when he opposed the Vietnam War.

Theodore Roosevelt called Addams a "Bull Mouse." During World War I, she was denounced as a radical and a Bolshevist, "the most dangerous woman in America." Because of its pacifism, the nationwide Catholic Worker movement shrunk to a few Houses of Hospitality during World War II, only to take on new life in the 1960s as the movement's nonviolent philosophy provided the moral underpinnings for opposition to the war in Vietnam.

Once, in 1936, when Dorothy Day saw 108 homeless Arkansas farmers living in tents by the roadside, her first response was to telegraph Mrs. Roosevelt to do something about it. Though Mrs. Roosevelt responded through the bureaucracy, she did so immediately. Somehow Day had sensed in her a kindred spirit. Meanwhile, anyone who admired Mrs. Roosevelt in her lifetime will remember how much she, like Addams and Day, was vilified as a radical, although her views were much more conventional than those of the other two. All three were reviled as busybodies and do-gooders because they were strong, independent, fearless women wielding political and moral influence in a world run exclusively by men.

Dorothy Day's influence will last, as Mark Massa documents in *Catholics and American Culture: Fulton Sheen, Dorothy Day, and the Notre Dame Football Team* (1999), because she builds on so many traditions that are foundational to modern Catholicism: the social encyclicals of Leo XIII and Pius XI, the French personalism of Emmanuel Mounier and Jacques Maritain, English distributists like G. K. Chesterton, the mysticism of St. Thérèse of Lisieux, and the American spirituality of the transcendentalists Emerson and Thoreau and abolitionists such as William Lloyd Garrison.

She will last because, with the French visionary Peter Maurin, she founded a movement that combines agrarianism, Christian philosophy, socialism, pacifism, anarchism, journalism, and strong personalities into a half-century of Catholic intellectual life that was both leftist and obedient to church authorities.

Her spiritual family includes Michael Harrington, author of *The Other America*; the Association of Catholic Trade Unionists; Daniel Berrigan, S.J.; John Cogley, an editor of *Commonweal* and the *New York Times*; generations of readers of the *Catholic Worker*; Cesar Chavez and the United Farm Workers; James Douglas, who helped draft the Vatican Council's statement on peace; countless draft resisters; and the thousands of poor people who have filed through her Bowery soup kitchen for a meal and a bed.

Her autobiography, *The Long Loneliness*, is by no means the whole story of her life, which she has told in several memoirs and an autobiographical novel. It is a "confession." She says, "Going to confession is hard. Writing is hard, because you are 'giving yourself away.' But if you love, you want to give yourself."

She begins with her Brooklyn childhood and ends with Peter Maurin's death; in between she recounts her pilgrimage—as a journalist, a Greenwich Village bohemian, a political agitator, a world traveler, and a convert. She passes over an abortion and a brief marriage, but dwells lovingly on her common-law marriage with Forster Batterman, whose child, Tamar, she bore, but whom she left so she and her daughter could become Catholics.

Rereading *The Long Loneliness*, along with a 1968 collection of articles from the *Catholic Worker* edited by Thomas C. Cornell and James H. Forest, *A Penny a Copy*, suggests that the word that best describes Day is *revolutionary*. Revolution is the reorientation and realignment of a whole system of values; Dorothy Day's contribution to such a shift of values helps her bridge the gap between generations and makes her a symbolic mother to much of the American church.

She loves the Mystical Body of Christ in all its attractive and unattractive parts—Eugene O'Neill reciting "The Hound of Heaven" to her in a Fourth Street saloon back room; Max Bodenheim taking refuge in drink because drink was easier to get than bread; Elizabeth Gurley Flynn, the communist whom Dorothy saw as fulfilling the first law of Christ. Day gave the word *Catholic* its fullest extension, and she has vastly expanded our concept of violence.

For Day, violence is President Truman "jubilant" over the deaths of 318,000 Japanese. "It is to be hoped they are vaporized," she wrote caustically in the September 1945 *Worker*, "our Japanese brothers, scattered, men, women and babies, to the four winds, over the seven seas. Perhaps we will breathe their dust into our nostrils, feel them in the fog of New York on our faces, feel them in the rain on the hills of Easton."

Violence, for her, was in the lay trustees of St. Patrick's Cathedral who broke the graveyard strike in 1949, who, as John McKeon wrote in the *Catholic Worker* (April 1949), "could not treat Catholic working men as human beings and brothers."

Although I knew several of her friends through my job at *Commonweal*, I saw her only a few times and met her only once. A few years before her death in 1980, she came to a memorial Mass at St. Joseph's Church in the Village for John Cogley, the most admired Catholic writer of his time, whose intellectual integrity and desire to be an Anglican priest led him to leave the church. I gave her communion and, with James O'Gara, *Commonweal* editor, talked to her after Mass. In *The Long Loneliness* she describes herself kneeling in that same church in her youth attending early Mass after a night in the taverns, not knowing what was going on at the altar but comforted by the lights and silence.

A secular historian might suggest that because we still have intercontinental nuclear missiles pointed at one another and the poor are still with us, her revolution has failed. Of course, this historian could say the same thing about Christianity itself. Dorothy Day's followers would answer that we still have time.

Edward Steichen

31   The Family of Man

1955

In THE FIRST MEDITATION OF THE second week in the Spiritual Exercises, St. Ignatius of Loyola helps us to prepare ourselves to contemplate the meaning of the Incarnation by asking us to call up an imaginary vision of the whole spread of the earth inhabited by many different nations. Today we could be sure he would use the marvelous first photograph taken by the astronauts from space of our planet, that splendid blue pearl floating in the universal sea.

We are to scan the surface of the globe, zoom in, and observe the human race in all its rich variety. "Some are white, some black; some at peace, and some at war; some weeping, some laughing; some well, some sick; some coming into the world, some dying," and some on the road to hell. We listen to what they say, then we try to picture God on his heavenly throne, and we hear the divine persons say, "Let us work the redemption of the human race."

When Ignatius wrote those lines, he probably had in mind the medieval illuminated manuscripts, stained-glass windows, or paintings of Brueghel and his contemporaries that depict in vivid detail the day-to-day business dealings of ordinary people— farmers bringing in wheat before a storm, the punishments of the damned, the heavenly banquet of the saved. We, with our cinematic minds, can conjure up every 1940s newsreel, the burning autos and plastic-bagged corpses of the TV evening news, for our own vision of a world waiting to be saved. Ignatius's point is that our contemplation must begin by concentrating on particular men and women—this one digging a ditch in the field, that one selling a chicken, or stealing it.

Edward Steichen, one of America's two greatest photojournalists—the other, his comrade Alfred Stieglitz, who shot *The Steerage*, the 1907 photo of immigrants huddled below deck on a luxury liner—probably never knew of Ignatius. His life's greatest work, however, was a 1955 photo exhibit presented at the Museum of Modern Art that has inspired our meditation on the unity of humankind more than any other artwork in modern memory.

For those who lived through World War II and fought for the Allied cause, the war years were a crusade for the "redemption of the human race." Steichen's understanding of the human race emerged from his experience as an immigrant, an artist, and a photographer in both world wars. After his birth in Luxembourg in 1879, his parents brought him to the United States in 1882 and raised him in Hancock, Michigan, and Milwaukee, Wisconsin. As a young photographer he experimented by mixing painting and photographic techniques, and he joined Stieglitz to found Photo-Secession, a group promoting photography as a fine art. They opened a gallery in New York that for the first time in America exhibited the work of Rodin, Matisse, and Cézanne.

His role during World War I as an aerial photographer turned him against impressionistic photography. He burned his paintings and concentrated on precise, clear realism. In the 1930s he gained a reputation as a fashion photographer for *Vogue* and *Vanity Fair* and produced striking portraits of John Barrymore, Paul Robeson, Katherine Hepburn, and his brother-in-law Carl Sandburg. But World War II, when the United States Navy commissioned him to document the war at sea, marked a turning point in how he saw his own mission as an artist.

As director of photography for the Museum of Modern Art, he knew he had seen enough war, including the Korean War, to despise it as a "monstrosity," a "butcher shop" that set civilization back "to the animal stage." He had attempted to shock the public into this realization through three exhibitions of contemporary war images, but the shock, he found, quickly wore off. The public would find the images "ghastly" then go out for some drinks. So he was inspired to try another approach, to present a *positive* image of the beauty and unity of the human family. He picked up Sandburg's biography of Lincoln and as he flipped through the pages, three words jumped out of the text of a Lincoln speech: "family of man."

So in 1952 he set out for twenty-nine cities in eleven European countries and wrote letters to photographers all over the world, determined to prove that "the art of photography is a dynamic process of giving form to ideas and explaining man to man." It was conceived as a mirror of the universal elements and emotions in the everydayness of life—as a mirror of the essential oneness of humankind throughout the world. He wanted the element of love to dominate and to communicate an optimism that gives us faith in ourselves. In his midseventies, he worked seven days a week, with a few assistants and a lot of advisers, sorting through over two million photos. He knew that he risked controversy. The cold war was at its height and the American public, cowed by McCarthyism, was not attuned to seeing the world as one. In 1954, the Atomic Energy Commission exploded the hydrogen bomb at the Bikini atoll in the Pacific and accidentally wounded nearly three hundred Americans and Japanese. Steichen's answer to these events would be 503 pictures from sixty-eight countries, some poetry quotes selected by Sandburg, and his own belief in man's inherent goodness.

The exhibit opened in New York in 1955, toured the world, and was seen by nine million people; the book, *The Family of Man*, sold over five million copies. The first image is a burst of sun breaking through clouds over a dark beach, with the caption from Genesis 1:3, "and God said, let there be light."

The photographs go on to portray life from birth to death—lovemaking, harvests, house building, music making, toil, famine, grief, war. Finally, there is the famous Eugene Smith picture of two children, a little boy and girl (actually his own children), walking off into sunlit woods as if the whole cycle of life were to begin again.

As Carl Sandburg says in his introduction, "If the human face is 'the masterpiece of God,' it is here then in a thousand fateful registrations."

The more than forty-five years that have passed since this exhibition give poignancy, and sometimes irony, to its contemporary impact. Its celebration of pregnancy and childhood is no less valid, yet today more than one million teenagers become pregnant every year, over 70 percent of them unmarried. In the underclass of American ghettos, children are having children. Boys imagine they are proving their virility, girls imagine they are filling a void in their lives, and infants emerge into a world that cannot or will not care for them. We also celebrate childbirth reminded of the more than one million American abortions every year.

We see the famine pictures every year, though now in color. Perhaps the most telling American photo of the twentieth century is Dorothea Lange's grim portrait of the migrant woman dressed in rags, her chin resting on her fingertips, her two children nestled on her shoulders with their backs to the lens, as she stares grimly ahead asking what tomorrow might bring.

Nor have we seen our last picture of a defiant teenager throwing a rock at a tank, or of a dead soldier, the back of his shirt torn open, a rifle stuck upright in the earth to mark the hole where his body sprawls, and the quote from Sophocles, "Who is the slayer, who the victim? Speak."

The Spiritual Exercises might last a weekend, or thirty days, or be spread out over several months. But ideally, the experience, like the impact of an artwork or a book, comes to life again every time a passage or a picture creates a presence that wasn't there before or raises a question one may have been trying to duck. And maybe we slow down and look at it again.

32 The Divine Milieu

1957, 1960

To some the world has disclosed itself as too vast: within such immensity, man is lost and no longer counts; and there is nothing left for him to do but shut his eyes and disappear. To others, on the contrary, the world is too beautiful; and it, and it alone, must be adored.

There are Christians, as there are men, who remain unaffected by these feelings of anxiety or fascination. The following pages are not for them. . . .

Why IS IT THAT IN RECENT YEARS—in contrast to the continuing influence of Thomas Merton, C. S. Lewis, and even G. K. Chesterton—we hear less of Teilhard de Chardin? A catalogue check in a college library shows that of fifty-four titles about Teilhard, the overwhelming majority were written in the 1960s, a decade after his principal works, *The Phenomenon of Man* and *The Divine Milieu*, appeared in English. Both of these books were written in the 1920s, but religious superiors would not allow Teilhard to publish in his lifetime. Somehow his principal themes—the unity of all creation, his spiritualization of the scientific theory of evolution, his optimistic reading of the destiny of the human race—spoke to the spirit of the 1950s and 1960s.

147

Is the twenty-first century less optimistic than the American 1960s? Has Teilhard's unique vocabulary become a greater obstacle than it was then? Has his mystical reconciliation of the sciences—biology, paleontology, geology—with theology become less palatable to our taste? Or did the 1960s sense a tension between materialism and the spirit, while today the stock market and the confidence in becoming a millionaire have won out?

"The look in his eyes when they met your eyes revealed the man's soul. His reassuring sympathy restored your confidence in yourself," writes his friend Pierre LeRoy, S.J. He was witty and convivial as well as brilliant; and, unlike many so-called important people, he was sincerely interested in others. He would listen to someone's ideas, and if they seemed extravagant, he would simply smile. Perhaps this "reassuring sympathy" explains his impact on thousands of readers who normally would never pick up a "spiritual" book. He wrote *The Divine Milieu*, he said, "for the waverers . . . those who, instead of giving themselves wholly to the Church, either hesitate on its threshold or turn away in the hope of going beyond it."

Teilhard was born in 1881, with the blood of Voltaire in his veins from his mother's side of the family. A stretcher bearer in World War I, a Jesuit, a teacher, a paleontologist, and a codiscoverer of Peking man, Teilhard fused Christian salvation history and Darwinian evolution in his spirituality. Reread today, *The Divine Milieu* strikes me as, among many other things, a spirituality of work, an encouraging reassurance to those sucked into the exhaustive, competitive vortex of law, medicine, teaching, social work, factory toil, farm labor, or raising a family. Understood correctly, this means that they are being sucked into God, not alienated from the source of all creation.

Teilhard's insistence that we find "rejuvenation" in "the perception of a more intimate connection between the victory of Christ and the outcome of the work which our human effort here below is seeking to construct" finds an echo in the last line of John F. Kennedy's inaugural address: "Here on earth God's work must truly be our own." So a generation on the eve of Vatican II was ready for the writer who anticipated the theme of *The Constitution on the Church in the Modern World*, that the future of humanity lies in the hands of those who are strong enough to provide coming generations with reasons for living and hope.

Sample his influence. Thomas Merton considered a key passage in *Milieu*, in which "the Christian is not asked to swoon in the shadow, but to climb in the light, of the Cross," "the finest contemplative page written in our century." Novelists such as Graham Greene and Flannery O'Connor have testified to his impact, as have political leaders such as Sargent Shriver, who quoted him at the Democratic Convention in 1972, and Mario Cuomo, who said that Teilhard had convinced him that "God did not intend this world only as a test of our purity, but rather as an expression of his love; that we are meant to live actively, totally, in this world and in so doing make it better for all whom we can touch."

That is the message of this short series of prayers, reflections, and notes for those who feel the world and God are pulling them in opposite directions. Teilhard wants to nourish a healthy love of both God and the world, not by teaching his readers to "purify" their intentions but by encouraging them to collaborate in God's continuing work of creation.

When we were in theology, a popular controversy was over the role of the "hyphenated priest": the hypothetical identity crisis brought on when priests dedicated to rebuilding the secular city also became doctors, lawyers, factory workers, congressmen, artists, and circus clowns, as well as preachers and professors. Somehow the debate died. Perhaps those who couldn't take the tension left. Others printed Teilhard's prayer on their ordination cards: "To the full extent of my powers, because I am a priest, I wish from now on to be the first to become conscious of all that the world loves, pursues and suffers . . . to become more widely human and more nobly of the earth than any of the world's servants."

Teilhard died suddenly of a stroke in New York City, where he had lived since 1951, on Easter Sunday of 1955, the same year I graduated from Fordham. I learned later that two of my favorite Jesuits, anthropologist J. Franklin Ewing, S.J., and philosophical psychologist Joseph Donceel, S.J., had been his friends, so surely Teilhard had visited the campus many times. Now I like to imagine that our paths crossed, or even that our eyes might have met. After two years in the antiaircraft artillery in Germany, I entered the novitiate at St. Andrew-on-Hudson. There, as part of our daily labor, I cut the grass in the graveyard, clipping around the base of a plain, gray stone marked, incompletely, "Teilhard," never guessing that beneath the sod this great mystic who had studied the earth so intimately and who had spiritualized matter in his philosophy, was now mingled with the clay from which we have all sprung.

Walter M. Miller Jr.

33 A Canticle for Leibowitz

1960

If the definition of a classic, as Robert Giroux put it in a talk at St. Peter's College on October 7, 1999, is a book that stays in print, a variation on the definition is a book that we keep talking about, whose main ideas retain relevance beyond the political circumstances that inspired it.

A Canticle for Leibowitz first appeared at the height of the cold war when people were talking about bomb shelters in their backyards. Critics compared it to *Brave New World, 1984*, and *On the Beach*; one reviewer, Walker Percy, said that though it was not as "good" as Katherine Mansfield, " . . . it is of more moment than Katherine Mansfield . . . and the better known sci-fi futuristic novels, *1984* and *Brave New World*." Now each republication seems to add to its reputation and to transcend the headlines of over forty years ago.

Canticle's last chapter poses a question about the future of humankind in space: It's A.D. 3700. We have made a thorough mess of things. We have consistently preserved enough knowledge to allow us to reconstruct our weapons of mass destruction out of the ashes of the previous era. What good would it do to transplant our civilization, several times destroyed by nuclear wars and half-rebuilt, to another world where we would probably not let it survive?

151

Since *Canticle* was published in 1960, we have transplanted human hearts, walked on the moon, photographed Mars up close, waged and lost a war in Vietnam, created "life" in test tubes, cloned sheep, come to the brink of several nuclear meltdowns, and watched a space shuttle blow up on TV. In our TV and cinema *Star Trek* and *Star Wars* worlds, the popular culture has created a whole imaginary universe that is as real to our children as are their grade-school teachers or schoolyard chums. Yet *Canticle* speaks with an authority beyond all these events.

Critical reception of *Canticle* was mixed, largely because some critics lacked the background to deal with Miller's ideas. The *Times Literary Supplement* observed: "Some critics have talked about this astonishing novel in terms of science fiction. That is an insult. Primarily and essentially it is religious and human." But it gained its vast reputation by becoming one of those books that friend passes to friend. Read this and tell me what you think.

The story begins a thousand years from now and spans seventy generations. The world is in ruins, reduced to barbarism by an accidental atomic war. In their Utah desert sanctuary, the monks of the abbey of blessed Leibowitz preserve the memorabilia, the last vestiges of human knowledge.

Their blessed founder had been an electrical technician until his wife was killed by fallout. Then he started a religious order of copyists and memorizers to rescue human culture from the new Dark Ages. But Leibowitz was martyred by the tribe of Simpletons—those who, seeing the havoc wrought by technology, feared a new Renaissance.

Somehow, as centuries pass and man regains mastery over nature, the split between church and secular culture widens. Secular rulers and scientists again turn science and weapons into gods. The faith, as personified by each generation of monastery abbots, becomes the increasingly isolated conscience of humankind.

When monsters—genetic victims of radiation—are born, the church alone demands that they be allowed to live. At the end of the book, when another Flame Deluge, nuclear war, is turning cities into puddles of glass and piling corpses by the millions, the last abbot spends his last breaths confronting the government

Mercy Cadres, who would administer the secular sacrament of euthanasia to the dying.

Of course in 1960, Miller had no idea of the sudden gulf that would separate the pre- and postconciliar church. His church of the future, which will protect itself against the gates of hell by sending a spaceship full of monk-scientists, children, nuns, and bishops (to preserve the apostolic succession) to another galaxy, retains, with all its learning, some of the worst aspects of the pre-conciliar church. Before the ship takes off, a monk slams the door and quips, "Sic transit mundus!"

New Rome deals with its friends and foes by concordats and interdicts, as if old Rome had learned nothing from history. As the intercontinental ballistic missiles leave their launching pads in the war between the Atlantic and Asian states, the pope stops praying for peace and sings the Mass in Time of War. In his conflict with the secular-humanist doctor who would put radiation victims out of their misery, the abbot can only reply with the Stoic dictum that nature imposes nothing on man that it doesn't prepare man to bear.

We would like to know more about Miller himself. Born in Florida in 1923, he attended the University of Tennessee, served in the army in Europe during World War II, participated in the shelling of Monte Casino, and received several medals. He came home sick over what he had seen. At the University of Texas, he poured all his energies into writing short stories, TV shows, and *Canticle*, which has been the basis of his national—and international—reputation.

I tracked him down personally in the 1970s to write a book review for *Commonweal* on a *Canticle*-like science-fiction novel, Thomas S. Klise's *The Last Western*, which he compared favorably to *Moby Dick*. Later, Notre Dame *Commonweal* writer John Garvey visited him in Florida for an interview and won his friendship. He told John that he had written *Canticle* while struggling, successfully, to save his marriage, but he had been unable to write since then because writers have to tell their own stories and he was too ashamed of his own story to put it on paper.

He had drifted away from post–Vatican II Catholicism into his own form of Buddhism; though he opposed nuclear weapons, he loved guns. The 1996 death of his wife, Anne, to whom he had been married for fifty years, was a terrible blow. There was no funeral, and friends were told to send no condolences. "If you want to do a good deed," Miller said, "kiss an enemy" (cf. Garvey ref.). A few months later, Miller picked up one of his guns and killed himself. Garvey wrote in *Commonweal* (April 5, 1996), "He was a complicated, difficult, and compassionate man. I liked him very much. God rest him."

Still we have his wonderful book. We can hardly expect him to solve the problems that Job and Dostoyevsky failed to put to rest. It is enough that he suggests that we will never be able to replant Eden because we would never give it a chance to grow. We are like the children in *Lord of the Flies*: even when we are rescued from the primitive barbarism we have created on a tropical island, we are brought into a larger context of sophisticated barbarism in war.

Since *Canticle* first appeared, some new words—such as Three Mile Island, Bhopal, *Challenger,* and Chernobyl—have entered everyday language with their own warnings about about our limited ability to control our technology. The end of the cold war tells us that nuclear missiles are not likely to fly between the Soviet Union and the United States.

But Walter M. Miller Jr. cautions us sadly that whatever we did wrong originally, we are likely to do wrong again.

154

J. F. Powers

34 Morte D'Urban

1962

I BELIEVE THAT THE WORLD will be saved by the
poor," Georges Bernanos once wrote; and his poverty-stricken
curé in *The Diary of a Country Priest* scribbled in his journal: "By
nature I am probably coarse grained, for I confess that I have always been repelled by the lettered priest. After all, to cultivate
clever people is merely a way of dining out, and a priest has no
right to go out to dinner in a world full of starving people."

In the first chapter of J. F. Powers's *Morte D'Urban*, a wealthy
Chicago businessman, Billy Cosgrove, drives the urbane Fr. Urban
around town, treats him to lunch, and leads him up to the roof of
a better-class apartment building from which they can gaze out
over Lake Michigan and the Chicago skyline. Urban has been
hoping for a big donation, and, to butter Billy up, has given him
some oak firewood from the novitiate property for his fireplace.
"This would be a prestige address for *any* concern," says Billy,
and Urban's heart sinks. He had wanted a gift, and now he thinks
Billy is trying to rent him a property.

But he's wrong. Billy will give the Order of St. Clement the top-
floor apartment in exchange for some more firewood. The order
accepts; but, to Urban's disappointment, they use it for their own
comfort, rather than as a sophisticated apostolic center.

We can see that the original rooftop scene is a subtle parody of Jesus' temptation, in which Satan shows him the world from a high place. The order has been corrupted—but just a little bit.

I would be surprised if Powers were not an admirer of Bernanos, but their priests move in very different circles. While the curé is soaking his hard bread in bad wine, Fr. Urban and a clerical or business pal are downing champagne in Chicago's Pump Room and remarking that Jesus also ate lamb. Both Bernanos and Powers are concerned with the mediocrity of the church's subculture, but for Powers's Fr. Urban, the fund-raiser for the Clementines, a religious order outstanding only for the pervasiveness of its mediocrity, poverty is most often having to cope with the stupidity and shriveled imaginations of his peers.

No novelist has so meticulously—nor hilariously—described the daily doings inside the average American rectory or religious community of men: the housekeepers and cooks who rule and possess their charges more absolutely than many wives, the petty power struggles and jealousies over apostolic turf, the once cozy recreation room overcome by the new TV. Within these small worlds seldom touched by the social conflicts of race and war, the priests try, within the limitations of a disintegrating way of life, to lead holy—or at least good—lives.

Fr. Urban, "fifty-four, tall and handsome but a trifle loose in the jowls and red of eye," is a whiz, a spellbinder in the pulpit and at small-town midwestern garden parties, the kind of popular priest who sees in every new face a soul to be saved and a potential benefactor to be cultivated—though not necessarily in that order. Sent in turn to a crumbling retreat house and a foundering parish, he revives one by building a golf course to attract a higher-class clientele and the other by conducting a census that demonstrates the need for a new church.

In one of the novel's funniest chapters, Urban plays golf with the bishop, a Presbyterian minister, and Fr. Feld, a stocky little champ whom the bishop has brought along to whip Urban in retaliation for trouncing the bishop a few months before. Urban has decided it will be good politics to allow the bishop his surrogate victory, until he sees the Clementine novices gathered on the hill to cheer him on. Another kind of Catholic novel gives the priest a more dramatic moral crisis—such as how to advise his unmarried sister who wants an abortion—but Powers sees integrity won and lost in little battles as well as grand ones.

The "death" Urban undergoes is the awful discovery that the line between himself and Sinclair Lewis's George Babbitt is a thin one. Urban has always argued that lambs can lie down with lions and live; but the shady businessman and rich widow he has pursued and pampered have brought him in their doors, bought him drinks and presents, and kept him there on their terms. The thirtyish rich woman who invites him for a nude midnight swim after drinks by the fireplace tells him: "You're an operator . . . and I don't think you have a friend in the world."

Powers, who died in 1999 at eighty-one, grew up in Illinois, left Northwestern University to work in a bookstore, as a pacifist refused induction in World War II, and was imprisoned for over a year in Minnesota. For several decades, he and his family lived in both Ireland and Minnesota, where he taught writing at St. John's University in Collegeville. He was a shy man who wrote with great difficulty, producing three short-story collections and two novels. A devout Catholic who did not like the changes in the church, his faith was tested by the death of his wife in 1988.

In 1966, writing in *America* on Crawford Power's reissued novel, *The Encounter,* about a Maryland priest who sees his own life mysteriously tied to that of a circus acrobat, I predicted that the "priest-novel for tomorrow's generation" would be written or inspired by the "movement"—"a priest student or seminarian who takes the Gospel so seriously that both the promise and corruption of modern society, the problems of race, peace, and poverty seem more than ever the priests' special province." It hasn't happened. The priest novels for today's and tomorrow's generations were written years ago.

35 The Other America

1962, 1971, 1981

G OOD AFTERNOON, ladies and gentleman." I cringe.
I am riding on a New York subway, deep in the bowels of the
earth, and this black man in rags and bandages and on crutches
has banged through the doors between the cars, demanding that
we lift our eyes from our magazines and pay attention to him. He
is homeless and poor and sick and wants money, and I am angry—
at him because he has forced himself on us, at society because it
has not solved the poverty problem, and at myself because I'm
not going to give him anything.

What would Michael Harrington do?

"I am a pious apostate, an atheist shocked by the faithlessness of
believers, a fellow traveler of moderate Catholicism who has been
out of the church for more than twenty years." So begins *Fragments
of a Century*, Michael Harrington's personal memoir of the 1950s
and 1960s. He declares himself a product of the middle-class Irish
ghettos of St. Louis and Holy Cross College, where the intellectual
decadence of rationalistic neo-Thomism, which forgot the complexity of the human soul, began to sour him on Catholicism.

Yet in 1971 he received a Holy Cross honorary degree and gave
the graduation address there. Many of those who have admired
Harrington's books and journalism for years still think of him as
part of the Catholic tradition, perhaps because some elements of
the faith are so deep in his bones. Today, his economic and political

values seem steeped in the Christian principles he absorbed in his years of living and working at the Catholic Worker House of Hospitality on Skid Row in 1951 and 1952. There he read the breviary daily and came face to face with the down-and-out poor who were to become the subjects of *The Other America: Poverty in the United States*, one of the most influential books in recent American history.

Harrington defined poverty in terms of "those who are denied the minimum levels of health, housing, food, and education that our present stage of scientific knowledge specifies for life as it is now lived in the United States." His dividing line, following the Bureau of Labor Statistics, was $4,000 a year for a family of four and $2,000 for an individual living alone. This meant that between forty and fifty million Americans, or about a fourth of the population, were poor—really hard put to get enough to eat. Then he explained how the poor have become "invisible." That good clothes were cheap hid the fact that those wearing them were not decently housed, fed, or doctored. More than eight million of the poor were over sixty-five years old, many sitting alone in rented rooms, without phones, and suffering from mental illness. The young poor were confined to their ghettos, sometimes advertising their poverty through lurid tabloid headlines about drugs, robberies, and gang killings.

Most of the poor he described were from large, established cultures of poverty—migrant farmworkers, the urban economic underclass of dishwashers and laundry workers not covered by the 1961 amendment to the 1938 minimum-wage law and earning about $45.50 a week, Appalachians no longer needed in the mines, farmers incapable of competing with the mechanized agribusiness of the Midwest, and blacks doubly impoverished by being born in a black ghetto. Then Harrington adds three other groups: the bohemian intellectuals, the rural poor who have migrated to the cities, and the alcoholics he came to know on Christie Street while working with Dorothy Day.

The Other America, at first little noticed, caught the eye of Dwight Macdonald, whose feature review in *The New Yorker* was reprinted as a pamphlet. It made its way along the grapevine to President John F. Kennedy, who decided to make it a theme of his next campaign. Lyndon Johnson made it the centerpiece of his War on Poverty until that war became the casualty of the other war in Vietnam.

After updating *The Other America* for the 1970s and 1980s, Harrington produced a sequel, *The New American Poverty* (1984), in which he grants some progress in public awareness of the poor, but warns about the danger of "scientifically" redefining poverty out of existence and of not noticing how it has changed: it had become "feminized," internationalized, and more violent than ever in the blood of drug wars.

In a sad chapter of the 1984 book, he returns to the old Bowery haunts where he had lived at the Worker thirty years before, only to find the old Bowery gone. Even the Catholic Worker had locked the door! Before, the door was always open and anyone could walk in. But now the drifter population is younger and angrier. There are fights in the food line, tension between blacks, Hispanics, and Anglos. The "homeless," many of them mental patients, can get nasty and violent. Even the local Franciscan church must bolt the door.

I met Harrington several times at lectures and parties and was much charmed by his eloquence and warmth. During the last phase of his life he led the Democratic Socialists, wrote books and articles, and delivered weekly commentaries on National Public Radio that, he told me shortly before he died, sometimes had more influence than his years of writing. If he were alive today, he might refer to the work of two journalists, Donald L. Barlett and James B. Steele, whose books, *America: What Went Wrong?* (1992) and *America: Who Stole the Dream?* (1996) have continued his work of documenting the growing gap between rich and poor and analyzing the economic and political causes for the gap. Barlett and Steele describe how government policies favoring the rich—such as tax breaks for the wealthy, increased immigration into the domestic job market, sending jobs abroad, decline in antitrust enforcement, and the decline of manufacturing—have created two classes that they call the have-mores, those with incomes over $75,000, and the have-lesses.

Chicago scholar Ed Marciniak has enumerated the new categories of poor in *Commonweal* (January 28, 2000) as the residents of big public housing projects, idlers, drug users, teenage unwed mothers, urban homeless, the hidden mentally ill, the disabled and chronically ill, the temporarily jobless, and the working poor who don't earn a living wage.

Other recent studies point out that the top 1 percent of the population now controls 40 percent of the nation's household wealth and that the gap widens, both economically and socially, as the new millionaires withdraw to private preserves, gated communities with walls and security guards, while the basic American dream of a nice home for everyone has become an illusion. The *New York Times* (February 20, 2000) reports that in Silicon Valley, California, "where millionaires are minted every day," more and more working people, some of whom make $50,000 a year, are becoming homeless. In a neighborhood of Ferraris and Mercedes-Benzes and columned mansions with swimming pools, the homeless working poor sleep on the public bus—as New Yorkers sleep in the subway—and beg meals at the church soup lines. "At the richest time in the richest region in the richest nation in the world, less than thirty percent of the households here can afford to buy a house."

Meanwhile, because I have met a beggar on the subway just about every time I've ridden it, I suppose I cannot expect ever to be left alone. Which is as it should be.

161

C. S. Lewis

36 The Four Loves

1960

Just as the central revelation of the Scriptures is that God, by nature and definition, is love, so the final week of St. Ignatius's Spiritual Exercises attempts to instill a constant disposition that enables us to be loving under even the most difficult circumstances. St. Thérèse's "little way" involves loving a fellow nun she doesn't even like; Myles Connolly's Mr. Blue shows love to someone whom no one else can stand; the North American Jesuit martyrs tried to love their Iroquois torturers while burning at the stake.

One of the qualities of some of the best books on love and friendship—such as Martin Marty's *Friendship*, Dom Aelred Watkins's *The Enemies of Love*, and C. S. Lewis's *The Four Loves*—is that they deromanticize complex relationships, silence the violins, so that love is seen not merely in terms of its emotions but as an extension of personal integrity which itself can grow only out of a lifetime of major and minor self-denials.

Of C. S. Lewis's more than forty books—such as the popular *Screwtape Letters*, in which an experienced devil gives advice to a young devil—that have sold over fifty million copies and that include literary criticism, children's literature, science fiction, autobiographical memoirs, and religious apologetics, some critics pass over *The Four Loves* as radio talks delivered in the last years of his life, while others list it among the handful of books on which

his greatness is based. All agree it has captured a wide reader-
ship, including the admiration of Pope John Paul II. In one
sense, its text draws on earlier works, such as *The Allegory of Love*
(1936), but he wrote it while he was learning through experience
what he had previously known about love mostly through books.

As those who saw the film *Shadowlands* (1993) know, in 1956
Lewis married Joy Davidman, an American divorcée with two
sons. They married first civilly, then sacramentally—first to save
her from being deported, then for Lewis to bring her into his
home as she faced death from bone cancer. He married her first,
he said, for friendship, then for love. She died in 1960, but the
two years during which she regained some strength were the
happiest of his life. They are also the years of his writing and
recording these talks on love for the American Episcopal Church
radio series in Atlanta, Georgia. Alas, the Episcopal authorities
found the chapter on Eros "too frank" and his English too British
for American listeners, but the book, like its author, found
friends around the world.

Lewis begins with some distinctions between Gift-love, by
which a person plans and works for the future of a family he or
she may die without seeing; Need-love, sometimes like a child's
love for parents or a person's love for God, and sometimes a glut-
tonous craving for affection; and Appreciative-love, the starting
point for our whole experience of beauty, which enables us to
rejoice in God's glory.

After discussion of what he calls "Sub-human" loves, such as
love of nature and patriotism, Lewis plunges into his conversation on Affection, Friendship, Eros, and Charity. We can see him
propped up in a big leather chair before the fireplace in his study,
waving his pipe (he also smoked sixty cigarettes a day) and staring at a distant spot on the bookshelf right below the ceiling. We
can also see him showing the manuscript to Joy and asking,
"What do you think if I say this?"

Under Affection—the "most instinctive," "most animal" of
loves—we meet those familiar distortions: Mrs. Fidget, who
"lived for her family" but imprisoned them in her possessiveness
(cooking hot meals on the hottest summer days and always waiting up for those who were out late) and Dr. Quartz, the devoted

teacher, who welcomed hero-worshiping students to his home until they dared to differ with the master and assert their own views. We can also imagine Cambridge tutor Professor Lewis, who would meet with his pupils, read their essays, and go after them vigorously, delighted when a student would fight back and defend a position.

On Eros, Lewis warns that sexual love, called Venus, is in danger of being taken too seriously; indeed, jokes about sex, in the long run, endanger Christianity far less than reverential gravity. Our sexual attitudes, he says, need less of Wagner and more of Mozart. Of the three views of the human body—of the pagans and Christians, to whom it is the tomb of the soul; of the neopagans and the nudists, to whom it is glorious; and of St. Francis, who called it "Brother Ass"—Lewis is with St. Francis: "The fact that we have bodies is the oldest joke there is."

Friendship, says Lewis, is the side-by-side relationship that originated in the hunting expeditions of primitive man, in which two persons discover the same truth together. Friendship has to be about some other love, such as tennis, running, politics, or music. Friends, according to Lewis, do not look into one another's eyes. True friendship, as a love, is rare, partly because so few experience it, and partly because some have a foolish fear that behind every firm and serious friendship lurks homosexuality.

To this Lewis replies: "Those who cannot conceive of friendship as a substantive love but only as a disguise or elaboration of Eros betray the fact that they have never had a friend."

I would have liked the Friendship chapter longer, less British, less smelling of the pipe smoke. Less masculine.

Lewis did not foresee the feminist revolution and one of its most positive effects, that men and women could more easily be friends. He could have said more about the cost, gladly paid, of lifelong friendships, and what we do as Christians to maintain them. We travel across the country or across the world every several years to keep friendships alive. We write long letters, send e-mails, make and take long phone calls late at night, drive hours through storms to weddings, wakes, and funerals, and hold hands at hospital bedsides.

We see one another through lost jobs, childbirths, broken marriages, rebellious children, and loss of faith. We run, swim, ski, climb mountains, exchange books, and put up with one another's quirks almost as though we were married. We drink beer with a friend for years and support him later when he says he's an alcoholic. Often we pray together. And sometimes we look into one another's eyes.

The final chapter on Charity—which is the Christian concept of *agape*, the disinterested willing of the other's good—challenges us to make our love, like God's love, selfless. It is the crowning spiritual conclusion to a discussion that, in the earlier chapters, could make sense to anyone. But Lewis's best moment is in his rejection of St. Augustine's suggestion in the *Confessions*, following the death of his friend Nebridius, that we should not give our hearts to anything we might lose:

> There is no escape along the lines St. Augustine suggests. Nor along any other lines. There is no safe investment. To love at all is to be vulnerable. Love anything, and your heart will certainly be wrung and possibly be broken. . . . The only place outside Heaven where you can be perfectly safe from the dangers and perturbations of love is Hell.

Christopher Dawson

37 The Historic Reality of Christian Culture: A Way to the Renewal of Human Life

1960

IT WAS HARD TO IMAGINE as we maneuvered and shoved our way through the multitudes descending on Times Square from all over the world in the afternoon of the last day of 1999, and that night watched on TV the staged celebrations from remote corners of the planet—Pacific Islanders decked out in "colorful native garb performing traditional dances"—and read the morning-after stories of festivities at the Pyramids of Giza and the Eiffel Tower, that all this had anything to do with the two thousandth anniversary of the birth of Christ.

Only the midnight scenes of the pope opening the "holy door" in Rome for the Jubilee Year and of New York's Cardinal John O'Connor at the altar of St. Patrick's Cathedral testified to this being a religious occasion; and, sadly, they projected images of feebleness and age, as if symbolic of a church increasingly marginalized by cultural forces with which it can no longer compete.

The promoters of the media events would call them "multicultural" and "celebrations of diversity." Henry Adams would have seen them as end products of civilization's rush toward multiplicity and disintegration that he anticipated, with horror, at the turn of the last century. Ironically, however, some would argue that today a new order of unity, absolutely secular, is emerging—the one brought about by economic globalization, the new computer technology, and the pervasive omnipresence of the electronic mass media.

As recently as a half century ago, when the leaders of the intellectual Catholic Renaissance—Jacques Maritain, Etienne Gilson, and Christopher Dawson—still had influence, it made sense to argue that Western Europe was the source and center of a system of values, fundamentally Christian, on which Western civilization could be rebuilt. Indeed, after World War II, Catholic political leaders in France, Italy, and Germany shared that vision.

Today these ideas survive on the reading lists for Catholic studies programs at a growing number of colleges and universities, such as St. Thomas University in St. Paul, Minnesota. The patron historian of the movement is Christopher Dawson, who was born in Wales in 1889, educated at Oxford, converted from Anglicanism to Catholicism in 1914, taught at several universities, and in 1958 was named the first Chauncey Stillman Professor of Roman Catholic Studies at Harvard University, where he lectured until 1962. Among his several books, such as *The Making of Europe* (1932) and *Religion and Culture* (1948), I'm focusing on *The Historic Reality of Christian Culture* for several reasons. It's relatively short (120 pages) and it comes toward the end of his active career (his health was poor for several years before he died in 1970). It may thus represent a distillation of his thought and give us the flavor of his Harvard teaching. And it appeared in 1960, the year of John F. Kennedy's election, a turning point in our history in which the fading Christian culture passed the torch to the Secular Man.

Reading Dawson today, though his book is written within the lifetime of many of today's readers, is, paradoxically, both like reading a much older book, such as Newman's *Idea of a University* or Adams's *Mont-Saint-Michel and Chartres*, and encountering a prophet who foresaw the current crisis and has insights—if not *the* answer—that we need. But we must not confuse his message with that of the medieval nostalgists who saw in the thirteenth century or in the image of the Virgin the ideal political or spiritual unity to which we should return. Dawson is a historian who looks above all to the future as he probes history's depths for constant resources we can tap and not for ancient solutions to modern problems. He says:

> Thus the movement toward Christian culture is at one and the same time a voyage into the unknown, in the course of which new worlds of human experience will be discovered, and a return to our own fatherland—to the sacred tradition of the Christian past which flows underneath the streets and cinemas and skyscrapers of the new Babylon as the tradition of the patriarchs and prophets flowed beneath the palaces and amphitheaters of Imperial Rome.

For Dawson, "Christian civilization was the principle of moral unity which gave the Western peoples their spiritual values, their moral standards, and their concept of a divine law from which all human laws ultimately derive their validity and their sanction." It was a living organism, "a *great tree of culture* which bore rich fruit in its season." Some vestiges of its influence remain, but they are fading, particularly as the public drifts away, not into paganism, which presumes devotion to a multiplicity of gods, but rather into a spiritual void—an allegiance to nothing at all. "For a secular civilization that has no end beyond its own satisfaction is a monstrosity—a cancerous growth which will ultimately destroy itself. The only power that can liberate man from this kingdom of darkness is the Christian faith."

This is not a sermon, but an interpretation of history that analyzes the past in terms of six ages, each lasting three or four centuries, and containing within each age three phases of growth and decay: a new apostolate that leads to cultural achievement, followed by assault, crisis, and loss. The ages include (1) the Apostolic Age and penetration of Hellenistic and Roman culture; (2) the age of the church fathers and the rise of Islam; (3) the spread of Catholicism to Western Europe; (4) the alliance between the monasteries and the papacy that led to internal reform, followed by St. Francis of Assisi in his imitation of "the poor life of Christ"; (5) Tridentine reform in response to the Protestant Reformation, the brief rise of a Catholic Baroque culture, followed by the French Revolution; and (6) the church's revival, as exiled French priests help carry the faith to America, where it thrives under a constitution that separates church and state. Thus, says Dawson, we live in this sixth age, with probably sixty more to go. What means do we have to meet the crisis of our age?

At the time when Dawson was writing, Christian civilization was embattled on two fronts: totalitarian communism, attempting to fill the masses' spiritual void with the rituals of the state; and secularism that, as yet, had no quasi-religious rites of its own. Now that communism, except in China, has more or less imploded, the opponents take new forms. Dawson takes issue with Arnold Toynbee's historical relativism, by which no civilization is better than any other, an approach that today survives in some forms of "multiculturalism." Nor is Dawson comfortable with John Dewey's philosophy that uses education as a training ground for democracy, thus tying schools to the goals of the state.

Dawson's hope for a renewal of Christian culture is in higher education. "The great obstacle to the conversion of the modern world is the belief that religion has no intellectual significance; that it may be good for morals and satisfying to man's emotional needs, but that it corresponds to no objective reality." The freshman survey course on contemporary civilization, he feels, is too amorphous; to restore a culture's internal unity, it is better to focus on that culture which was—and may again become—a source of unity. It is a manageable subject, directly relevant and genuinely interesting. And yes, he would emphasize the twelfth and thirteenth centuries—the era of St. Thomas and Dante.

We can imagine Dawson's regret that the process in the late 1960s that separated the control of most American Catholic universities from religious orders and the curriculum revisions that cut theology and philosophy requirements to accommodate more science and social science have made required courses on specifically Christian culture less likely. Meanwhile, consumerism and the advertising and entertainment industries have rushed to fill the void once occupied by religious values. If he had lived to see video games in which children compete to dismember human beings in explosions of blood and gore and to see TV reports of teenagers bringing guns to school to blow away their classmates, he would probably not have been surprised. Nor would he have given up hope.

For him Christianity "is essentially the religion of the Incarnation," which means it can enter and reenter any period of human history and once again be a spiritual and cultural creative force.

38 The Edge of Sadness

1961

P ART OF THE ATTRACTION of Edwin O'Connor's brief life—he died in 1968 at forty-nine, at the height of his career—is its wholeness, its clear continuity and fittingness. He grew up in a Catholic family in Woonsocket, Rhode Island, attended LaSalle Academy in Providence, and then in 1935 went to Notre Dame because he was impressed by a Holy Cross priest who preached a mission in his parish church. In those days, Notre Dame, like other Catholic universities, found football more satisfying than a rigorous intellectual life; but it nevertheless had some superb teachers, such as Professor Frank O'Malley, whose courses in freshman composition and on modern Catholic writers such as Charles Péguy and Paul Claudel could give a student a sense of being part of a coherent tradition, especially as a would-be writer trying to get a focus on life.

From then on, O'Connor wrote, wrote, wrote. In the Coast Guard for a while during World War II, he warmed up with an un-published memoir on his experiences. In Boston, he worked as a radio announcer, reviewed radio and TV for the *Boston Herald,* and frequented the *Atlantic Monthly* office, making friends and accepting their rejection slips until they printed his series of humorous criticisms of radio programs. He loved Fred Allen's Sunday night show and edited both an anthology of Allen's wit and his autobiography. Basically, O'Connor was a humorist, a

171

———

satirist with an amazing eye and ear for the language and behavior of the Boston Irish, gained not from his childhood, because his family was upper-middle class, but from later associations with politicians and priests.

Financially, O'Connor's breakthrough came with *The Last Hurrah* (1956), and the movie version with Spencer Tracy as Frank Skeffington, the pleasantly corrupt old Boston mayor who was to be replaced by a perhaps slightly more "clean" but certainly less colorful political establishment. With his new prosperity, O'Connor bought a Beacon Hill apartment where he could entertain his friends as generously as they had entertained him when he was poor, and he indulged a fancy for foreign cars. His bedroom, however, still had just a simple pallet and a crucifix on the wall. The year *The Edge of Sadness* won the Pulitzer Prize, he married Veniette Caswell Weil. His old friend, the journalist Monsignor Francis Lally, who performed the ceremony, said: "O'Connor was always, as I remember him, a happy man, though not without his moments of Irish melancholy. After his marriage, however, happiness shone out of him as if he had swallowed the sun."

Popular as *The Last Hurrah* may have been, *The Edge of Sadness* will endure longer. His portrait of this one fallible being who is both the victim and exemplar of the Catholic subculture is so powerful that I found myself praying for him as if he were a living priest in the parish down the street.

O'Connor does for the Boston Irish Catholic what Thoreau proposed for the American individual—he drives life into a corner, reduces it to its lowest terms, and does not shrink from the "meanness" he discovers there. Yet, this confrontation with the self in the corner is the occasion of grace. Like Bernanos, O'Connor has created a simple, weak, and holy man who narrates his own story and whose holiness is often a secret from himself.

We meet fifty-five-year-old Hugh Kennedy, once driven into depression, loneliness, and alcoholism by his father's death, and now, after four years of therapy, a better but still withdrawn priest and pastor of a representatively changing, crumbling parish. Kennedy had begun his priesthood in a flurry of apostolic zeal, but had discovered, after neglecting his interior life for too long, that he had become nothing but a cheerleader with a Roman collar.

Now he is simply marking time and passively behaving himself, allowing his bubbling young Polish curate to hustle around getting to know the people.

We catch the satirical influence of Fred Allen here in the Polish priest's enthusiasm for a former classmate known as the "Whistling Priest," who, as his apostolate, whistles "Ave Maria" sandwiched in between "How Much Is That Doggie in the Window?" and the commercials on TV. Meanwhile, Fr. Hugh is praying and not drinking—but not really living either.

One day his past breaks through his solitude: he accepts an invitation from the eighty-four-year-old Charlie Carmody, an old neighbor and wealthy real-estate operator and rent gouger whom Hugh's father had once described as "as fine a man as ever robbed the helpless," to join his family for Charlie's birthday dinner. What does Charlie want?

It is an Irish family recognizable to anyone who has attended alumni banquets and President's Club dinners at Boston College, Holy Cross, or Fordham—an extended clan of four generations including the tyrannical, manipulative, wily old chief; the long-suffering daughter Mary who stays home to care for him; another daughter Helen, to whom Hugh feels close, but who is stuck in a barely tolerable marriage to a dull doctor; Fr. John, the priest who loathes his parishioners; the black-sheep brother Dan, always trying to rope friends into a fast-buck scheme; and handsome, young grandson Ted all set to run for Congress. And each has his or her own story to pour into the weary ear of fragile Fr. Hugh.

But Fr. Hugh, who had earlier desired little more than his own peace but is now drawn into the lives and pain of this family, discovers in midlife his almost snuffed-out power to empathize and to love. And also to teach. In my favorite scene, young Ted, preparing his election campaign, stops in on Fr. Hugh, allegedly for advice. As the conversation develops, it seems that candidate Ted is really interested in meeting the voters in the parish. In a line stunning in its insensitivity, he blurts, "I could even break the ice, I imagine, by doing something like passing the basket at the collection at Mass—just so they'd have the feeling I wasn't coming up cold to them on the church steps."

Stung and disappointed, like any priest who discovers cynicism in the young, Fr. Hugh tells Ted about the distinction between ends and means, that the Mass is a prayer: "You can't use it for anything else."

Again, as in life, the novel's main moral crisis comes over a seemingly minor matter. The apparently dying crank, old Carmody, aware that he is a hated old man but grasping for one sign of respect, asks Fr. Hugh what Hugh's father really thought of him. He's pleading for a last minute pat on the back he doesn't deserve.

It is fitting that O'Connor dedicated *The Edge of Sadness*, his best book, to his best teacher: Frank O'Malley. Nothing makes a writing teacher happier—even in the next life—than to see a student write a great book.

39 "Letter from Birmingham Jail"

1963

IT WAS GOOD FRIDAY, April 12, and Martin Luther King Jr. didn't want to go to jail. But the Birmingham project was not going well. First, the planned economic boycott, restaurant sit-ins, and demonstrations had been postponed for several weeks to allow the city to elect a more "moderate" mayor, defeating Bull Connor, the brutal police chief famous for his attack dogs. Then, local black support was lukewarm, a lethargic populace was not lining up to get themselves arrested, and both local and national press coverage had faded. The city had gotten an injunction against further marches.

Finally, the Southern Christian Leadership Conference was running out of bail money. King, reluctant to lead protesters into prison if he could not get them out, was considering leaving Birmingham for another national fund-raising trip. But what would happen to the movement while he was away? At a gloomy staff meeting, his own father advised caution and the Rev. Ralph Abernathy, pleading that he was needed at his home church for Easter, would not commit himself to marching to certain arrest with King.

King withdrew into his own room alone, prayed, and came out a few minutes later dressed, for the first time, in denim work clothes. "I don't know what will happen. I don't know where the money will come from," he said. "But I have to make a faith act." Abernathy got a substitute for Easter.

The march started small, but by the time they confronted the police barricade a thousand singing, shouting protesters were with them. A detective grabbed King by the back of his belt and threw him into the paddy wagon. At the jail, they sealed him off from the others and tossed him in "the hole"—solitary confinement, a dark room with no mattress or linens, just an iron bed.

The next day, King was stunned to read in the *Birmingham News* a manifesto from a group of otherwise "liberal" white clergymen praising the calm of the police and opposing King's confrontational though nonviolent tactics. Incensed, he began to scribble his reply in the margins of the newspaper, and smuggled the document out in stages to an aide who typed it up. Though the press would not notice it for a month, it would become known as the historic "Letter from Birmingham Jail."

Prison has a way of focusing a man's thoughts. For years, King had developed a theology and a strategy of nonviolent resistance that didn't satisfy anyone very much. The conservative clergy, to avoid the unpleasantness of confrontation, preferred to leave it to "time" to solve the racial crisis. Younger militants, such as the Student Nonviolent Coordinating Committee, concentrated on voter registration, whereas the Black Muslims proposed a separate black nation and called the white man a "devil." King poured out both his frustrations and his philosophy in this letter to the Christian ministers, loading it with theological arguments and citations that they should recognize—St. Augustine, St. Thomas Aquinas, Reinhold Niebuhr, the Book of Maccabees, Thomas Jefferson, Jesus Christ, and St. Paul.

To a degree that King himself might not have grasped at the time, the civil rights movement was at a turning point. The cause had not yet captured the attention of middle America, and the Kennedy administration, though it gave occasional gestures of sympathy, saw no political advantage in backing black demonstrators in the South. King's rhetoric was aimed at breaking this let's-not-go-too-far-too-fast indifference.

If he's from Atlanta, why is he in Birmingham? Because "injustice anywhere is a threat to justice everywhere. We are caught in an inescapable network of mutuality, tied in a single garment of destiny."

Birmingham is probably the most thoroughly segregated city in the United States and its ugly record of police brutality is known in every section of the country. Its unjust treatment of blacks in the courts is a notorious reality. There have been more unsolved bombings of black homes and churches in Birmingham than in any city in the nation.

Why direct action? Only tension—nonviolent pressure—gets results. "We know from painful experience that freedom is never voluntarily given by the oppressor; it must be demanded by the oppressed." "Wait" almost always means "never." King invokes the picture of a father telling his little daughter why she cannot go to the whites' amusement park, the black family driving across the country looking in vain for a motel that will accept them, the humiliating addresses of "boy," "colored," and "nigger." "There comes a time," he says, "when the cup of endurance runs over."

Why must we break laws? We break *unjust* laws and we take full public responsibility for breaking them in order to demonstrate their injustice. King reminds his readers that everything Hitler did in Germany was "legal" and everything the Hungarian freedom fighters did in Hungary was "illegal."

Then he comes to his hardest point:

I must make two honest confessions to you, my Christian and Jewish brothers. First, I must confess that over the past few years I have been gravely disappointed with the white moderate. I have almost reached the conclusion that the Negro's greatest stumbling block in the stride toward freedom is not the White Citizen's Counciler or the Ku Klux Klanner, but the white moderate who is more devoted to "order" than to justice; who prefers a negative peace which is the absence of tension to a positive peace which is the presence of justice; who constantly says, "I agree with you in the goal you seek, but I can't agree with your

methods of direct action." . . . Lukewarm acceptance is much
more bewildering than outright rejection.

Weary of trying to explain that he is not an extremist, he takes
some satisfaction in the accusation. Jesus was an extremist: "Love
your enemies." Lincoln was an extremist: "This nation cannot
survive half slave and half free."

Second, he is disappointed in the white church's leadership.
He has heard them ask their congregations to comply with desegregation because it is the *law*, when they should be saying it is
morally right. For too many, social and economic justice are
mere social issues for which the gospel has no concern.

I have traveled the length and breadth of Alabama, Mississippi
and all the other southern states. On sweltering summer days
and crisp autumn mornings I have looked at her beautiful
churches with their lofty spires pointing heavenward. I have be-
held the impressive outlay of her massive religious education
buildings. Over and over again I have found myself asking:
"What kind of people worship here? Who is their God?"

King did not live long enough to get a satisfactory answer. The
Birmingham demonstrations went on for months and assumed a
dimension he had not foreseen. When he recruited one thousand
children to march, Bull Connor turned his dogs on them and
blasted them with fire hoses. The pictures went around the
world, and Europe and Africa, as well as the American heartland,
asked, What kind of a country is this? Bombs that exploded in
King's brother's house and in his own former motel sent blacks
into the streets throwing rocks, and police retaliated with random beatings. It dawned on Birmingham's civic leadership that
they should take some steps toward desegregation. Suddenly,
Kennedy worried that he could not lead the "Free World" if
Americans were not obviously free. It was time for a civil rights bill.

In mid-May, the *New York Post* discovered the eight-thousand-
word text of "Letter from Birmingham Jail," first published by
the American Friends Committee as a pamphlet. They ran a two-
page excerpt, which was followed by publication in a host of

178

smaller magazines such as *The Christian Century* and *Liberation*, and inclusion in King's third book, *Why We Can't Wait.*

Yet many black people and white people who long for a desegregated society are waiting still.

40 Everything That Rises Must Converge, "Revelation"

1965

T HE IDEA OF THE "CATHOLIC AUTHOR" as some-how a member of a distinct species of writers came into clearer focus in the 1950s when the "Catholic Renaissance"—the reassertion of Christian values in the wake of the disillusionment following World War I—focused on writers, especially those in France, who upheld basic Christian principles.

They were considered Catholic authors no matter how obscurely religious the principles that emerged from their novels and stories. For many of them—such as Georges Bernanos, François Mauriac, and Jacques Maritain—who remembered World War I, less than twenty years in their past, their Catholicism and their social policy were woven into the same cloth. For some, such as Evelyn Waugh, Catholicism seemed tied to a social class. For others, such as Graham Greene, religious themes permeated their plots without the authors becoming spokespersons for the church.

Flannery O'Connor was, paradoxically, a writer who gloried unapologetically in her Catholicism yet, except in essays, lectures, and letters, wrote only rarely about the Catholic Church. However, as her letters, published as *The Habit of Being*, and the essays found in the *Collected Works* attest, she loved to talk about religion and the mysterious workings of divine grace. Some of her correspondents were Robert Lowell, who she prayed would return to the faith; John Hawkes, whose students were debating the role of grace in her story "A Good Man Is Hard to Find"; Fr. James H. McCown, S.J., of whom she humbly asked permission to read André Gide and Jean-Paul Sartre for a discussion group when they were on the church's *Index of Forbidden Books*; and Alfred Corn, a college freshman who wrote to her about losing his faith and to whom she sent words of patient encouragement and advice. She reminded him of Gerard Manley Hopkins's admonition to "Give alms," and in that way experience charity rather than debate philosophy.

To an unnamed woman, "A" (later identified as Betty Hester), whom she led into the faith and sadly watched lose it, O'Connor wrote in 1961:

> But let me tell you this: faith comes and goes. It rises and falls like the tides of an invisible ocean. If it is presumptuous to think that faith will stay with you forever, it is presumptuous to think that unbelief will. Leaving the Church is not the solution, but since you think it is, all I can suggest to you, as your one-time sponsor, is that if you find in yourself the least return of a desire for faith, to go back to the Church with a light heart and without the conscience raking to which you are probably subject. Subtlety is the curse of man, it is not found in the deity.

Flannery O'Connor told Elizabeth Bishop that she did not want to be labeled a Catholic writer if that meant she "had an axe to grind," but she told "A" that Waugh's definition of a Catholic novel as "a novel that deals with the problem of faith" was too narrow. "I'd rather say a Catholic mind looking at anything, making the category generous enough to include myself."

O'Connor produced an extraordinary collection of stories and short novels—including *Wise Blood*, *A Good Man Is Hard to Find*, *The Violent Bear It Away*, and *Everything That Rises Must Converge*—all bursting with religious imagery and themes but not with the standard "Catholic" material such as the lives of priests and nuns, the traumas of parochial schooling, guilt, and rebellion against sexually oppressive clerical authorities. Rather, we see religiously obsessed southern Protestants, unsaintly, violent misfits who serve as instruments of grace.

Mary Flannery O'Connor was born an only child in Savannah, Georgia, in 1925. She was educated in Catholic grammar schools, and after moving to her mother's hometown of Milledgeville, where she would spend much of the rest of her life, she attended the public high school and the local Georgia State College for Women (now Georgia College & State University). Her father died of lupus in 1941. From early childhood, O'Connor was determined to be an artist or a writer or both. She submitted cartoons and stories to national magazines, and in 1945 she won a graduate journalism scholarship to the University of Iowa and its famous Writers' Workshop. During her student days there, she began to read ravenously and extensively, everything from medieval theologians to the Catholic Renaissance Europeans to her American contemporaries.

After some months at the Yaddo writers' colony in Saratoga Springs, O'Connor moved to New York, following friends Robert Lowell and Elizabeth Hardwick and Robert and Sally Fitzgerald, with whom she lived while finishing her novel *Wise Blood*. In 1951, she was diagnosed with lupus, and she eventually resettled in Milledgeville. For the rest of her life she wrote fiction, won prizes, and, supported by her crutches, lectured at colleges all over America, made a trip to Lourdes, and kept her friendships alive until 1964, when her disease claimed her, as it had her father.

A 1955 letter to "A" records the anecdote about O'Connor's Catholicism that to some is better known than her stories. Robert Lowell and Elizabeth Hardwick had taken O'Connor to dinner with novelist Mary McCarthy, who had written *Memories of a Catholic Girlhood*, about her leaving the church at age fifteen. O'Connor did not open her mouth the entire evening until McCarthy, having turned the discussion to the Eucharist, said that "she thought of it as a symbol and implied that it was a pretty good one." O'Connor then said, in a shaky voice, "Well, if it's only a symbol, then to hell with it." That was all she could say, "except that it is the center of existence for me; all the rest of life is expendable."

But O'Connor's stories are not mostly about the Eucharist, although in them God and his grace appear in similarly humble and concrete forms. Her stories are about poor southerners, most of them white, with blacks, called "niggers" by the whites, as the secondary characters. Her characters are often physically grotesque, ugly, odd, sometimes insane, and subject to visions, epiphanies that burst uninvited, like fire and lightning, into their lives.

In her stories, strangers confront one another in moments of irrational violence and see in the other person a revelation of themselves. Her prose is tight, blunt, and gritty, and some found her shocking. When *Life* magazine complained in 1957 that American novelists didn't write enough about the strong economy and "the joy of life," O'Connor told a Notre Dame audience that the Christian writer sees distortions in modern life that are repugnant, and the writer is forced to take violent means to get this vision across to a hostile audience.

Let's look at some stories.

In "A Good Man Is Hard to Find," a wanted criminal, called the Misfit, encounters a family on vacation, and when they recognize him, he determines to kill them. The grandmother, who up to this time has been a selfish irritant, pleads with the killer as his friends execute the family one by one. Suddenly she sees into his heart and says, "Why, you're one of my babies. You're one of my own children." He shoots her three times in the chest. In a line that has had literature classes debating for thirty years, he says, "She would of been a good woman, if it had been someone there to shoot her every minute of her life." For O'Connor, these two strangers—like all strangers—are connected to one another, unwitting channels of grace in their best and worst moments.

In "The Displaced Person," a Polish family is hired to work on a southern farm after World War II. The narrow-minded widowed farm owner is irritated that foreigners who don't share advanced American culture, religion, and language are intruding on local social and racial taboos. She feels no responsibility for the death camps and stacked-up corpses in Europe that she has heard about. The Polish father is the best, most efficient worker she has ever had. He is killed. To understand the story, the reader must keep his or her eyes on the glorious peacock that parades around the farm while keeping in mind what it means for any person to be displaced.

A key story in *Everything That Rises Must Converge*, which is titled after Jesuit mystical paleontologist Pierre Teilhard de Chardin's phrase for the emerging spiritual unity of all human-kind, is "Revelation," which was completed just before O'Connor's death.

In the story, Mrs. Turpin, a fat woman of cheerful disposition, accompanies her farmer husband to the doctor's office. She amuses herself by passing judgment in her head on the others in the waiting room, and, like the Pharisee in the Gospel, she thanks God that she is not like the lower class, white trash, ugly charac-ters in the room. She ranks classes in her head, with "white trash" even lower than "niggers." She engages the other waiting patients in chitchat, many of her comments laced with insults to blacks.

Suddenly a fat, ugly, sullen, acne-scarred Wellesley College student named Mary Grace, who has been reading a textbook on human development, hurls the book at Mrs. Turpin, beans her over the left eye, and whispers as she is subdued on the floor, "Go back to hell where you came from, you old wart hog."

Mrs. Turpin is a hog farmer, and she consults her hogs, in ef-fect, as to what this means. Her hogs respond with sounds that lead her to a vision based on the Teilhardian vision of the future of humanity. Obviously, Mary Grace is well named. Consistent with O'Connor's themes, she is an unlikely channel of grace, but in her is God breaking through.

Alex Haley

41 The Autobiography of Malcolm X

1964

WATCHING SPIKE LEE'S FILM *Malcolm X* on TV recently, I was struck by how apt Denzel Washington was for the role. I have seen Washington in person, talking to Fordham–Lincoln Center students about his role in *The Hurricane*, a film that tells the story of another black criminal whose life turned around in prison. Though twice their age, Washington kidded with the students as though he were one of them and worked in some spiritual advice about God's role in their lives. Now I saw how both Malcolm X and Washington were genuinely funny men.

But during his lifetime and for years after his death, very few white people thought of Malcolm X and laughed—or even smiled. They knew his anger and his alienation. They had not heard the recordings of his speeches, with his satirical riff on what he called the plantation "field nigger" who toils in the sun and the "house nigger" who has a nice inside job and identifies with his white master more than with his fellow slaves. When the master takes sick, the house nigger says, "Boss, *we* sick!"

There is not much humor in his autobiography, other than his ironic observations on the Negro's invisibility, a frequent theme in black literature. The white man is unable to see the black man right in front of him, because if he isn't a person he isn't really there.

185

Today there are dozens of books on Malcolm X, including some for children, and recent scholarship has raised some critical questions about the factual accuracy of both the late Alex Haley's *Roots* and the *Autobiography*, which is based on interviews and written by Haley in Malcolm's voice. Nevertheless, Malcolm X's story remains a milestone in American religious history and in the emergence of a new black consciousness.

To the central themes of American black literature—what it means to be a black American and the struggle to express that identity in an often hostile white urban culture—*The Autobiography of Malcolm X* brings the added dimension of another prominent American phenomenon: the conversion experience.

In *Native Son*, Richard Wright shocked America with his portrait of Bigger Thomas, a young Chicago black man who accidentally kills a young white woman in a moment of passion and fear, murders his own girlfriend, and then goes to his execution affirming his crime, refusing the consolations of both religion and ideology.

Bigger's rage was articulated more subtly in Ralph Ellison's *Invisible Man* in the 1950s and with renewed heat in James Baldwin's essays and novels in the 1960s. Both Ellison and Baldwin were Wright's literary sons, but Malcolm X, though he was not a murderer, best captured what Bigger Thomas represented: the black man as a threat. He frightened whites, excoriating them with his eloquence and wit, and his followers loved him for it.

At the same time, his autobiography is in the tradition of *The Education of Henry Adams*, in that it attempts to capture a life pulled along by historical forces in a world of fast-paced change, and of Jane Addams's *Twenty Years at Hull House*, in that it explains to an admiring public what brought this individual to the point of becoming a model for other Americans. For Addams, it was the childhood influence of Abraham Lincoln and a quasi-mystical insight at a bullfight in Spain that she was wasting a life that should be spent in the service of others. For Malcolm X it was the discovery of Allah.

On a walk through Harlem a few years ago, I stopped in the Liberation Bookstore and found an old poster of Malcolm standing by a window, brandishing a submachine gun. The quote beneath the picture was from one of his speeches: "By any means necessary." The image probably represented him not leading an armed struggle against whites but protecting himself from the black assassins who later gunned him down in the Audubon Ballroom on February 21, 1965. We remember the photograph of his body, with thirteen holes in his chest, and we also remember that many good white people felt relieved when he was gone.

Shortly before his death, Malcolm X had predicted that the white press would identify him with hate. Yet today, readers of the *Autobiography* see not a hater but a pilgrim. With its pattern of fall, grace, redemption, and death, this work is a religious testimonial consistent with Karl Rahner's thesis that anyone who courageously accepts life has already accepted God, for anyone who really accepts *himself* accepts a mystery in the sense of the infinite emptiness that is man.

At the same time, the book is an indictment of American private morality. Speaking mainly of so-called respectable upper classes, he writes, "As I got deeper into my own life of evil, I saw the white man's morals with my own eyes. I even made my living helping to guide him to the sick things he wanted." Nevertheless Malcolm was an extremely intelligent young man looking for meaning in his life and discovering his deepest self in the very quality that had made him an object of hatred—his blackness.

Born Malcolm Little in Omaha, Nebraska, in 1925, Malcolm decided in eighth grade that he wanted to be a lawyer. His teacher told him he was a "nigger" and should stick to his carpenter's bench. His father, he says, was murdered (though this has been questioned), and his mother, overwhelmed by the strain of caring for the family, was hospitalized. Malcolm saw these events as society penalizing its members who could not stand up under its oppressive weight. "Big Red," as he was called because of his reddish hair, became a pimp and an armed robber and was sentenced to prison.

In prison, Malcolm read constantly: the dictionary, encyclopedias, Will Durant, George Mendel, Spinoza, Shakespeare. He became convinced that black people had a glorious history that white historians had suppressed. He heard of Chicago's Elijah

Muhammad, Messenger of Allah, the Shepherd of the Nation of Islam in the Wilderness of the United States (Nation of Islam followers are commonly known as Black Muslims) and adopted the Nation of Islam's moral code.

He learned to pray. "I had to force myself to bend my knees. And waves of shame and embarrassment would force me back up. For evil to bend its knees, admitting its guilt, to implore the forgiveness of God, is the hardest thing in the world." He turned to Elijah Muhammad very much as James Baldwin had in *The Fire Next Time*, in search of a father, in search of his own name. But unlike Baldwin, who rejected Muhammad for his simple dogmatism, Malcolm X became his prophet.

After his release, Malcolm became Elijah Muhammad's most successful organizer, but his very success seemed to jeopardize Elijah Muhammad's authority. In March of 1964, disillusioned by Muslim aloofness from the civil rights struggle and by what he had learned about Elijah Muhammad's personal life, Malcolm broke away. At this time of personal upheaval, he made a pilgrimage to Mecca, where he was shaken by the further realization that the "white devils" he had learned to hate could also be his brothers. The new Malcolm, aware of a plot to kill him, continued to travel in Africa and the Middle East, internationalizing the American racial issue, planning to bring it before the United Nations, rethinking his previous beliefs, and groping for a new identity in the new society he wanted to help create.

The Liberation Bookstore also displayed an announcement for a rally to celebrate Malcolm's memory. Today the *Autobiography* is being accepted as a classic and is a standard on college reading lists, but America is still far from comprehending the significance of this too brief life. The black middle class has grown, and more blacks go to predominantly white colleges and universities and have moved into political and business leadership. More blacks have also gained prominence and popularity as sports stars and entertainment celebrities, but the American racial gap is still wide, and the social forces in the ghetto still destroy families and send young black men to prison.

Meanwhile, the most important fact about Malcolm X is that he changed.

He came to know, without flinching, the evil in himself and in the world. He opened his soul enough to cleanse it and to glimpse the previously invisible bonds that linked him to men and women of all classes and colors.

Expecting to die at any minute, Malcolm clung to life so that something could be achieved by his perseverance in his last days. "I know," he wrote,

> that societies often have killed the people who have helped them change those societies. And if I can die having brought any light, having exposed any meaningful truths that will help to destroy the racist cancer that is malignant in the body of America—then, all of the credit is due to Allah. Only the mistakes have been mine.

When both Martin Luther King Jr. and Malcolm X were alive, it was common to contrast the styles of the movements they led— one southern and Christian, the other urban and militant. Today we ask what shape the movement toward racial equality will take twenty years from now.

Perhaps we will talk less about racial movements. Gradually, with increased immigration from Asia and Latin America, with the astonishing population shifts in the big cities and the increased intermarriage that will follow as new citizens move through the work force and the professional classes, talk about race will fade. Whether or not they foresaw it, Martin and Malcolm will have paved the way.

Shusaku Endo

42 Silence

1966

> We priests are in some ways a sad group of men. Born into the
> world to render service to mankind, there is no one more
> wretchedly alone than the priest who does not measure up to
> his task.

In Shusaku Endo's *SILENCE*, Sebastian Rodrigues, a
twenty-nine-year-old Portuguese Jesuit, sits huddled in a shack
on one of the remote southern islands of Japan, hiding out and
not yet secure enough to explore his little village. Each night he
meets with a handful of secret Christians to teach them prayers,
forgive their sins, and offer a furtive Eucharist.

It is around 1640, and Japan's short, hundred-year (1549–1650)
first encounter with Christianity is plunging to a bloody end. It
began with the arrival of St. Francis Xavier, who after baptizing
many with great enthusiasm (although, not speaking Japanese,
he had inadvertently preached on a popular sun god rather than
the Trinity), died on an offshore island on his way to the greater
mission of converting China.

For a while, the missionary enterprise thrived, reinforced by
Japan's desire to profit from trade with Portugal and by the strategy of converting local rulers, who would then bring their whole
realms into the church. By 1614, more than half a million

Christians lived in Japan. But in a long-range political movement to unify Japan and shut out foreign influence, missionaries were banished and a campaign to exterminate Christianity began.

Rodrigues and his two companions had endured a perilous two-year journey from Lisbon to Goa to Macao, a trip they knew could lead to martyrdom, fired up with the zeal of Xavier and private pious ambition. Word had reached Portugal that their revered seminary professor, Christovao Ferreira, after undergoing the torture of "the pit"—being hung upside down over a hole filled with excrement, his blood draining slowly from a slight slit in his neck—had apostatized. They refused to believe this. They would go and find him. And if he had defected, they would atone for his infidelity.

Young Rodrigues, consistent with Jesuit tradition, used his first days in hiding to write long letters home. He described their voyage, their having to leave behind their seriously ill third member, and their high hopes for these Japanese, whom Xavier had described as ideal Christian converts. Deep down, he began to deal with his fears that he might not "measure up to the task" and then with the even deeper question of whether or not Christianity really belonged in Japan.

Endo's gloomy picture of the sad, wretched, and lonely priest has familiar echoes of Graham Greene's whiskey priest, Bernanos's country curate, Brian Moore's inept Jesuit missionary to the North American savages in *Black Robe*, and even the dark moments of loneliness in the essentially comic novels of J. F. Powers and Edwin O'Connor. The plot of *Silence* parallels that of Greene's *The Power and the Glory* in several scenes. In *Silence*, the troops who raid the peasant villages to flush out the fugitive priest offer their rewards and take their hostages as the parishioners sacrifice themselves for their pastor, and a miserable, pathetic Judas figure trails the priest from village to village, asking him to forgive his sins, and then hands him over to the authorities. The theme of betrayal, on several levels, knits together all the scenes.

But Endo is no mere Japanese version of Graham Greene. While both deal with the unpredictability of grace, Endo asks whether the Western and Eastern images of God can ever be reconciled. Greene and Moore put flawed but good men in bad situations and allow them a spiritual triumph through martyrdom. Endo's Jesuits virtually court martyrdom as if it were a seventeenth-century Catholic version of the Congressional Medal. But rather than spiritual triumph, they experience a terrible shame and learn another kind of spiritual lesson: that maybe this whole hundred years of sacrifice has not been a good idea. Perhaps it is not even God's will.

Born in Tokyo, Endo spent his early years in Manchuria before returning to Japan, and after his parents separated, he moved with his mother into the home of his Catholic aunt. His mother became a Catholic and induced Shusaku, age eleven, to accept baptism also. Because he had simply gone through the motions and had not really embraced the faith, a deep sense of betrayal—by both his mother and Christ—haunted Endo and his creative writing for years. This inward struggle enabled him to both commit himself deeply to Catholicism and develop his own felt image of Christ, not as the triumphant judge of Western Christology but as one who suffers and forgives. As a result, some of the Christians in *Silence* are men who move in and out of the faith, who go through the motions, who suffer and forgive.

The guards raid Rodrigues's village and take as hostages three Christians who have harbored the Jesuits. In the ritual tortures, the authorities order their captives to trample on the *fumie*, a sacred image of Jesus Christ or the Virgin Mary, as a sign of their apostasy or to face horrible death. Rodrigues begins to waver; he urges his benefactors to "Trample! Trample!" but is ashamed. When one of the captives asks, "Why has Deus Sama imposed this suffering on us?" he cannot answer. He is beginning to sense the "silence of God." He writes:

> Already twenty years have passed since the persecution broke out; the black soil of Japan has been filled with the lament of so many Christians; the red blood of priests has flowed profusely; the walls of the churches have fallen down; and in the face of this terrible and merciless sacrifice offered up to Him, God has remained silent.

He watches as the Christians are martyred by being tied to stakes in the surf where the tide will come in and drown them. He had often seen splendid martyrdoms in his dreams.

> But the martyrdom of the Japanese Christians I now describe to you was no such glorious thing. What a miserable and painful business it was! The rain falls unceasingly on the sea and the sea which killed them surges on uncannily—in silence.

Rodrigues and his friend, Fr. Garppe, split up, and Rodrigues begins a long journey on foot through beautiful mountains in search of another village where Christians will welcome him. He has some satisfying days of ministry, but of course he is betrayed and arrested.

The samurai who heads the persecution is, on the surface, not a monster but a genteel, reasonable fellow who presents Rodrigues with a moral dilemma that reaches into the heart of Rodrigues's doubts. They will torture the ordinary Christians in the pit until the priest apostatizes. Thus, by their logic (and, it seems, Endo's), the priest, by his silence, is causing their torment. That the barbaric Japanese authorities are alone responsible for their cruelty is not suggested.

In a brilliant climax, based on historical fact, Rodrigues does finally find his old professor. Ferreira has been given a wife and a family and a Nagasaki home and is brought in to convince his old pupil to follow his example.

Silence is one of the most depressing novels I have ever read. But I've read it three times.

Gustavo Gutiérrez

43 A Theology of Liberation: History, Politics, and Salvation

1988; FIRST PUBLICATION IN SPANISH, 1971

IN THE MIDDLE OF THE NIGHT on November 16, 1989, a military death squad invaded the campus of the University of Central America (UCA) in El Salvador, dragged six Jesuits and their two women housekeepers into the yard, and blew their brains out with automatic rifles. The method of execution was deliberate. They were attacking an idea that they imagined was located in the Jesuits' brains and thus could not live if their brains were destroyed. Their brains were the enemy of the power of the state. They were killed, said their colleague Jon Sobrino, because through their intellectual research they told the truth about the "massive, cruel, and unjust poverty of the mass of the people . . . because they believed in the God of the poor and tried to produce this faith through the university."

But you can't kill an idea with a bullet.

As David O'Brien wrote in his classic study of Catholic identity, *From the Heart of the American Church,* "the event sparked outrage, expressions of solidarity, and renewed attention to academic responsibility for poverty, violence, and injustice."

The ideal way to approach the theology of liberation is to fly to Lima, Peru, walk for a few days through the shantytowns that spring up overnight on the outskirts of the city, watch the water truck churn through the dust, and realize that the thousands of human beings who live here have no other water. The idea is to experience the lives of the poor, whose hopeless living conditions forced a group of pastors and theologians in the 1960s to rethink the relationship between the gospel and the poor and between the church and the political and economic leaders of the state.

My friend Jeff Thielman, coauthor with me of *Volunteer: With the Poor in Peru*, was overwhelmed and depressed by the suffering of the street children in Tacna, Peru, where he worked as an International Jesuit Volunteer after graduating from Boston College. Then he discovered the "base communities," small groups of poor people who meet in homes and pray at liturgies about the Gospels from the point of view of their daily struggle. At the same time, he read the story of four American churchwomen who had been raped and killed by the army of El Salvador. Now he had both a philosophy and the inspiration to stay and build a center that would nurture and educate the working-class children.

Liberation theology is a system of thought best understood as coming from a specific historical situation—the church's loss of the Catholic Latin American poor—and a strategy to win them back. As a well-developed theology, it has universal application, but it is particularly applicable to areas of the developing world such as India, Africa, and Asia and to the Bronx and Boston as well.

Historically, the roots of liberation theology are in the Spanish and Portuguese conquests of Latin America and the alliances formed between the church and the governing classes there. During the liberal revolutions of the nineteenth century, the church, for its own protection, sided with the wealthy class. It adopted, for the most part, a lifestyle that, until the mid-twentieth century, alienated it from the poor. Then a series of events—the Cursillo movement, the activities of worker-priests in Europe, the Cuban Revolution of 1956–1959 and the spread of its ideology, an influx of foreign missionaries, Vatican II, and the social encyclicals of Popes John XXIII and Paul VI—laid the intellectual groundwork for a new awakening. Finally, the 1968 meeting of the Latin American bishops in Medellín, Colombia, inspired a series of documents wherein the church examined its conscience and confessed its complicity in the staggering oppression of the lower classes.

Gustavo Gutiérrez, a parish priest in Lima, was trained in philosophy and psychology at Louvain and in theology in Lyon, France, and the Gregorian University in Rome. As a professor at the Catholic University in Peru, he introduced what at the time was a new way of doing theology, "a critical reflection on Christian praxis in the light of the world." *Praxis* means activity—specifically, a transforming activity guided by theory. But it also has connotations of Ignatian spirituality's "contemplation in action," Vatican II's "reading the signs of the times," and Marxist philosophy.

It means that doing, thinking, and praying are intimately related and that the objects of the reflection—the people—participate in the reflection as well. The new theology expressed itself with a special vocabulary.

The church engages in what it calls *conscienticizing evangelization,* sharpening the moral awareness of the true nature of sin, which is no longer merely an individual's guilt but sin embodied in *oppressive, sinful social and economic structures* in which all, including the church, participate. This awareness *empowers* the lower classes to participate in the *class struggle.* Does this struggle legitimize the use of violence by the oppressed? Actually, the poor are already victims of *institutionalized violence,* violence inflicted by the capitalists who control the economy and rob the poor of their just share in the country's wealth. Catholic social teaching does admit that violence can be used as a last resort. In the late 1960s and early 1970s, many priests argued that a new form of *socialism* would be a better answer to Latin America's problems than "developmentalism" controlled by North American capitalists.

Underlying these ideas is a biblical theology of "salvation history," which is based on an interpretation of Exodus as God's entering history to liberate his people from slavery in Egypt; on the prophets such as Isaiah, Jeremiah, and Amos, who condemned the rich for their exploitation of God's beloved poor; and on the political implications of Jesus' life and death.

"Peace, justice, love, and freedom are not private realities; they are not only internal attitudes," says Gutiérrez. "They are social realities, implying a historical liberation. A poorly under-stood spiritualization has often made us forget the human conse-quences of the eschatological promises and the power to transform unjust social structures which they imply."

Jesus was not a political leader in the sense that some of his Zealot disciples were. Yet all his public life he confronted groups in power, such as Herod and the Sanhedrin and, in his option for the poor, the wealthy class. He died at the hands of political au-thorities, a victim of the Roman state and of the "sinful situation" he had exposed.

Thirty years after the idea was born, the voice of liberation theology is less strong than it was, partly because Vatican authorities, perhaps with European Marxism rather than the Latin American situation in mind, have reprimanded theologians, restaffed or closed seminaries, and appointed bishops who don't share the thinking of Gutiérrez and his colleagues. But Latin America has changed too. Few of the old dictatorial regimes remain, and the new church is no longer so clearly identified with those in power. Above all, the idea that the church must express its "solidarity with the poor" is no longer a radical idea but an accepted fact. That it would take martyrs to get us this far was clear from the beginning.

Gutiérrez's 1988 edition refers to an earlier version that says:

> In today's world the solidarity and protest of which we have been speaking have an evident and inevitable "political" character in-sofar as they imply liberation. To be with the oppressed is to be against the oppressor. In our times and on our continent to be in solidarity with the "poor," understood in this way, means to run personal risks, even to put one's life in danger.

In the 1988 edition, Gutiérrez notes the murder of Archbishop Oscar Romero in El Salvador. The day before Romero was shot down at his altar, he uttered an anguished cry to the Salvadoran army: "In the name of God and of this suffering people whose wailing mounts daily to heaven, I ask and beseech you, I order you: stop the repression." Earlier he had told his congregation, "This week I received a warning that I am on the list of those to be eliminated this week. But it is certain that no one can kill the voice of justice."

Today, those authorities most responsible for the murders of Archbishop Romero, the American churchwomen, and the six Jesuits and their two housekeepers have yet to be brought to justice.

But, through a historical process that I think Christopher Dawson would appreciate, American Catholic universities are incorporating the lives and deaths of these men and women into their self-understanding. The question, what is a Catholic university today? will never again yield a quick answer such as, owned by the Catholic church. But more and more the universities answer that it is one in which the lives of those martyrs, inspired by liberation theology, are celebrated to inspire the young.

Jonathan Schell

44 The Fate of the Earth

1982, 2000

I N AUGUST 1985, on my first day in Vienna, I hurried
up the grand stairway of the opera house with my ticket for the
last available seat for a concert called "Journey for Peace."
Thousands gathered in the square outside to watch the concert on
a movie screen. It was the Hiroshima Peace Concert—featuring
Beethoven's Leonore Overture no. 3, Fumiko Kohjiba's
"Hiroshima Requiem," Mozart's Violin Concerto no. 5, and
Leonard Bernstein's Symphony no. 3 ("Kaddish")—with Leonard
Bernstein and Eiji Oue conducting. The orchestra was the
European Community Orchestra, made up of young people who
had been drawn from all over Europe to express unity through
their art.

The concert marked the end of Hiroshima Week, the fortieth
anniversary of the days on which, as Radio Moscow and Radio
Warsaw reminded us daily in their short-wave newscasts, the
United States of America dropped the atom bombs on Hiroshima
and Nagasaki. So, after Bernstein whipped and leaped and danced
his way with these youths through a triumphant Leonore—as
thrilling a hymn to humankind's free spirit as we know—and
rewarded them with hugs and kisses, Oue, who was born in
Hiroshima in 1957, conducted the "Requiem," a stirring, mourn-
ful piece. Then, little violinist Midori, who was born in Osaka in
1971, softly performed the Mozart piece, hunched over, leaning

199

into it, and finishing to the standing ovation she has been receiving for years.

It occurred to me that these young performers were both our shame and our hope: born twelve years after the bomb, did the smiling, cherubic Oue carry the effects of our radiation in his system? But were not the combined brilliance of Oue and Midori lyric testimony that one generation can somehow assimilate history's genius and outlive its crimes? And what about the young musicians in the orchestra: how do they react differently from their brothers and sisters at Holy Cross, Fordham, Loyola, or Saint Peter's College—or at American secular or state institutions—when they hear of the Holocaust and the bomb?

That night in Vienna comes back to me when I read the books of Jonathan Schell, especially the 2000 edition of *The Fate of the Earth*, which also includes the sequel, *The Abolition*.

Schell begins *The Abolition* with a quote from Pope John Paul II's speech in Hiroshima in February 1981:

> In the past, it was possible to destroy a village, a town, a region, even a country. Now it is the whole planet that has come under a threat. This fact should fully compel everyone to face a basic moral consideration: from now on, it is only through a conscious choice and then deliberate policy that humanity can survive.

Schell's use of the pope's speech is typical of his writing, not because he tends to invoke a religious authority to fortify his arguments, but because his worldview is based on the understanding that nuclear war, even after the cold war, could mean the end of the human species. It is a worldview that religiously committed persons in this age should share.

His work is, to borrow from strategic and Christian terminology, a call for a policy of "preemptive repentance." We must repent of the crime of extinguishing the species with nuclear weapons before we commit it, and in that repentance we must find the will not to commit it. To Schell, the only acceptable policy of deterrence is what he calls moral deterrence, in which we are deterred by the realization of what we would do to the enemy "and to countless innocents, including all potential future generations of human beings" with nuclear weapons.

Schell has his critics. Theodore Draper, in the *New York Review of Books*, calls *The Fate of the Earth* "political fantasy and millennial daydreaming" and a "disguised counsel of despair." Today, when we read both *The Fate of the Earth* and *The Abolition*, we should remember that when they appeared, the Berlin Wall still stood and the cold war and Soviet threat were still the political and moral basis of our nuclear strategy.

Few books have been more successful in alerting the public to the effects of nuclear war and in forcing a radical rethinking of nuclear policy than *The Fate of the Earth*. It is, in many ways, the *Uncle Tom's Cabin* of the antinuclear movement. When it first appeared serially in three issues of *The New Yorker*, readers were stunned by the implications of Schell's analysis and passed the articles, then the book, to their friends, strengthening the "new peace movement" that challenged the idea that nuclear weapons are here to stay.

In *The Fate of the Earth* Schell does three things, each of them the topic of one of the essays in his book. First, he describes the nature of a nuclear explosion and its five distinctive effects: initial nuclear radiation; the generation by gamma radiation of an electromagnetic pulse that can destroy communications systems; the wave of blinding light and intense heat; the blast wave that flattens buildings; and radioactive fallout. In doing so, he demonstrates that the United States could not survive a nuclear attack by the Soviet Union. Indeed, the human species would not survive a nuclear war.

Second, he draws on philosophy, literature, art, and theology to explain the historical and metaphysical unity of the human species—dead, living, and yet unborn. We must see ourselves as parents of the future.

Third, he demonstrates the failure of deterrence as a strategy. In essence, he states that it is immoral to threaten to do what we cannot morally do. It would be immoral to use nuclear weapons first, so it is also immoral to threaten to do so. And once we have been attacked, to retaliate would merely be an act of revenge, an insane action that would multiply the destruction already inflicted on the globe.

In Schell's view, if deterrence fails to prevent a nuclear attack, the only rational response is "to get on the hotline and try to stop the whole debacle as soon as possible." Obviously, any writer who says that the response to a nuclear attack should be a presidential phone call is not going to win acceptance in America today, even if he's right.

In *The Unfinished Twentieth Century*, Schell rethinks the meaning of the twentieth century, called the "short century" because it really began with World War I in 1914 and ended with the failure of the hard-line Communist coup in Moscow in 1991. The century's distinguishing characteristic, he says, is its people's willingness to exterminate entire classes of people. First, there was genocide, the destruction of a people; second, the extermination of social classes, as practiced by Stalin, Mao Zedong, and Pol Pot; and third, the extermination of cities and their populations, as in Churchill's bombing of Hamburg and Hitler's plans to destroy Moscow and Leningrad. The totalitarian crimes set the scene for Hiroshima, in which a "liberal civilization" acted on the power to exterminate the species, to undo the work of Genesis.

We are asked to imagine what civilized people would have said if Hitler had used the atom bomb. They would have said that the decision was the product of an immoral system. But we did it. We have tried to justify nuclear weapons on the grounds that bombing Hiroshima shortened the war and aiming missiles at the Soviet Union kept the peace. Now, if we fail to get rid of them, it will show that we used them not to face an extraordinary danger that has now passed, but because they are really intrinsic to our civilization. We have become the apt pupil of totalitarian power.

As Ivan Eisenberg pointed out, commenting in *The Nation* on Schell and the influence of the threat of the nuclear holocaust on music, what used to give death meaning was the continuity of humankind, and now that is in question. In "Late Night Thoughts on Listening to Mahler's Ninth Symphony," biologist Lewis Thomas says that he once took Mahler's final movement as a tranquil reassurance that death was a peaceful experience. He had once thought of the earth as one organism, renewed in its cycle of living and dying. Now, with what he knows about the various weapons systems capable of destroying life on any continent, he envisions the actual end of humanity itself. "I cannot hear the same Mahler. Now, those cellos sound in my mind like the opening of all the hatches and the instant before ignition."

The cold war is over. The weapons are still in place.

We don't know how Cain killed Abel, but he probably used a weapon. The ax or club made murder more efficient, safer for the killer. It was history's first recorded use of technology. Succeeding generations improved on the club with the spear, the sword, the crossbow, dynamite, the musket, the cannon, the Colt 45, the machine gun, the tank, the plane, napalm, the B-17, the cluster bomb, the smart bomb, the hydrogen bomb, and the missile. We can annihilate millions made "in God's image," whose images we have never seen. As it was in the beginning, the fate of the earth is in our hands.

Karl Rahner, S.J.

45 The Love of Jesus and the Love of Neighbor

1983

To select one work by Karl Rahner, S.J., the great German theologian who died in 1984, as most representative could never do justice to either the reader or Rahner's life and thought.

A scholar, a theologian who incorporated the insights of existentialism into Thomistic theology, a teacher and spiritual mentor, a courageous thinker who applied his theological method to pastoral problems, and a loyal churchman who suffered Rome's censures in the late 1950s, Rahner loved the church enough to criticize it. His more than four thousand essays and talks are collected in the multivolume *Theological Investigations.* He was the church's greatest intellectual of the twentieth century. He was also a holy and humble man who said that the best way to learn to pray was to fall on one's knees.

Excellent one-volume anthologies of Rahner's work include *The Practice of Faith,* a compilation of his thoughts on the spiritual life, and *A Rahner Reader,* edited by philosopher Gerald McCool, S.J. But his fundamental work is *Foundations of Christian Faith: An Introduction to the Idea of Christianity* (1978). This work, to an extent, sums up his philosophy and theology, and an ambitious reader might want to compare it to Hans Küng's *On Being a Christian,* which reached out both to educated priests (whom he thought his book would most greatly influence) and to marginal believers at a time when educated people were yearning to have Jesus Christ explained in a frank and intelligent way.

In *Foundations of Christian Faith*, Rahner addresses himself "to readers who are educated to some extent and who are not afraid to 'wrestle with an idea,'" and he hopes that he will "find readers for whom the book is neither too advanced nor too primitive." It's a rewarding workout, perhaps best read systematically in a discussion group or slowly over several months.

As one who is not a professional theolgian, I would like to discuss three aspects of Rahner's impact on Christian thought for the men and women of my generation.

The first is the idea of the *anonymous Christian.* Rahner offers a "theological anthropology" in which, through an analysis of our own experience and of our openness to ultimate reality, that is, to God, we free ourselves from the long-held artificial distinction between nature and grace, between the so-called natural and supernatural realms of existence. Rather, we learn that, as Fr. Richard McBrien expresses the idea in *Catholicism*:

> God is not "a" Being separate from the human person. God is Being itself, permeating the person but transcending the person as well. Because God permeates as well as transcends us, there is no standpoint from which we can "look at" God objectively, in a detached manner, as it were. God is always present within us, even before we begin the process, however tentatively and hesitantly, of trying to come to terms with God's reality and our knowledge of God.

This understanding of how God is present to all persons is the basis of Rahner's extremely influential and controversial idea of the "anonymous Christian," wherein even an atheist could be considered a Christian, because everyone's experience of the transcendent, of "absolute mystery," is an experience of God:

> The person who accepts a moral demand from his conscience as *absolutely* valid for him and embraces it as such in a free act of affirmation—no matter how unreflected—asserts the absolute

being of God, whether he knows or conceptualizes it or not, as the very reason why there can be such a thing as an *absolute moral demand* at all.

Of course, this idea that one's Christian commitment may be "anonymous," that one can be Christian without being "religious" in the traditional sense, was revolutionary in that it gave impetus to "secular Christianity," the pursuit of religious goals in the secular world and on secular terms.

Naturally this concept also had an impact on missiology. If unbelievers in remote lands can reach God merely through their openness to him in experience, should missionaries intrude on radically different cultures and even risk their lives to baptize those content with their own spirituality, primitive as it may seem?

The second is the idea of *Christ our brother.* Writing in *Commonweal* (January 31, 1986), theologian Robert Imbelli calls *The Love of Jesus and the Love of Neighbor* "one of Karl Rahner's last gifts to his fellow believers, the mature simplification of a life's journey." It is here that Rahner—echoing his idea that sometimes the best way to discover prayer is to fall on one's knees—says: "You are only really dealing with Jesus when you throw your arms around him and realize right down to the bottom of your being that this is something that you can still do today." As Imbelli explains, "It is not the idea of Jesus which saves. It is the person who loved and was crucified and is risen who is the Savior of the world."

Although at first glance it might seem that there are few men more distant from each other than Rahner and Thoreau, both build their systems of thought on the principle that is at the center of American spirituality: the close, sometimes ruthless analysis of personal experience. As Rahner says, we cannot understand words like *love* and *fidelity* on first hearing; we can do so only by "gathering together our life experiences while listening to them—slowly, patiently, ever and again listening to our own lives—just as someone might collect fresh spring water in a beaker as it wells up slowly out of the earth."

This leads us to how we commit ourselves to others; how we can love a person who is far away; how love can overcome time and space; how we can read Scripture in the way that two lovers gaze at each other; and how Jesus, through the Spirit, presents himself as our model and our friend.

Rather than his divinity making Jesus more remote, in Rahner's theology Jesus' divinity is in his messiahship: "'Messiah' means the vehicle and bearer of a definitive message . . . in which God definitively 'commits himself.'" In Jesus, God invites us to love one another with the same love Jesus has given us. Thus, love of neighbor is an antecedent for love of God, and there is no love of God that is not, in itself, already a love of neighbor. In short: "God is not in competition with human beings."

In a practical coda, Rahner spells out the consequences of this love for the modern world. He shows how Christian communion generates a political responsibility, rejoices that modern communication increases opportunities for human nearness, welcomes the breaking down of religious individualism, and slaps the wrists of ecclesiastical power people who have abused their authority in the defense of orthodoxy. "Could a Teilhard de Chardin really not have been dealt with in a more brotherly fashion in Rome?" he asks.

The third is the idea of how to *prepare for death.* Saul Alinsky, the famous Chicago activist of the 1960s and the community organizer who taught neighborhoods to unite against oppressive power structures, often told his followers that he attained true freedom when he accepted the fact that he was going to die. At that moment, he knew that none of his enemies could frighten him. Alinsky, whose friend Jacques Maritain called him a saint, was a Jewish Marxist who liked working with poor Catholic parishes. His attitude exemplifies Rahner's idea that how we die sums up who we are—accepting death determines our stance toward life, so that in our last moment we are what we have always been.

When Rahner's mother died in 1976 at the age of 101, friends found a handwritten page in her missal quoting the prayer of Teilhard de Chardin: "It is not enough that I should die while communicating. Teach me to treat my death as an act of communion." Rahner himself composed several prayers in preparation for his own passing. In a talk he gave in Freiberg, his birthplace, in 1984, he concluded: "Eighty years is a long time. However, for each one the life span allotted to him is but a brief moment in which what should be becomes."

Elisabeth Schüssler Fiorenza

46 In Memory of Her: A Feminist Theological Reconstruction of Christian Origins

1983

W HEN POPE JOHN PAUL II offered a ritual apology during Lent 2000 on behalf of the church for any wrongs done throughout history to women, not everyone was satisfied with the breadth or specificity of the proclamation.

From the standpoint of one school of feminist criticism, the oppression of women began with the creation account in Genesis in which Eve was blamed for humankind's fall and condemned to bear children in pain, and it continued in the structures of Old Testament patriarchal society. The Catholic Church in particular, according to this line of argument, denied women their autonomy through its opposition to divorce, abortion, and birth control, a moral code imposed by a priestly class of celibate men who, by excluding women from ordination, had denied them voice and status in the church.

A standard response to this critique is that historically Christianity has elevated the status of women in Western civiliza-tion; that the church has protected the family in which women, as mothers, are fulfilled; that the prohibitions of abortion and birth control are inescapable consequences of the natural law; and that although the church's unbroken theological tradition prohibits

209

the ordination of women, the cult of the Blessed Virgin Mary and the glorious lives of women saints and religious demonstrate the church's high esteem for women.

Another school of feminist criticism, whose adherents include prominent theologians within the church, approaches the issue of oppression in a different way. Clearly women, with some exceptions—great saints such as Catherine of Siena and founders of religious orders such as Teresa of Ávila—have been frozen out of the decision-making process. There is little doubt that women bishops and cardinals, if they did not approve of abortion, would offer different pastoral insights on how to deal with the problem. Meanwhile, feminist theologians such as Elisabeth Schüssler Fiorenza of Harvard and the University of Notre Dame and Elizabeth Johnson of Fordham, author of *She Who Is*, have reexamined the Scriptures, approaching them from the point of view of modern women who have experienced the women's liberation movement.

Theologians of this school break through the convention that these texts were written, for the most part, by men who shared the presuppositions of a patriarchal society, a mentality that man is the ideal human being and maleness is symbolic of the divine and that women are inferior to men and represent a lower, more carnal, reality. Historically, the Greco-Roman society in which Christianity emerged assumed that the male was in charge: depending on his political status, he might rule over his slaves, his serfs, his wife, his children, and if he had religious authority, his parish or diocese.

Feminist theologians have discovered that in the Old Testament, particularly in the Wisdom Literature, feminine characteristics are attributed to God. In the New Testament and in the history of the early church, there is evidence that women were much more central to the church's founding than we had supposed. Through this method of reexamining, Scripture becomes a resource in the liberation of women and other subordinated people.

The logic is clear: if the New Testament teaches equality among rich and poor, free and slave, Greek and Jew, and men and women, and if women were leaders in the early church—and indeed, Christianity could not have spread without wealthy women patrons who provided their homes as church centers—women should share equally in the leadership today.

Among the many excellent feminist theologies, Elisabeth Schüssler Fiorenza's *In Memory of Her* is an exemplary mainstream scholarly study that is both meticulous in its method and ardent in its purpose. She takes her title from Mark 14:3–9, the anointing at Bethany, in which an unnamed woman approaches Jesus at the house of Simon the leper two days before Jesus' death and anoints him with a costly ointment of nard. Some present, specifically Judas Iscariot, scold her for this waste of money, but Jesus defends her: "She has done what she could; she has anointed my body beforehand for its burial. Truly I tell you, wherever the good news is proclaimed in the whole world, what she has done will be told in remembrance of her."

Ironically, says Fiorenza, the name of Judas has lived on, but the name of this woman has been forgotten. Thus, Professor Fiorenza will restore this unnamed woman—and all women like her—to the prominence Jesus promised. In doing so, she will draw on the insights of liberation theology, one of which is that "all liberation theologies, including feminist theology, is the recognition that all theology, willingly or not, is always engaged for or against the oppressed. Intellectual neutrality is not possible in a world of exploitation and oppression."

Part of Fiorenza's method is to examine a series of troublesome texts, such as 1 Peter 2:18–3:12, in which slaves are told to be submissive to their masters and women to their husbands, and to explain them in their fuller contexts. As a political and social subgroup, Christians were already considered subversive to the patriarchal Roman society. New Christians, including many women and slaves, considered themselves "liberated" from ancestral customs and pagan gods. This attitude clearly threatened the harmony of households in which the husband was still a pagan, and it opened Christians to the charge of sedition. Peter's strategy suggests winning over the master with charity and patience; it does not intend to reinforce patriarchy, even though, in time, that was one of the results.

Ephesians 5:21–33, however, in comparing Christian marriage to the relationship between Christ and the church, does reinforce patriarchy rather than equality. The husband is compared to Christ, and the bride is subordinate to Christ, though the dominance of the husband is "Christianized" by its command of love. (In performing weddings today, I notice that the couples never select readings that admonish the bride to obey her husband.)

Gradually, in the first and second centuries, as the structures of the church more and more came to resemble those of the Greco-Roman society, the patriarchy of civil society was imposed. Women were praised for their humility and submission. The apocryphal, or noncanonical, texts tended to give more prominence to women, particularly Mary Magdalene, who was described as a competitor with St. Peter. These texts were pushed out of mainstream discussion by the formation of the canon. Meanwhile, the role of prophets, many of whom were women, was downplayed, partly in response to the Montanists, who had women prophets among their leaders. Gradually, patristic writers excluded women from influence—they could not teach, be intellectual leaders, or write books. Authority became centralized in the episcopacy.

The more authentic tradition, Fiorenza says, is preserved in the Gospels of Mark and John. In Mark, the four male disciples—Peter, James, Andrew, and John—are portrayed as failures who don't understand Jesus and desert him at the end, whereas the four women—Mary Magdalene, Mary the mother of Joses, Salome, and Mary the mother of James the younger—stand beneath the cross as true followers.

John emphasizes the role of the disciples, both men and women, beyond the first group of twelve; then he presents Mary the mother of Jesus, Mary Magdalene, and the Samaritan woman at the well as equals and as exemplary disciples. Finally, at the resurrection of Lazarus, the scene that establishes Jesus' identity, John gives "the primary articulation of the community's Christological faith," according to Fiorenza, to Martha: "Yes, Lord, I believe that you are the Christ, the son of God, who is coming into the world" (John 11:27).

In Memory of Her is professional, rather than popular, theology. But a reader who finds the detailed scriptural commentary slow reading will still find Fiorenza's epilogue a stirring statement of her personal spirituality. She rejects the two images that, she says, have dominated the American women's movement for two hundred years: the Eden-home motif that proclaims the homemaker vocation to be the woman's fulfillment, and the Exodus image, which compels women to leave behind community, family, children, and religion and flee into the desert. She prefers to define women's relationship to God not through men or patriarchal structures but through "the experience of being called into the discipleship of equals, the assembly of free citizens who decide their own spiritual welfare."

Christian spirituality means eating together, drinking together, sharing with each other, talking with each other, experiencing God's presence through each other, and, in doing so, proclaiming the gospel as God's alternative vision for everyone, especially for those who are poor, outcast, and battered. As long as women Christians are excluded from breaking the bread and deciding their own spiritual welfare and commitment, *ekklesia* (the kingdom) as the discipleship of equals will not be realized and the power of the gospel will be greatly diminished.

47 Black Robe

1985

W<small>HAT WE KNEW BEST</small> about them was how they died. From grammar school, through St. Joe's Prep School and Fordham, where our dorm was called Martyrs Court—for Isaac Jogues, John Lalande, and René Goupil—to the Novitiate of St. Andrew-on-Hudson, where October's North American Martyrs was the biggest feast, the tortures they endured were heroic tales that rivaled the passion of Christ.

Francis X. Talbot, S.J.'s biographies of Jogues, *Saint among Savages*, and Jean de Brébeuf, *Saint among the Hurons*, were in steady circulation, and the most gruesome chapter was usually the last. In *Saint among the Hurons*, the Iroquois and Huron captors competed with one another to break de Brébeuf's spirit, while he resolved not to cry out or give in. They tied him naked to a stake and burned him with red hot hatchets, cut off his nose, hacked off a piece of his tongue, poured boiling water over him in mockery of baptism, burned him again, gouged out his eyes, cut strips of his flesh to eat, scalped him, and then pulled out his heart, licked off the blood, roasted it, and ate it.

Brian Moore discovered these Jesuit giants while reading a Graham Greene essay on Francis Parkman's nineteenth-century historical classic, *The Jesuits in North America*, which Parkman had based on *The Jesuit Relations and Allied Documents*, volumes of extremely detailed reports sent home to France by the seventeenth-century Jesuit missionaries. Greene quotes a passage from Parkman:

> [Father] Noël Chabanel came later to the mission for he did not reach the Huron country until 1643. He detested the Indian life—the smoke, the vermin, the filthy food, the impossibility of privacy. He could not study by the smoky lodge fires, among the noisy crowd of men and squaws, with their dogs and their restless, screeching children. He had a natural inaptitude to learning the language, and labored at it for five years with scarcely a sign of progress. The Devil whispered a suggestion in his ear: Let him procure his release from these barren and revolting toils and return to France where congenial and useful employments awaited him. Chabanel refused to listen: and when the temptation still beset him he bound himself by a solemn vow to remain in Canada to the day of his death.

The words *solemn vow* struck Moore as "the voice of a conscience that, I fear, we no longer possess." So he read Parkman and *Jesuit Relations* and wrote a powerful, popular novel that has none of the glory that we have been raised to associate with martyrdom and little of the hope we associate with saints—but all of the terrible pain.

Born to a Catholic family in Belfast in 1921, Moore separated himself as a young man from all ideological allegiances, whether socialist or Catholic. Somehow, however, like James Joyce, to whose *Dubliners* Moore's first novel, *The Lonely Passion of Judith Hearne*, has been compared, and Graham Greene, who considered Moore his "favorite living novelist," Moore kept returning to the ethical questions that Catholicism, in both its valid insights and its wrongheaded dogmatism, raised.

Moore, who became a Canadian citizen in 1948 and later moved to Malibu, California, where he spent the rest of his life, published nineteen novels. He died at seventy-seven, and toward the end of his writing career his novels dealt increasingly with situations in which characters in Northern Ireland, Haiti, and France were confronted with moral dilemmas.

Carefully plotted to keep readers hanging by their fingernails, his novels competed well for slots on the best-sellers list and for the literary prizes he often won. *Black Robe* captivates the reader through the sensationalism of its torture scenes (no worse than Fr. Talbot's), the army-sergeant and street-punk, f-word-littered vocabulary attributed to the Indians, and the apparently obligatory sex scenes between the Jesuit's young assistant and an Indian girl (Fr. Talbot is shaking his head).

It is 1635. Young, slender, thin-bearded, and intellectual, Paul Laforgue, S.J., from Normandy, is sent from Quebec into the Canadian wilderness around the southern end of Lake Huron, to a remote mission where one or both of the Jesuits may be sick or dead. He is to take their place. A party of Indians, including warriors and their families friendly to and paid by the French, are to guide Laforgue and his twenty-year-old assistant, Daniel, up the river, over the rapids, and within safe distance of the mission.

Because the Catholic French and Indian—called Savage—cultures are so far apart, tragedy awaits upstream. The Savages are naked; the Blackrobes hide their bodies. The Savages share everything; the French keep private property to themselves. The Savages kill a moose, tear him up, and eat him half-cooked; they sleep on top of one another, sometimes copulating, snoring, sweating, and stinking. Jesuit missionaries usually do not. The Savages are guided ultimately by dreams and sorcerers, the Jesuits by directives from religious authorities.

Young Laforgue is motivated by his burning desire to baptize all these Savages. In the theology of his time, he is convinced that they will never see heaven if he cannot get to them at the last moment, sprinkle them with melting snow, and recite a formula that the Savages standing by will interpret as a curse. Young Daniel, who Laforgue thinks is destined for the priesthood, is driven by his sexual passion for a Savage maiden.

In the course of the journey, Laforgue and his companions suffer the torments that Jogues and de Brébeuf suffered, and Moore does not hesitate in spelling out the details. In one paragraph, Daniel's lover's little brother is dismembered, cooked, and eaten before their eyes.

When Laforgue finally makes it to the mission, he finds the dead body of one of the Jesuits rotting in the chapel, the superior suffering from a stroke, and the Indian villagers dying from a plague. The Indians seem willing to accept baptism because they think that the Jesuits' superior sorcery will save them from the plague. The superior is murdered; now Laforgue must decide. To baptize them under these conditions, when they neither believe nor understand what the sacrament means, would be to give in to the very superstition that Catholicism is intended to replace.

When he resists, the Huron chief asks:

"Do you love us?"

Today the whole mind-set that moved seventeenth-century missionaries to heroism is no longer in effect. We no longer believe that a basically good person who has not been baptized is not saved; our "missionaries" enter into alien cultures to identify with the people and learn from them rather than to introduce them to a superior system of belief. Some interpret the early Jesuit efforts in North America as an intrusion, a violation of a superior, primitive way of life. They believe that the Iroquois who tortured the Jesuits to death were not Savages or Indians but Native Americans defending their own culture.

Brian Moore knows this and, without detracting from the love that brought Paul Laforgue from Normandy to the Canadian woods, allows us to reach these conclusions. John Breslin, S.J., in an *America* article (March 20, 1999) following Moore's death on January 10, 1999, sums up his career well:

> Moore's conviction . . . that love trumps all other spiritual values, is consonant, ironically, with the deepest truth of the Gospel and with a soupy humanistic sentimentalism. What saves it here and elsewhere is the crucible of passionate commitment and intense suffering from which it emerges. Thus Laforgue joins the other renegade clerics of twentieth-century Catholic fiction: Greene's whiskey priest, Bernanos' curé, Endo's Jesuit missionary—not bad company for a character or a novelist.

Helen Prejean

48 Dead Man Walking: An Eyewitness Account of the Death Penalty in the United States

1993

O<small>NE OF THE STRANGEST TRAITS</small> of the American character—in the most prosperous, technologically advanced, idealistic, Christian, church-going country in the world—is its love affair with violent death.

Perhaps this is the heritage of the frontier, or of the mythical frontier of film—from *The Virginian* to *High Noon* to *The Magnificent Seven*—in which "real men" settle their differences by shooting it out in the middle of the street.

Or maybe it is film and TV's romantic treatment of Mafia gangsters, in which murder is absorbed not as a sin but as a natural fulfillment of a family code. *Of course we eliminated him. What did you expect?*

In that sense, the code of the street has become the code of the state. Dating back to centuries before Christ, the most primitive of ancient moral norms—an eye for an eye—hangs on as the rule of the most modern, liberal, democratic state, the only government in the free world to still execute its citizens.

In a string of articles in *America* and the *National Catholic Reporter*, Robert F. Drinan, S.J., Georgetown law professor and former Massachusetts congressman, spells out the anomaly of a

218

church that, in recent decades, through papal exhortations and statements from American bishops, has made its opposition to capital punishment clear, while its membership, along with the other 60 percent of the American public, approves as more and more men and women—overwhelmingly poor black and Hispanic males—are sent to the lethal-injection chamber or the electric chair. This is the last step of a judicial process that, because they are poor, never gave them a fighting chance. Referring to New York's court-appointed lawyers, Kevin Doyle, the New York State capital defender, told the press: "Basically these folks are sent into battle underequipped, undertrained, and undercompensated." As a result, a good number of their innocent clients aren't able to prove their innocence in court.

Between 1976 and 1993, for example, 225 men and 1 woman were put to death. Southern states led the way, with 31.55 percent in Texas, 14.2 in Florida, and 9.3 in Louisiana. Meanwhile, 455 death-row inmates were freed by last-minute evidence that proved their innocence. Close call! More recently, the governor of Illinois suspended executions because of the state's record of wrongful convictions, and in *Actual Innocence* (2000), authors Jim Dwyer, Barry Scheck, and Peter Neufeld use DNA evidence to note the innocence of sixty-five men who are condemned to prison and/or death.

Ironically, the public enthusiasm for the death penalty coexists with the popularity of prison films about innocent men, played by attractive movie stars, who are victimized by a corrupt judicial system and saved from the electric chair by another movie star at the last moment. Somehow the viewing public cannot move to the next conclusion: maybe we shouldn't be so quick to kill. And meanwhile, no one dares to run for political office, much less the presidency of the United States, without making it clear that he or she is as ready as—or more ready than—the other guy to pull the switch.

In New Orleans, where I taught at Loyola University, I also said Mass at the city jail. We went right into the cell block and spread the altar cloth on the same table where they had just wiped up spilled coffee and grits, and twenty or thirty of the inmates gathered around to sing and pray. All were young, and 99 percent were black. All came up for communion, and as I placed the host on each outstretched tongue, a voice within me told me that what I saw at this moment was the real person, a prisoner of poverty and broken hopes whose true self was reaching out to taste the sacred bread.

Another voice told me that if this young man were released, he might return to his neighborhood—a crime-ridden housing project a few blocks away—blow away his own brother in a family spat over drugs, be sentenced to death, and get shipped to the state prison at Angola.

And there he would meet Sister Helen Prejean.

Helen Prejean, long one of Louisiana's secret virtues, has moved her two linked causes—abolition of the death penalty and support for victims of violent crimes—to a new level of national consciousness, thanks to *Dead Man Walking* and the film version of her book. She believes that Americans support the death penalty mainly out of ignorance. They support it because politicians who should (and do) know better exploit the public's fear of violent crime. They support it because no one has explained to them the death penalty's cruelty, its unfairness, its cost in taxpayer dollars, and above all, its degrading impact on those who relish the satisfaction that another "scum" has "fried."

In 1980, when her religious community, the Sisters of St. Joseph of Medaille, made a commitment to "stand on the side of the poor," Sister Helen Prejean moved into New Orleans's St. Thomas housing project, a hellhole symptomatic of a state where half of the adult population has not completed high school and one in every three babies is born to an unwed mother. Louisiana consistently ranks among the top three states with the largest percentage of residents in prison. In 1982, Sister Prejean became a pen pal of an Angola death-row inmate—Elmo Patrick Sonnier, who with his brother Eddie (in Angola on a life sentence), had kidnapped, raped, and murdered a teenaged girl in 1977. As a spiritual adviser, Sister Prejean also began a series of personal relationships with prisoners. These relationships transformed her life, and as the impact of *Dead Man Walking* grows, they may transform America.

Based on a journal she kept over a dozen years, *Dead Man Walking* is rich with detailed observations and enlivened with re-constructed dialogues. It is several books at once: the spiritual journey of a southern woman who came late to the realization that the politically "neutral" nun was actually "on the side of the oppressor"; a portrait gallery of inmates, their victims, and the Louisiana politicians who profit from the suffering of both; and a well-documented theological and sociological case that speaks against capital punishment. In the last words of rapist-murderer Robert Willie, "It makes no difference whether it's citizens, countries, or governments. Killing is wrong."

Killing is wrong, for one thing, because it does not deter crime. Death-penalty states have the highest level of violence. The death penalty disproportionately affects blacks and the poor, and people are often sentenced to it out of a wrongful conviction. In the United States in the twentieth century, 417 people were wrongly convicted of capital crimes, and 23 of those were executed. Executions cost more than life imprisonment. And because even criminals are human beings, executing them debases us all.

One critic has compared Prejean's indictment of capital punishment to that of Albert Camus. I suggest other parallels: both Thoreau's *Civil Disobedience* and Rachel Carson's *Silent Spring* appeal to the conscience and are based on a combination of personal experience, eloquence, and research. Since *Dead Man Walking* first appeared in 1993, Helen Prejean has been on the road talking to anyone who will listen. Maybe that 60 percent of the public who do not listen to the pope will listen to her.

Peter Ackroyd

49 The Life of Thomas More

1998

$\mathbf{M}$ANY OF US KNOW St. Thomas More best from Paul Scofield's portrayal of him in Robert Bolt's play and 1966 film, *A Man for All Seasons*. But since historical drama inevitably rearranges and recreates history for dramatic effect, we know the image—or the idea—rather than the man.

Or we know the other image, that inscrutable, slightly sad face in Hans Holbein's 1527 portrait of the lord chancellor of England, splendid in his gold medallion and fur robe with red silk sleeves, beneath which, since the age of eighteen, he had worn a hair shirt to temper his pride and contain his sexual desires.

What a wonderful ideal these images represent—the incorruptible individual, the man who would rather die than compromise his integrity—today found more often in plays and films than in public life.

Peter Ackroyd, the prizewinning biographer of T. S. Eliot and William Blake, would hardly classify himself as a spiritual writer even though he is drawn to religious subjects. Yet the modern reader in search of spiritual food hungers for a life story of Thomas More, who embodied the humanism of the sixteenth century as well as the dual Christian commitment to family life and public service that is often invoked but so desperately missed in the twenty-first.

More's theological, polemical, and devotional writings fill twenty-one volumes in *The Complete Works of St. Thomas More*, but aside from *Utopia*, which is subject to multiple interpretations, it is his life rather than his books that captures the contemporary imagination.

Ackroyd brilliantly evokes the full atmosphere of More's world: the contrast between More and his nemesis, Martin Luther, as representatives of the old faith and of the religious revolution of Protestantism; the richness of medieval liturgy and ceremonies at court; and the balance of worldly power and domestic asceticism that permeated the lord chancellor's routine at court and in his Chelsea home.

More's first wife, Jane, died at twenty-two, perhaps in childbirth, after bringing forth four children—Margaret, Elizabeth, Cecily, and John. A month later, thirty-three-year-old More married Alice Middleton, a wealthy widow eight years his senior who had a daughter from her first marriage. Over the years, More took in several wards, and his children married well, so he presided over a large and diverse household that, in some ways, he administered like an academy, teaching Latin and Greek to his children and a dozen wards and grandchildren, making him a pioneer in the education of women.

In his new house, he built both a library and a private chapel to be faithful to Thomas à Kempis's rule that you must "enter thy secret chamber and shut out the tumults of the world." He went to bed at nine o'clock, rose at two in the morning, attended Mass, and set to work. He ate little, drank water, read Scripture at dinner, and got the family to talk about what they had heard. At his little twelfth-century parish church, All Saints, he served Mass and sang in the choir.

It is important to realize that Ackroyd's book is the scholarly biography of a saint rather than a *vita sancti*, as in *Butler's Lives of the Saints*, which is written for edification. Though More was from the beginning good and pious, he was not always right, and he was not a "saint" until that awful moment when his conscience said no to power when nearly everyone else had said yes.

The fascination in watching his life unfold, knowing how it will end, is in seeing this brilliant young courtier rise. The son of a prominent lawyer, Thomas More was born on February 7, 1478, and named for Thomas Becket, the twelfth-century archbishop of Canterbury. Becket was born just a few yards from More's house and was slain at the altar for defying his king. As a child at St. Anthony's school, Thomas daily crossed the square where criminals were beheaded and burned.

More considered a monastic life but instead became a lawyer, an undersheriff of London, an impartial judge and friend of the poor, a diplomat and secretary for Henry VIII, a supervisor of the Exchequer, and a speaker of the House of Commons. Every morning he would nod in respect to Cardinal Wolsey, the second most powerful man in England, who rode to the palace daily on a mule as a sign of humility but did so resplendent in crimson and jewels. When Wolsey fell from favor, Henry named More chancellor of England.

Thomas More served at the heart of a royal household that was profoundly corrupt and ready to kill its adversaries. That it killed them according to the law made them no less dead and their executions no less cruel.

The title "man for all seasons" was bestowed on More by his friend Erasmus, the greatest humanist and the author of *In Praise of Folly*, which he wrote as a guest in More's house. More was not a man for all seasons, however, as much as he was a man of and for his own times. For him, heretical ideas such as Luther's undermined the basic unity of civil and ecclesiastical society; their influence could mean, says Ackroyd, "the end of the world," at least as More had known it.

As chancellor, More set up a network of spies and raided meetings in which suspected heretics could be caught with forbidden books. The heretics would then be thrown into the Tower of London and sometimes burned. More approved of burnings. Ackroyd describes the executions: "People watch from open windows as the body of the condemned man, charred and melted by the flames, topples forward from its chain into the fire." One heretic took forty-five minutes to die. As Ackroyd says, More "epitomized, in modern terms, the apparatus of the state using its power to crush those attempting to subvert it. His opponents were genuinely following their consciences, while More considered them the harbinger of the devil's reign on earth."

Ironically, as he carried out his purge in loyalty to the king, the king and his would-be-wife, Anne Boleyn, were passing heretical pamphlets around the court.

As Henry VIII's perfidy became more obvious, More was stuck in the sixteenth-century version of today's "influence trap." The secretary of state knows the president's policy in Africa is wrong, perhaps even immoral. But he doesn't tell the president this because he's afraid the president won't listen to him anymore. He goes along with a bad policy, hoping that later the president will listen. But it ends up being too late.

Privately, More knew that Henry's case for nullifying his son-less marriage to Catherine of Aragon was baseless, but he dissembled in public "for the sake of the greater struggle ahead." Finally, his refusal to attend the coronation of Anne Boleyn, whom Henry married in 1533, sealed his fate.

In February of 1534, the Act of Succession declared the marriage of Henry and Catherine null and void and claimed that no power on earth—meaning the pope—had the authority to declare otherwise. It further ordered that all the king's subjects must take an oath to support the supremacy of the king. Thus it declared the king's authority as above the pope's, even in church affairs. By April, every member of Parliament had so sworn, and More was summoned to Lambeth Palace. He read the act and the oath and said he could accept the act, but to swear the oath would be to lose his soul. He could not support the schism that denied the pope's jurisdiction over England, something that, apparently, most English people could easily accept.

On April 17, Thomas More was imprisoned in the Tower of London. A few days later, a visionary nun and five priests who had opposed the marriage were taken from their cells. The nun was hanged. The priests were hanged, revived, and castrated, their intestines were pulled out and boiled, and their hearts were plucked out while they were still conscious. Then they were beheaded. More's friend John Fisher, bishop of Rochester, was also arrested, condemned, and beheaded. To prepare himself until they took away his books, More wrote *De Tristitia Christi* (*The*

Sadness of Christ,) a commentary on Christ's agony in the garden the night before his death. Then More was tried and condemned to beheading.

As much as he loved his family, particularly his brilliant daughter, Margaret Roper, who was considered one of the best-educated women in Europe, they could not give him the comfort of understanding what he was doing. Margaret visited him in his cell and urged him to take the oath as she had done. His wife, Alice, pleaded with Henry that her husband was suffering from a scruple, "a devilish fantasy." He was truly alone. But he was alone with his conscience, which to him represented the communion of saints, the whole history and tradition of the church, the duty and law he loved and would die for.

In his last days, More knew that although he would die alone—surrounded by a curious crowd but with his family kept away—in another sense, later generations would watch and remember his final moments. So he bore himself, says Ackroyd, as an actor in a medieval mystery play. The king, fearing the effect of More's last address to the crowd, sent an order that he "should not use many words." Obedient to the end, from the scaffold he told the on-lookers that he "died the King's good servant, but God's first."

More has long been considered the patron of lawyers. Recently he has been proposed as the model for politicians as well. I try to imagine a future TV debate between presidential candidates in which each candidate is asked to comment on what he or she most admires in their patron saint.

His willingness to die rather than compromise?

Robert Ellsberg

50 All Saints: Daily Reflections on Saints, Prophets, and Witnesses for Our Time

1997

IN RECENT YEARS, the concept of sainthood, rather than fall out of vogue like other pre–Vatican II devotions, seems to have expanded in two ways. First, Pope John Paul II has zealously promoted the cult of the saints by proclaiming more than seven hundred beatifications and more than two hundred canonizations during his pontificate. That's more than those proclaimed over the last two centuries by all his predecessors combined and close to more than all those proclaimed by pontiffs since the sixteenth century, when records of such things were first kept. As Lawrence S. Cunningham pointed out in *Theological Studies*, the pope announces these new "friends of God" as he travels around the world, a sign that he sees the proliferation of saints as an instrument of evangelization.

Second, other commentators have developed the concept of the communion of saints, that transcendent union of all believers in heaven, in purgatory, and on earth, to emphasize the solidarity, the mutual dependence, of all those touched by grace, including those whose lives are linked to ours by love or common ideals whether or not they are or were formal members of the church.

With this in mind, Robert Ellsberg has compiled a list of 365 men and women whose lives "speak to the spiritual needs of our day," and he has written short essays about each of them. He has assigned each one a calendar date so that each day we may be challenged, he hopes, to expand our notion of what holiness can mean.

Roughly a third are the standard monks and nuns and martyrs from *Butler's Lives of the Saints* (plus Alban Butler, 1710–1773, himself), but the rest are a fascinating—and occasionally startling—collection of modern martyrs, novelists, intellectuals, rebels, heretics, artists, musicians, poets, pacifists, Jews, Hindus, and people who may not have even existed but who have appeared in Scripture or in pious folklore. Veronica, who wiped Jesus' face with her veil, and Noah are two such examples.

I have enjoyed reading about people whom I knew personally, even if only briefly, and who deserve the attention this book can give them, such as *National Catholic Reporter* journalist Penny Lernoux; theologian John Courtney Murray, S.J.; Jesuit superior general Pedro Arrupe, S.J., who was treated shabbily by the Vatican in its attempt to "reform" the Society it feared he had failed to control; and interracial apostle John LaFarge, S.J., whose Mass I served when he was on retreat.

Ellsberg includes writers who appear among these fifty spiritual classics: Ven. John Henry Newman, Karl Rahner, Martin Luther King Jr., Dietrich Bonhoeffer, Pierre Teilhard de Chardin, Thomas à Kempis, Henry David Thoreau, Job, G. K. Chesterton, St. Thomas More, Georges Bernanos, Flannery O'Connor, St. Augustine, François Mauriac, Albert Schweitzer, Dante Alighieri, St. Thérèse of Lisieux, St. Luke, Dorothy Day, Thomas Merton, and St. John.

Ellsberg's mother, a Christian, introduced him to the communion of saints, and his father, Daniel Ellsberg, the author of the Pentagon Papers who later leaked them to the press, pointed him toward Gandhi and nonviolent struggle. As the editor of Orbis Books, which specializes in liberation theology, Ellsberg naturally finds his heroes—as do I—among those who risk their lives and reputations on behalf of the weak and poor or those who simply have an idea that has a right to be heard, but whom authorities would rather slander, torture, silence, or kill than let the idea spread.

To our shame, we can commemorate Jan Hus, reformer and martyr, whom the church, after a "canonical lynching," burned for heresy in 1415. Giordano Bruno, cosmologist and martyr, suggested that the universe was infinite and that some day human beings might travel through space and visit other worlds; he was burned for heresy in Rome in 1600. Antonio Rosmini-Serbati, leading scholar and founder of the Institute of Charity, lost not his life but his career and reputation for writing *The Five Wounds of the Church* (1848). These wounds were the division of the clergy from the people in worship, the defective education of the clergy, the disunity among the bishops, the nomination of bishops by secular powers, and the enslavement of the church by riches.

To our relief, more persons than we realized stood up against Hitler and paid the price: Franz Jägerstätter, conscientious objector and martyr; Edith Stein, Jewish convert, Carmelite, and martyr; Alfred Delp, Jesuit and martyr; and Hans and Sophie Scholl, Munich students in their twenties and members of the White Rose. The Scholls published pamphlets that said:

> Man is free, to be sure, but without the true God he is defenseless against the principle of evil. . . . We must attack evil where it is strongest, and it is strongest in the power of Hitler. . . . We will not be silent. We are your bad conscience. The White Rose will not leave you in peace.

Until they were beheaded.

Among the surprises and challenges are some names that we have learned to revere as "great," famous, or intriguing, but not immediately as saints: Mozart, Vincent van Gogh, Héloïse, Oskar Schindler, Walker Percy, Albert Camus, and finally, Etty Hillesum, a Dutch Holocaust victim whose diary, *An Interrupted Life: The Diaries, 1941–1943*, I considered for this fifty classics list but decided against.

Let's think about some typical and atypical saintly lives on their feasts:

January 14: Martin Niemoeller (1892–1984). A highly decorated U-boat commander during World War I and a Lutheran pastor, Niemoeller was at first an anti-Semite and a Hitler supporter, but when he saw the evils of Nazism and the Jewish persecution, he helped found the Confessing Church, to which Karl Barth and Bonhoeffer belonged, to distance the church from National Socialism. Though he was convicted of "urging rebellion," the judges refused to sentence him because he was a World War I hero, so Hitler ordered him to Dachau as his "personal prisoner." After the war, he led a movement to confess the crimes against the Jews and traveled throughout the world speaking against nuclear arms and in defense of human rights.

April 18: Cornelia Connelly (1809–1879). This is one of the craziest stories in the history of American Catholicism. In 1839, Cornelia and Pierce Connelly, the parents of four children, were teaching in Catholic schools in rural Louisiana. Following the deaths of two of the children, Pierce decided he wanted to become a priest. Pope Gregory XVI agreed to grant his request on the condition that Cornelia, who had just given birth to her fifth child, would take a vow of chastity. Looking for something to do with her life, she founded a religious congregation for the education of girls. Pierce, tired of the priesthood, tried to take over her congregation and sued her in an Anglican Church court to force her back into the marriage. He lost the suit but kidnapped the children, and she never saw them again. For the rest of her life, suffering from skin disease in her last years, she established and directed schools in England, America, and France as superior of the Society of the Holy Child Jesus.

August 31: John Leary (1958–1982). Son of a New England Irish working-class family and inspired by the lives of Dorothy Day and Thomas Merton, John spent his Harvard years and two years after graduation working with prisoners, the homeless, and the elderly. A member of Pax Christi, he protested against the military draft, capital punishment, abortion, and a lab that did military research. He graduated with honors in religious studies, went to daily Mass, including liturgies in the Byzantine and Melkite rites, shared his apartment with street people, read the Bible, said the rosary, made retreats at a Trappist monastery, and never took himself too seriously. He was a runner, and while running he would recite to himself the Jesus prayer: "Lord Jesus, Son of the Living God, have mercy on me, a sinner." Running home from work one afternoon to his room at the Catholic Worker house in Boston, he dropped dead.

Many of us can look at our lives and realize that we have had friends who were very much like him. And that's why this book is so good.

Conclusion

I HAVE LIVED WITH THESE fifty writers on various levels of intimacy over many years.

Perhaps I knew Augustine first without reading him because his is my middle name. Then late at night, before I could read, I listened to Sigrid Undset through my father's voice as he read *Kristin Lavransdatter* to my mother as she worked on her knitting. Then Dante through the sensational Doré illustrations. And *Death Comes for the Archbishop* was always on our library shelf, and I would read the title almost daily and wonder who the Archbishop was and how and why he died. I presumed that he was murdered. And speaking of murder, among the volumes I have saved from my parents' library is a beautiful 1933 *Brothers Karamazov* with illustrations by Boardman Robinson.

Other writers—such as the Evangelists, Thoreau, Greene, and Joyce—I have read again and again at different stages of my life because I am either teaching their books or writing about them, and this has often been the test. Do I love this book enough to reread a hundred pages or so several times a week and walk into a classroom bursting to share what I know with young men and women who might well be angry that I have given them so much to read?

My other test is a more difficult one. One of the more disturbing assertions in these pages is Cardinal Newman's opinion—expressed in the devastating metaphor that one cannot cut stone with a razor blade—that liberal education cannot make us better persons. If I believed that for a moment I'd have to quit all my jobs of teaching, preaching, and writing.

We grow morally by confronting the virtues—and vices—in our fellow men and women. Page Smith, in his provocative history of American education, *Killing the Spirit* (1990), challenges teachers to impart the virtue of courage to their students by demonstrating it in their lives. Can we achieve that at least partly by assigning a book? If we read deeply enough and allow the author and the characters he or she creates to break through our distractions and defenses, that encounter can be the moral equivalent of a confrontation with a living person. No, it does not achieve the sensation of the friend's living embrace or the shock of a fraternal admonition; but it is real and true.

Saint John says in the prologue of his Gospel, "No one has ever seen God" (1:18). But if we keep reading we'll soon come to know him. I have never met Myles Connolly, but I have been loved by friends. Though I lived in France for a year, I did not meet a poor country priest. Now I have. As this is written, I am reading Dostoyevsky's *Crime and Punishment* for the first time in order to teach it in an ethics of criminal justice course, and I'm preparing to teach *The Brothers Karamazov* in a theology course next week. I am tingling with excitement at the prospect. Dostoyevsky, I think, invites his readers to learn courage, the courage he learned in his own life in prison as he came to terms with his own guilt and, challenged by the New Testament and the life of Jesus, probed his own demons, endured his epilepsy, and gave us his vision of the world.

Like Augustine, Dorothy Day, Malcolm X, Thomas Merton, John Henry Newman, Abraham Lincoln, and others, he let a book bore into his soul.

—St. Peter's College, 9 March 2001

Selected Sources

The Book of Genesis

Although the multivolume Anchor Bible (Doubleday, 1964–2000) is a
treasure trove for scholars, the most useful scholarly one-volume reference is *The New Jerome Biblical Commentary* (Prentice Hall, 1999),
eds. Raymond E. Brown, S.S., Joseph A. Fitzmyer, S.J., and Roland E.
Murphy, O.Carm.

See also Robert Alter, *Genesis, Translation and Commentary* (W.W.
Norton, 1996) and Pauline A. Viviano, *Genesis*, Collegeville Bible
Commentary (Liturgical Press, 1985).

The Book of Job

The classic reference work by John L. McKenzie, S.J., *Dictionary of the
Bible* (Bruce, 1965), has a good essay on Job—and on everything else.
Also, Moshe Greenberg, "Job," in Robert Alter and Frank Kermode,
eds., *The Literary Guide to the Bible* (Harvard, 1987).

See also "The Impious Impatience of Job" by Cynthia Ozick in *The
American Scholar*; reprinted in *The Best American Essays 1999*
(Houghton Mifflin, 1999).

**Robert Alter, *The David Story : A Translation with Commentary of 1 and 2
Samuel***

Robert Alter, *The David Story: A Translation with Commentary of 1 and 2
Samuel* (W.W. Norton, 1999).

See also John L. McKenzie's *Dictionary of the Bible* and *The New Jerome
Bible Commentary.*

The Gospel of Luke

My Luke sources are: Joseph A. Fitzmyer, *The Gospel According to Luke*, 2
vols., The Anchor Bible (Doubleday, 1981); Luke Timothy Johnson, *The
Gospel of Luke*, Sacra Pagina (Liturgical Press, 1991); and G. B. Caird,
The Gospel of St. Luke, Penguin New Testament Commentaries (Penguin,
1964).

The Gospel of John

The preeminent scholar on John is Raymond E. Brown, S.S., especially
in the Anchor Bible series; but the older commentary, which I love

for its style and pastoral analysis, is John Marsh, *Saint John* (Penguin, 1968). For the latest scholarship see Francis J. Moloney, S.D.B., *The Gospel of John*, Sacra Pagina (Liturgical Press, 1998).

St. Augustine, *The Confessions*

St. Augustine, *The Confessions*, trans. Maria Boulding, O.S.B. (Vintage, 1998).

Before reading the *Confessions*, read Garry Wills's short *Saint Augustine* (Viking, 1999), then try Peter Brown, *Augustine of Hippo: A Biography* (University of California Press, 1967). See also *St. Augustine* (1933) by Rebecca West, in *Rebecca West, a Celebration* (Penguin, 1978).

Dante Alighieri, *Inferno*

Contemporary critics who put Dante in a modern perspective are David Denby in *Great Books: My Adventures with Homer, Rousseau, Woolf and Other Indestructible Writers* (Simon and Schuster, 1996) and Harold Bloom in *The Western Canon: The Books and Schools of the Ages* (Harcourt Brace, 1994). Wallace Fowlie, whom I knew personally as a *Commonweal* contributor and visiting scholar at Holy Cross, has written *A Reading of Dante's Inferno* (University of Chicago Press, 1981). Otherwise, go to the shelves. The millennial book list was in the December 3, 1999, issue of *Times Literary Supplement*.

Michael Walsh, *Butler's Lives of the Saints*

Butler's Lives of the Saints, ed. Michael Walsh. Concise edition, revised and updated (HarperSanFrancisco, 1991).

To understand the formal process by which someone "becomes" a saint, read Kenneth L. Woodward, *Making Saints: How the Catholic Church Determines Who Becomes a Saint, Who Doesn't, and Why* (Simon and Schuster, 1990). To read a big fat scholarly but lively life of a saint that we all loved in the Jesuit novitiate, get James Brodrick, S.J., *Saint Peter Canisius* (Loyola Press, 1962).

Thomas à Kempis, *The Imitation of Christ*

Thomas à Kempis, *The Imitation of Christ in Four Books*, rev. ed. Trans. Joseph N. Tylenda, S.J. (Vintage, 1998).

The introduction by Joseph N. Tylenda, S.J., to the Vintage edition of the *Imitation*, perhaps with an encyclopedia article on the *devotio moderna*, is sufficient background. Then turn to those who have been influenced by this unusual book, such as Thomas Merton and Dorothy Day. But here—because I say go to the shelves—I should mention a quirky little volume, Albert Mordell's *Dante and Other Waning Classics* (Kennikat Press, 1915), in which he debunks Dante, Milton, Bunyon, à Kempis, St. Augustine, and Pascal. Their religious content, he says, keeps them from being really good books.

Ven. John Henry Newman, *The Idea of a University*

John Henry Newman, *The Idea of a University*, ed. Frank M. Turner (Yale University Press, 1996).

In the *New York Times* (February 24, 2001) commemoration of the 200th anniversary of Newman's birth, Peter Steinfels writes that "no self-respecting anthology of English prose can be without passages from Newman's *Apologia pro Vita Sua* (1864) or other works." But, for a contemporary study of what happened in America to the idea of "Catholic identity" in the universities, see Philip Gleason, *Contending with Modernity* (Oxford University Press, 1995).

Henry David Thoreau, *Walden*

Henry David Thoreau, *Walden and Civil Disobedience* (Penguin, 1983).

There are many collections of essays on *Walden*, but my favorite resource is *The Annotated Walden*, ed. Philip Van Doren Stern (C. N. Potter, 1970). Then see Richard Ruland, ed., *Twentieth Century Interpretations of Walden* (Prentice-Hall, 1968).

Abraham Lincoln, "The Second Inaugural Address"

Besides Alfred Kazin, see David Herbert Donald, *Lincoln* (Simon and Schuster, 1995).

Fyodor Dostoyevsky, *The Brothers Karamazov*

Fyodor Dostoyevsky, *The Brothers Karamazov*, foreword by Manuel Komroff (Signet Classic, 1999).

Read Dostoyevsky's *Crime and Punishment* (Penguin, 1991). It will chill your bones. See also A. Boyce Gibson, *The Religion of Dostoevsky* (Westminster Press, 1974); René Wellek, ed., *Dostoevsky: A Collection of Critical Essays*. Twentieth Century Views (Prentice-Hall, 1962); and Geir Kjetsaa, *Fyodor Dostoyevsky: A Writer's Life* (Viking, 1987).

St. Thérèse of Lisieux, *The Story of a Soul*

Dorothy Day would say to read about the "other" Saint Teresa, the sixteenth-century mystic and reformer, in *The Life of Teresa of Jesus: The Autobiography of Teresa of Ávila*, ed. E. Allison Peers (Doubleday, 1960). See also Peter-Thomas Rohrbach, *The Search for Saint Thérèse* (Hanover House, 1961).

Henry Adams, *Mont-Saint-Michel and Chartres*

Henry Adams, *Mont-Saint-Michel and Chartres*, in *Novels, Mont Saint Michel, The Education* (*Literary Classics of the United States*, 1983).

For more Adams, read *The Education of Henry Adams* (1907) in *Novels, Mont Saint Michel, The Education*, plus Elizabeth Stevenson's biography. James Joseph Walsh's *The Thirteenth, Greatest of Centuries* (Fordham, 1907) is now considered a period piece, but it was a favorite of Theodore Roosevelt and still has its attractions.

G. K. Chesterton, *Orthodoxy*

Maisie Ward, author of *Gilbert Keith Chesterton* (Sheed and Ward, 1943), knew the great man well. Chesterton's *St. Thomas Aquinas* (Sheed and Ward, 1933) is still respected by scholars.

James Joyce, *Dubliners*

James Joyce, *Dubliners*, intro. by Brenda Maddox (Bantam Classics, 1990). Of course read Joyce's *A Portrait of the Artist as a Young Man* (1916) for its famous account of the hero's horrifying high school Jesuit retreat. After Edna O'Brien's short biography, *James Joyce* (Viking, 1999), the standard biography is Richard Ellmann's *James Joyce*, rev. ed. (Oxford University Press, 1982). Very helpful for allusion and symbol hunters is W. Y. Tindall, *A Reader's Guide to James Joyce* (Noonday Press, 1959).

Sigrid Undset, *Kristin Lavransdatter*

Sigrid Undset, *Kristin Lavransdatter* (Knopf, 1929).
See also Carl F. Bayerschmidt, *Sigrid Undset* (Twayne, 1970); J. C. Whitehouse, *Vertical Man: The Human Being in the Catholic Novels of Graham Greene, Sigrid Undset, and Georges Bernanos* (St. Augustine's Press, 1999); and Deal W. Hudson, ed., *Sigrid Undset on Saints and Sinners* (Ignatius Press, 1993).

François Mauriac, *Thérèse*

François Mauriac, *Thérèse* (Penguin, 1995).
See also Maxwell A. Smith, *François Mauriac* (Twayne, 1970) and Robert Speaight, *François Mauriac: A Study of the Writer and the Man* (London: Chatto and Windus, 1976).

Willa Cather, *Death Comes for the Archbishop*

Willa Cather, *Death Comes for the Archbishop* (Modern Library, 1993).
See also Paul Horgan, *Lamy of Santa Fe: His Life and Times* (Farrar, Straus, and Giroux, 1975); Willa Cather, *On Writing* (Knopf, 1949); and Joan Acocella, *Willa Cather and the Politics of Criticism* (University of Nebraska Press, 2000).

Myles Connolly, *Mr. Blue*

Myles Connolly, *Mr. Blue* (Macmillan, 1928).
There is not a lot of scholarship available on Connolly or Walter M. Miller. Visit the library and consult *Contemporary Authors* (Gale Research, 1981), *Contemporary Literary Criticism* (Gale Research, 1973), *Current Biography* (H. W. Wilson), and the *Catholic Encyclopedia*.

Albert Schweitzer, *Out of My Life and Thought: An Autobiography*

Albert Schweitzer, *Out of My Life and Thought: An Autobiography* (Henry Holt, 1990).

See also James Brabazon, *Albert Schweitzer: A Biography* (Putnam, 1975) and Albert Schweitzer, *The Quest of the Historical Jesus* (Johns Hopkins University Press, 1998).

Georges Bernanos, *The Diary of a Country Priest*

Georges Bernanos, *The Diary of a Country Priest* (Macmillan, 1937).
See also Robert Speaight, *Georges Bernanos* (Liveright, 1974) and William Bush, *Georges Bernanos* (Twayne, 1969).

Graham Greene, *The Power and the Glory*

Graham Greene, *The Power and the Glory*, intro. by John Updike (Penguin, 1995).
See also *The Portable Graham Greene*, ed. Philip Statford (Penguin, 1977); Norman Sherry, *The Life of Graham Greene*, Vol. I, 1904–1939 (Penguin, 1990); and Graham Greene, *The Lawless Roads* (Longmans, Green and Co., 1939).

Rebecca West, *Black Lamb and Grey Falcon: A Journey through Yugoslavia*

Rebecca West, *Black Lamb and Grey Falcon: A Journey through Yugoslavia* (Penguin, 1995).
Rebecca West, a Celebration (Penguin, 1978) contains her greatest works, including *Greenhouse with Cyclamens* (1989) on the Nuremberg trials, and *The New Meaning of Treason* (1964). A good biography is Victoria Glendinning, *Rebecca West, A Life* (Knopf, 1987).
See also Bonnie Kime Scott, ed., *Selected Letters of Rebecca West* (Yale University Press, 2000).

Evelyn Waugh, *Brideshead Revisited*

Evelyn Waugh, *Brideshead Revisited*, Everyman's Library (Knopf, 1993).
See also David Lodge, *Evelyn Waugh* (Columbia University Press, 1971) and Frederick L. Beaty, *The Ironic World of Evelyn Waugh: A Study of Eight Novels* (Northern Illinois University Press, 1992).

Alan Paton, *Cry, the Beloved Country*

See also Allister Sparks, *The Mind of South Africa* (Alfred A. Knopf, 1990); Edward Callan, *Alan Paton* (Twayne, 1968); and Alan Paton, *Towards the Mountain: An Autobiography* (Scribner, 1980).

Thomas Merton, *The Seven Storey Mountain*

Thomas Merton, *The Seven Storey Mountain* (Harcourt, Brace, 1948).
Paul Wilkes, ed., *Merton: By Those Who Knew Him Best* (Harper and Row, 1984); Michael Mott, *The Seven Mountains of Thomas Merton* (Houghton Mifflin, 1984); and William H. Shannon, *Silent Lamp: The Thomas Merton Story* (Crossroad, 1992).

Dietrich Bonhoeffer, *Letters and Papers from Prison*

Dietrich Bonhoeffer, *Letters and Papers from Prison* (Macmillan, 1967).

See also G. Leibholz, "Memoir," in Bonhoeffer's *The Cost of Discipleship*
(Touchstone, 1995); Eberhard Bethge, *Bonhoeffer, Exile and Martyr*
(Seabury, 1975); William Kuhns, *In Pursuit of Dietrich Bonhoeffer*
(Pflaum, 1967); and David H. Hopper, *A Dissent on Bonhoeffer*
(Westminster, 1975).

Dorothy Day, *The Long Loneliness*

Dorothy Day, *The Long Loneliness: The Autobiography of Dorothy Day*
(Harper San Francisco, 1997).

The major biography is William D. Miller's *Dorothy Day: A Biography*
(Harper and Row, 1982). Jim O'Grady's *Dorothy Day: With Love for the
Poor* (Ward Hill Press, 1993) is written for young people. See also
Mark S. Massa, *Catholics and American Culture: Fulton Sheen, Dorothy
Day, and the Notre Dame Football Team* (Crossroad, 1999) and Allen F.
Davis, *American Heroine: The Life and Legend of Jane Addams* (Oxford
University Press, 1973).

Edward Steichen, *The Family of Man*

Edward Steichen, *The Family of Man* (Simon and Schuster for the
Museum of Modern Art, 1955).

Compare Steichen to his greatest contemporary in Dorothy Norman,
Alfred Stieglitz: An American Seer (Random House, 1973). See also
Penelope Niven, *Steichen: A Biography* (Clarkson Potter, 1997).

Pierre Teilhard de Chardin, S.J., *The Divine Milieu*

For more Teilhard, read *The Phenomenon of Man* (Harper, 1959) and
Letters from a Traveller (London: Collins, 1962). A pioneer work in
Teilhardian studies is Christopher F. Mooney, S.J.'s *Teilhard de
Chardin and the Mystery of Christ* (London: Collins, 1966). See also
Thomas M. King, S.J., *Teilhard's Mysticism of Knowing* (Seabury, 1981).

Walter M. Miller Jr., *A Canticle for Leibowitz*

See note on Myles Connolly.

J. F. Powers, *Morte D'Urban*

See also John V. Hagopian, *J. F. Powers* (Twayne, 1968); J. V. Long,
"Clerical Character(s)," *Commonweal* (May 8, 1998); Andrew M.
Greeley, "J. F. Powers, R.I.P.: Catholic Storyteller," *Commonweal* (July
16, 1999); and Ross Labrie, *The Catholic Imagination in American
Literature* (University of Missouri Press, 1997).

Michael Harrington, *The Other America*

Michael Harrington, *The Other America: Poverty in the United States*
(Penguin, 1992).

See also *Fragments of the Century*, Michael Harrington's personal memoir
of the 1950s and 1960s (Simon and Schuster, 1977); Harrington's
Other America sequel, *The New American Poverty* (Holt, Rinehart, and

Winston, 1984); and Maurice Isserman, *The Other American: The Life of Michael Harrington* (PublicAffairs, 2000).

C. S. Lewis, *The Four Loves*
C. S. Lewis's most popular other works include *Mere Christianity: Comprising the Case for Christianity; Christian Behavior and Beyond;* and *The Screwtape Letters.* See also William Griffin, *Clive Staples Lewis: A Dramatic Life* (Harper and Row, 1986).

Christopher Dawson, *The Historic Reality of Christian Culture*
Christopher Dawson, *The Dynamics of World History* (Sheed and Ward, 1957).
As a follow-up on this essay, consider Dawson's *The Crisis of Western Education* (Sheed and Ward, 1961), which includes an appendix by John J. Mulloy with a program of study, book lists of Christian classics, etc., for those who would implement Dawson's ideas.

Edwin O'Connor, *The Edge of Sadness*
Edwin O'Connor, *The Edge of Sadness* (Little, Brown, 1961).
Arthur Schlesinger Jr. edited *The Best and the Last of Edwin O'Connor* (Little, Brown, 1970), which includes selections from his novels as well as his critical essays. See also Hugh Rank, *Edwin O'Connor* (Twayne, 1974).

Martin Luther King Jr., "Letter from Birmingham Jail"
Martin Luther King Jr., "Letter from Birmingham Jail" in James M. Washington, ed., *A Testament of Hope: The Essential Writings of Martin Luther King Jr.* (Harper and Row, 1986).
See also Taylor Branch, *Parting the Waters: America in the King Years, 1954–63* (Simon and Schuster, 1988) and Stephen B. Oates, *Let the Trumpet Sound: The Life of Martin Luther King Jr.* (Harper and Row, 1982).

Flannery O'Connor, *Everything That Rises Must Converge,* "Revelation"
Flannery O'Connor, *Everything That Rises Must Converge,* "Revelation" in *Flannery O'Connor: Collected Works* (Library of America, 1988).
See also Flannery O'Connor, "The Church and the Fiction Writer," *America* (April 17, 1999) and Harold Bloom, ed., *Flannery O'Connor,* Modern Critical Views (Chelsea House, 1986).

Alex Haley, *The Autobiography of Malcolm X*
Alex Haley, *The Autobiography of Malcolm X* (Grove Press, 1965).
See also Peter Goldman, *The Death and Life of Malcolm X* (University of Illinois Press, 1979).
There are two collections of Malcolm X's speeches: George Breitman, ed., *By Any Means Necessary* (Pathfinder, 1970) and *Malcolm X Speaks: Selected Speeches and Statements* (Grove, 1965). For other black

American writers, don't miss the essays of Alice Walker and of James Baldwin, particularly Baldwin's *Notes of a Native Son*.

Shusaku Endo, *Silence*

Shusaku Endo, *Silence*, trans. William Johnston (Taplinger, 1979). Follow with Endo's short stories, *Stained Glass Elegies: Stories*, trans. Van C. Gessel (Dodd, Mead, 1985).

Gustavo Gutiérrez, *A Theology of Liberation: History, Politics, and Salvation*

See also Jon Sobrino, *Christology at the Crossroads: A Latin American Approach* (Orbis, 1978); Arthur F. McGovern, *Liberation Theology and Its Critics: Toward an Assessment* (Orbis, 1989); and Jeff Thielman and Raymond A. Schroth, S.J., *Volunteer: With the Poor in Peru* (Paulist, 1991).

Jonathan Schell, *The Fate of the Earth*

See also Jonathan Schell, *The Unfinished Twentieth Century* (Verso, 2000); Michael Walzer, *Just and Unjust Wars: A Moral Argument with Historical Illustrations* (Basic Books, 1977); and John Hersey, *Hiroshima* (Alfred A. Knopf, 1946).

Karl Rahner, S.J., *The Love of Jesus and the Love of Neighbor*

Karl Rahner, S.J., *The Love of Jesus and the Love of Neighbor* (Crossroad, 1983).
Rahner's *The Practice of Faith: A Handbook of Contemporary Spirituality* (Crossroad, 1983) is a wonderful collection of excerpts from his major writings. His *Foundations of Christian Faith: An Introduction to the Idea of Christianity* (Seabury Press, 1978) is a major summing up of his theology. For background, the best complete presentation of Catholic theology is Richard P. McBrien, *Catholicism* (Winston, 1980). I have the Teilhard de Chardin prayer for a good death, in Rahner's mother's handwriting, courtesy of Leo O'Donovan, S.J., who received it from Rahner himself.

Elisabeth Schüssler Fiorenza, *In Memory of Her: A Feminist Theological Reconstruction of Christian Origins*

Prof. Fiorenza has edited *The Power of Naming: A Concilium Reader in Feminist Liberation Theology* (Orbis, 1996). See also Elizabeth A. Johnson, *She Who Is: The Mystery of God in Feminist Theological Discourse* (Crossroad, 1992).

Brian Moore, *Black Robe*

Read some more Moore, such as *The Lonely Passion of Judith Hearne* and *The Statement*. Then return to *Black Robe*'s sources: *The Jesuit Relations: Natives and Missionaries in Seventeenth-Century North America*, ed. Allan Greer (Bedford/St. Martin's, 2000) and Francis X. Talbot, S.J., *Saint among Savages* (Harper and Bros., 1935).

Helen Prejean, *Dead Man Walking: An Eyewitness Account of the Death Penalty in the United States*

See also Jim Dwyer, Barry Scheck, and Peter Neufeld, *Actual Innocence: Five Days to Execution and Other Dispatches from the Wrongly Convicted* (Doubleday, 2000) and Raymond A. Schroth, S.J., "Sister Helen Prejean: On Death Row," *Commonweal* (October 6, 2000).

Peter Ackroyd, *The Life of Thomas More*

The Complete Works of St. Thomas More (Yale University Press, 1963–1997). See also Louis L. Martz, *Thomas More: The Search for the Inner Man* (Yale University Press, 1990) and Michael J. Moore, ed., *Quincentennial Essays on St. Thomas More* (Appalachian State University, 1978).

Robert Ellsberg, *All Saints: Daily Reflections on Saints, Prophets, and Witnesses for Our Time*

Robert Ellsberg, *All Saints: Daily Reflections on Saints, Prophets, and Witnesses for Our Time* (Crossroad, 1997).

I must add two favorite books at the end: John W. O'Malley, S.J., *The First Jesuits* (Harvard University Press, 1993), the best available story on the early Society of Jesus; and Paul Johnson's lively and provocative *History of Christianity* (Atheneum, 1976).

For a book that recommends good books, turn to *The Reader's Catalog*, founded by Jason Epstein and edited by Geoffrey O'Brien (Reader's Catalog, 1997). It has 40,000 annotated entries and 1,968 pages, more than 100 of which are devoted to books on religion and philosophy. *Commonweal, National Catholic Reporter, America,* and *Crisis* all devote space to major articles on religious culture and to reviewing religious books.